In Great
WATERS
The Story of the Portuguese Fishermen

They that go down to the sea in ships,
That do business in great waters;
These see the works of the Lord,
And his wonders in the deep.

— *Psalm 107: 23 - 24*

In Great WATERS
The Story of the Portuguese Fishermen

JEREMIAH DIGGES
with a foreword by
Donald W. Davidson

THE PENINSULA PRESS
Cape Cod, Nantucket & Martha's Vineyard

Copyright ©2014 by The Peninsula Press
Cover background image derived from the United States Department of Commerce
Chart No. 70 of the East Coast: West Quoddy Head to New York (1935)
All photographs used on the cover and the interior are courtesy of the United States Library of Congress.

IN GREAT WATERS
The Story of the Portuguese Fishermen

is published by
The Peninsula Press · Cape Cod 02670 USA
WWW.CAPECODREADER.COM

All rights reserved.
No part of this publication may be reproduced or transmitted in any form or by any means, electronic or mechanical — including on-line, photocopy, recording, or any information storage and retrieval system now known or to be invented — without prior written permission of the publisher.

Library of Congress Control Number: 2014932711
Digges, Jeremiah.
IN GREAT WATERS: The Story of the Portuguese Fishermen
The Peninsula Press, ©2014.
ISBN: 978-1-883684-03-7

Manufactured in the United States of America
1 2 3 4 5 6 7 8 9 0 / 23 22 21 20 19 18 17 16 15 14

*To
Uncle Harry*

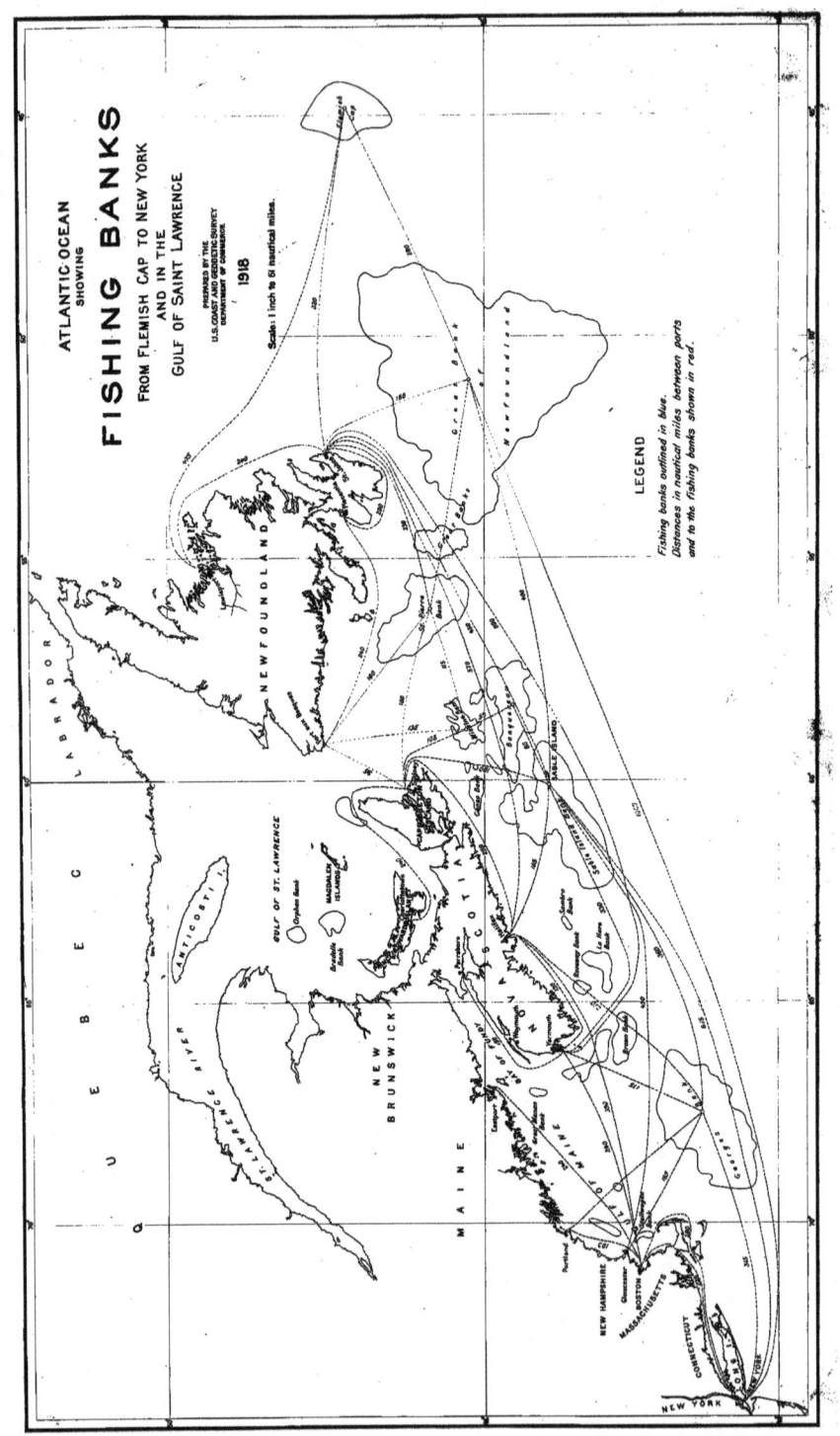

Contents

Foreword
Donald W. Davidson
— 11 —

List of Illustrations
— 9 —

Introduction
Jeremiah Digges
— 13 —

Chapter I
Bacalhao
— 24 —

Chapter II
Admirals in Shirt Sleeves
— 31 —

Chapter III
Ghost Town
— 41 —

Chapter IV
Land of the Free
— 48 —

Chapter V
Ports of the Grand Bankers
— 58 —

Chapter VI
Success Story
— 73 —

Chapter VII
'Tis Men's Lives
— 86 —

Chapter VIII
The Ghosts of Georges Bank
— 99 —

Chapter IX
Boreas Strains a Lung
— 113 —

Chapter X
Mist on the Western Banks
— 126 —

Chapter XI
Big Wind on the Grand Banks
— 138 —

Chapter XII
The Crowning of Captain Joe
— 149 —

Chapter XIII
Flying Fishermen
— 161 —

Chapter XIV
Tollgates of Davy Jones
— 179 —

Chapter XV
Nets and Trawls and Six-Inch Guns
— 193 —

Chapter XVI
Today
— 211 —

List of Illustrations

Atlantic Fishing Banks
U.S. Coast & Geodetic Survey (1918)
National Oceanic and Atmospheric Administration
Historical Map & Chart Collection
— 6 —

Bound for Georges Bank
Farm Security Administration - Office of War Information Photograph Collection
Library of Congress
— 11 —

Provincetown Harbor Chart
U.S. Coast & Geodetic Survey (1922)
National Oceanic and Atmospheric Administration
Historical Map & Chart Collection
— 21 —

Provincetown fishing trawler at low tide alongside Higgins Lumber Pier
Farm Security Administration - Office of War Information Photograph Collection
Library of Congress
— 22 —

Bow of a dory towed by the fishing boat *Alden* out of Gloucester
Farm Security Administration - Office of War Information Photograph Collection
Library of Congress
— 40 —

Handling a cargo from the Grand Banks, Gloucester
Detroit Publishing Company Photograph Collection
Library of Congress
— 70 —

During a mackerel chase, a dory is towed by the *Alden* of Gloucester
Farm Security Administration - Office of War Information Photograph Collection
Library of Congress
— 93 —

Gloucester Harbor Chart
U.S. Coast & Geodetic Survey (1912)
National Oceanic and Atmospheric Administration
Historical Map & Chart Collection
— 111 —

Foreword

I'M THE FIRST TO ADMIT that these next two pages are the kind that most readers have no problems skipping over to get to the "real" book in hand. After all, this is just the "foreword," which is something a lot of folks tend to misspell as well as to misunderstand. And then, in order to get to the first page of the first chapter, those readers still have to decide whether or not to look at the "introduction." That's where the author attempts to set you up for the rest of his work; here, though, I'm supposed to offer up some sort of credible opinion as to why you should read along any further at all. So, here I am to say, "Believe me. If you love Cape Cod, then you'll love this book." Now, let me tell you why.

For one thing, I think Joe Berger's writing is very good. And by that I don't mean that Joe knows how to spell and punctuate. I mean it's "good," because his style is very comfortable, and this reads more like a good story than like a good history. Now that I think of it, I suppose that's why he decided to subtitle this book "The Story of the Portuguese Fishermen" rather than "The History of the Portuguese Fishermen."

That said, this book is about a lot more than just a people who came to this corner of the planet in search of food. It is about their place in the history of the world and this nation, as well as their place in the history of the Cape and the Commonwealth alike. Whew! I know that's quite a claim to back up, but it's true, and Joe Berger's the one who can prove it. With names that he can bring to life with story after story rather than with date after date. Here you will find that history is not a matter of what damn thing following another; here you will find that the daily life.

"I am never happier than when gathering this kind of material, which means digging into old, obscure books and manuscripts, and ship logs and family papers, and -- best of all -- listening to men talk," Joe admitted to a Provincetown reporter back in April of 1938. "When men talk on Cape Cod, sitting on a wharf, or a fish shed, or in the fo'cs'le of a flounder-dragger, it is just so much talk to them; but to a fellow in my line of business -- why, it's very often pure gold which they are tossing around so carelessly! So, I keep my mouth shut and let them toss. And when I get home, I run it through the mill on my typewriter, and see what comes out."

What comes out of Joe's typewriter is not much at all about love letters in the sand or lobster stew with an ocean view. Instead, it is a look at life

And all the while, there are various elements of that thing they call "progress," whose endless tramping can always be felt in the background and it is always marching closer and closer. Always there are bigger boats, faster boats, newer charts, newer markets, newer modes of transportation, newer ways of preserving fish, newer modes of communication. And always there is the ocean, timeless and moody, as well as the weather, the so-called "elements" themselves. And there is God and country and war.

Josef Berger, who chose to call himself "Jeremiah Digges" in print, first published this book in 1941, a half a year prior to the bombing of Pearl Harbor. And so, his story of the Portuguese fishermen ends before the Second World War, but the story of the Portuguese fishermen continued on and endures.

In the aftermath of World War II and with the technologies that it had spawned, the fishing grounds of the world became even more accessible to more and more nations.

Introduction

IT IS A HARD LIFE.

That is the way they put it, the dark, weather-worn fellows who go shuffling in long seaboots up and down the streets of any Yankee fishing village. If you ask them how they are getting along, that will be the stock answer. But if you go with them into the cold, the fog, and the fury of the waters where they spend most of their time, then truly from these men you will need no answer. The sea, and their own nightmarish struggle for a subsistence from it, will tell you what no word, no shrug of bent shoulder, no sigh of man's breath, can.

Yes, a hard life, such as the sea has always held out to those who go down to it for their keep. If anyone should stack up all the ships' logs, the sailors' journals, newspaper stories and other non-fiction – all the writings into the workaday record of the sea – gather them in one big pile and then compare them with anything that has ever been imagined of the doings of men ashore, the saltwater account would assay more violence to the ton, more convincing hardship, more real human misery.

But not enough, it seems to me, has been set down about the kindliness of men, the bigness of heart, which I for one have found against this same harsh background. My own experience has been limited to the trips I have made to the banks with Portuguese fishermen, but I have no reason to doubt that with other humble laborers of the sea it would be the same. There would come out, perhaps in other ways, the same open-handedness, the same humor and sympathy, which made it possible for me to find the makings of this book.

I remember how seasick I became on my first day out in one of their vessels, in which they were taking me to the Western Banks – how *awfully* seasick – and I can imagine how I must have looked, lying there in my bunk and wondering with each new roll and pitch why the world wasn't made of solid granite. And I remember that while I was at my

13

INTRODUCTION

worst, Cook blew the dinner whistle. Down came the "first-table gang," to take their places at the reeling, slopping board.

One member of this crew was old João, a huge Azorian, who had been friendly to me from the moment I stepped on board. João had told me he stood six feet three, weighed two hundred and sixty-five pounds, and was sixty-six years old. Now he took his seat, which was directly thwartships from my bunk. Eagerly he loaded up his plate with the beloved sausage known as *linguiça*, and with potatoes, cabbage, and a great pile of other stuff – all he could lay on without losing cargo in that kind of sea. Then he looked over at me. Slowly he wagged his great head, and not knowing that I could understand Portuguese, remarked in that language:

"Poor fellow, I guess he hasn't much of a stomach!"

But Cook, who had asked me what my business was, and who had been duly impressed when I told him I was a writer – or perhaps unduly so – now objected.

"João" – also in Portuguese – "any time you can trade that big belly of yours for his brains, you do it. That fellow *writes books!*"

João looked at me again. Then he looked down at his plate. And once more at me. And then, with a grand flourish of his fork, he declared:

"No, by Jesus Christ, I keep my belly!"

At that moment I noticed the engineer looking me over rather carefully, and with no great show of favor. And still in the Portuguese, he spoke up.

"Writes, eh? Writes books. H'm-m! You wouldn't think it to look at him. He doesn't look very smart."

"Be careful what you say, José," Cook cautioned him. "He understands a little Portuguese."

José was immediately stricken.

"Ai," – in a very loud tone – "I did not say, Henrique, he was *not* smart! I only said he did not *look it!*"

And I have reason to believe that poor José was later given a private talking-to by the skipper himself, for fear that my feelings might be injured again through such poor manners. For they are like that. I was their guest; and to a guest whom they could tolerate at all, they were so generous, so kind that it was all but embarrassing. Later, when I demonstrated how inept I could be with a gaff, or with a pair of oars, this barrier was overcome.

15

But to get down to the real business of introductions, I would point out that of all the Portuguese, or of the persons of Portuguese descent, in America, numbering around 80,000, the fishermen and their families make up only a very small fraction. All told, they are between 5,000 and 6,000. The heaviest immigration of Portuguese came in the ten years 1911-1920, and most of those newcomers found work in the textile mills and other manufacturing plants of New England, and on the farms of California.

Yet it has been in the business of the sea that the Portuguese stand out here as a people with a story all their own, just as it was in that same hard calling that their country once had achieved greatness among the nations of the world. They have an affinity with the sea, these men, which I shall not attempt to explain, because I cannot. They are at home on the sea. They are at ease there. Or perhaps it is truer to say that they are less at their ease anywhere else.

Maybe I can point up my own impression of them by mentioning here a word used constantly by the Azorians to describe their own state of mind; for most of the fisher people are from the Azores. The word, then, is *saudade*, and it is one of those terms for which we have no exact English translation. If you ask one of these islanders what he means by it, he will say that he is sad, but something more than sad – homesick, and yet not only homesick; that he has a longing to go "back," yet not back to the islands which were his home – for even in the Azores people have the *saudade!* Yes, he *is* homesick, but for a home that no longer exists, and in his own life never did exist; he longs for something "again," and the longing is so acute that it hurts and saddens – yet he cannot tell you what it is that he longs for! And that, as nearly as he is likely to explain it, is the *saudade*.

The sea does not satisfy such yearnings. I shall be glad to eat any book of romantic fiction or poems about the sea which proves to my own satisfaction that it does. And yet, I think I can understand how there would be some false promise in it, some illusion of easement to be found there – there and nowhere else in the world.

Certainly, for this reason or for some better, the affinity between these men and the sea lives on. On the decks of homely little fishing boats out of Gloucester and Provincetown I have seen it, recognized it again and again, felt its realness today as surely as it shows through the romantic

INTRODUCTION

retrospect of centuries, from the time of da Gama, Magellan, and the others who put Portugal on the map of a new and bigger world. And it is this small minority of the Portuguese in America, the seafaring men, that I am setting off in this book from the whole ethnic group. Their career is my story.

In its beginnings, that career was unique in the history of American immigration. Unlike the incoming masses from other lands, these Portuguese did not buy tickets and crowd the steerage quarters of passenger vessels. They began, almost without exception, working their way across as whalemen, on the ships of New Bedford and Nantucket and other whaling ports.

That was a hard life, too – so hard and so cruel that Yankee skippers couldn't find enough men at home who were willing to sail with them. Young fortune-seeking Americans of the 1820's preferred the risk of sudden death in the untamed West to that of slow starvation on the high seas. On the frontier there was at least a chance of finding the fortune. The New Bedford waterfront tried to sweep aside this bashfulness with the ancient device known as the shanghai; but the brutality of the whaling masters had become such an old story that within a few years even the bums and floaters alongshore were wary of the traps set for them in water-front dives.

To solve the problem of their labor shortage, Yankee skippers now had either to treat their crews more humanely – feed them a little more and beat them a little less – or to look elsewhere for their men. They chose, of course, to look elsewhere. To the Azores and the Cape Verde Islands they sailed their vessels with skeleton crews; and from those little archipelagos, possessions of Portugal, they picked up eager young greenhorns, whole crews of them, at something less than a dime a dozen.

These island youths were perfect material. They made good sailors and good whalemen, especially the tall, black, graceful Cape Verders, who were superb in such work: they took Yankee beatings as all good "furriners" should, and to most of them starvation was nothing new. Back in New Bedford the word quickly went the rounds of the countinghouses, and shipowners of that pious city, catching up on their lost sleep, once more were able to rise in time for morning devotions.

The islanders also learned that whaling with the Americans was a hard life. But it was a way of getting to America – the only way they saw open

17

to them – and new recruits were always ready to take the places of their countrymen who had quit ship on reaching America. Many such voyages lasted more than two years; and in working their way "across," the boys usually had to work several thousand miles around.

By 1850, however, this strange 'fore-the-mast immigration was in full swing; and from that time to the end of the century, thousands of Azorians and Cape Verde Islanders were landed in American ports.

The Cape Verders, on whom the *saudade* weighed even more heavily than it did on the Azorians, generally stuck to whaling. Early in the game they became boat steerers and harpooners, and later many of them were mates and even captains in the New Bedford fleet. To most Azorians, however, that initial whaling voyage was merely a route of escape from a woeful existence at home – an evil, indeed, but the lesser of two. When these young men had gone through their ordeal and had stepped ashore at last in America, they turned at once to other work.

In the fifties many went to California, joining the gold rush. In order to get there, hundreds signed on with New Bedford whaleships, which were then working in the Arctic from bases in Alaska – sailing 18,000 miles around Cape Horn and up the west coast, through the Bering Strait and on to Point Barrow, Herschel Island, and other points on the Alaskan coast, near the newly discovered bowhead whaling grounds.

Whalebone brought big prices in those days, and bowhead whales carried tons of this commodity in their heads. Therefore when the Sag Harbor whaling bark *Superior* dropped anchor in Honolulu in the autumn of 1848, and her skipper made it known that he had discovered great schools of bowhead whales up in the far north, the word was spread through the whole South Seas whaling fleet, and almost as quickly back to New Bedford.

When they heard there was gold in them ice floes – oily, bony gold, sporting about on the far corner of the continent – skippers and shipowners of the home port were eager to chance the long voyage. Their only problem was to find crews, men willing to face the hardships of whaling in the Arctic, and under ordinary conditions that would have been difficult, because the fo'mast hands, long familiar with the Yankee shipowners' way of "going shares," knew better than to expect any of this new-found wealth for themselves. The old New Bedford jingle already had been learned by heart:

INTRODUCTION

>An aught's an aught, and two is two,
>All for me and none for you.

But as luck would have it, gold – grainy, yellow gold – was discovered in that year in California. Within a few months the great 1849 gold rush was under way. Landlubber and seaman alike wanted to get to the coast, by any route that offered. As the sailorman figured it, San Francisco was a way port on the long route to the Arctic whaling grounds; and thus if a man were to sign on with a whaling skipper, and then desert at Frisco, he would have his free passage and be right on hand for the bonanza!

Suddenly the whaling firms found themselves besieged with applicants – even experienced sailors, who ordinarily avoided whaling like the pox – and another jingle gained smiling lip service along the New Bedford waterfront:

>Who jumps his ship may go to prison,
>But all the gold he gits is hisn.

The gold fever of those times registered its highest temperatures in New England. And with traffic already well established between New Bedford and the Azores, via whaleship, the talk of California gold also spread over the islands. There, among the simple fishermen of Pico and the farmers of Fayal, those California nuggets attained the length of a codfish, the girth of a cantaloupe. And Yankee whalemen, still needing men in their fo'c's'les, solemnly verified all such dimensions.

Of the whaleships' recruits who planned to desert at Frisco while en route to the Arctic, not all were successful. But for several years the runaways went on, and among them were enough Azorians to found permanent settlements on the west coast. Between 1850 and 1860, the number of Portuguese (mostly Azorians) living in California jumped from 109 to 1,459. Passing through the disillusionment and recovery from gold fever, these people went into farming. Their communities drew more of their fellow countrymen from New England and from the homeland to join them on their farms or to go out with the tuna fishing fleet of southern California. Thus by 1930 California had more than 100,000 Portuguese, or almost as many as Massachusetts, the leading state, with its 109,000; today there is constant travel and much letter writing between these people of the two states, for many members of the same families live in each.

To those island greenhorns, fresh out of whalers' fo'c's'les in the 1850's, three main choices were open as they stepped ashore and wandered through the bewildering streets of New Bedford, or of Provincetown at the tip end of Cape Cod: they could sign on for another whaling voyage, they could go West and hunt gold, or they could try earning a living here in Massachusetts. Having had a taste of whaling, many preferred to choose between the unkown terrors of the other two.

Provincetown was then a big fishing port, and so was Gloucester. They were different, these towns, from anything at home on the islands. Yankee fishermen were not like the codfishers of the old country; their vessels were different, and so was the gear they used; everything was strange. But here was work the islanders knew they could do; these were ways of the sea, and therefore – however strange – ways they knew they could learn. And so, from New Bedford the new New Englanders were drawn to the two fishing ports, one on Cape Cod, the other on Cape Ann, and there began to make their homes.

Of all that has happened to these men and their families, I do not pretend to tell. There is overweight of hardship there, of struggle, and of death. Broken by the jagged lines of dangerous living, the design of life itself becomes elusive – as elusive as the meaning of that *saudade* which has ever hung over it. Even the pretense of a detailed, comprehensive account, were it possible to compile one, would be of no wide interest. Death and danger repeat themselves too often; the copybook rules of narration are swept aside by the February gales of Georges Bank.

Rather than use up these pages, therefore, with the cataloguing of tragedy, or even for a full complement of the minor statistics, dates, and other matters of local knowledge that may properly go into an ethnic study in its conventional form, I am passing along the story as it has come to me, and as it must have come to anyone undertaking it at first hand. I am choosing out a few highlights, and letting it tell itself around them.

Thus many of the incidents and characters in these pages are only samples, fragments of that story, included here to represent, rather than to account for in full. Many a Portuguese skipper's rise to success in the New England fleet was as full of adventure as that of Captain Tony King, whom I have taken for example; the loss of Captain Sou'west's son Manuel should be multiplied by a thousand, to apply to the life of the dory fishermen; and gales like that which blew the schooner *Joseph P. Johnson* across the ocean have been blowing on, through the years.

Introduction

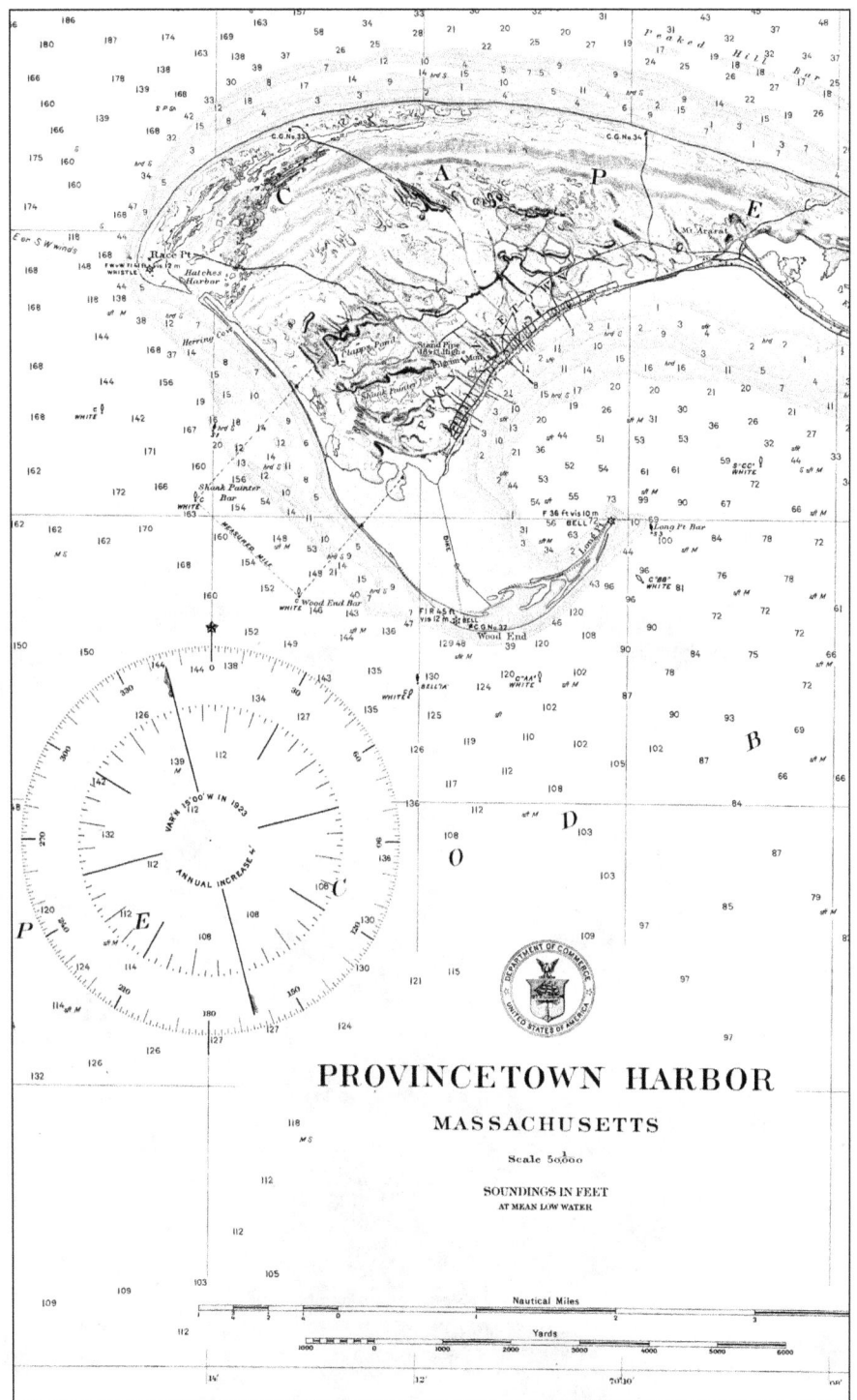

Introduction

He who would tell this tale in full must have lived long – and must wait, yet a while longer.

For their hospitality and generous aid, I am heavily indebted to the fishermen of Gloucester, Provincetown, and New Bedford. They have welcomed me into their homes, they have taken me to sea in their vessels, they have done all they could to help me.

For the chance to see them at their work, I am especially indebted to Captain Joseph Rose of schooner *Magellan*, Captain Joaquim Gasper of schooner *Elvira Gasper*, the late Captain Lawrence Santos of schooner *Mary P. Goulart*, and to skippers of many smaller craft.

For their first-hand accounts of incidents recorded here, I am grateful to Joseph Telles, who was cook of the trawler *Rush* when she was destroyed by a submarine; to Sebastião Rose, who was in the crew of the schooner *Mary P. Mesquita* when she was rammed and sunk by an ocean liner; to Captain Antoine Joaquim Souza, one of the rescue crew who were awarded Congressional medals for their lifesaving feat in the "*Portland* Gale;" and to members of the families of Captain Marion Perry, Captain Joseph Mesquita, and others who figure in these pages.

For other valuable assistance, I wish to express my appreciation to Rilla Silva Alexander, Manuel P. Domingos, Manuel de Pinho, and John Marshall.

JEREMIAH DIGGES
Provincetown, Massachusetts
October, 1940

Chapter I
Bacalhao

OLD BACALHAO BRUSHES HIS NETS from the two backless chairs nearest the stove. With his bandanna he makes a few dainty passes at the smudges of tar left on the seats. Then he lifts a mackerel keg from a corner of the shack, blows apologetically across the head of it, and sets it near the stove too. Now all three ladies can sit down.

But the ladies don't sit. They are Yankee ladies, who call themselves "The Old Stock," and it is hard to tell when such ladies will sit and when they will not sit. Bacalhao gives them a smile, and with his most cordial gesture, urges them:

"Seet down, seet down! I feeneesh the nets by 'm by – no trouble!"

The Yankee ladies slowly sit.

All three are wearing black fur coats, which they keep buttoned chin-high; for it is a rugged winter that Cape Cod is having in this year of 1912, and at the moment a "white nor'wester" is keeping the windows adance in Bacalhao's rickety "fish store."

Old-stock Yankee ladies of Cape Cod are not in the habit of visiting such "stores" – little gray-shingled waterfront shanties where Province-town's fishermen store the gear they use in their trawling and gill-netting, and wherein dories can be hauled up through wide doorways that face the beach.

Now Bacalhao, in his limited personal experience with Yankee ladies, has found always that they are after something; and he takes it for granted that when they venture into such a place as his store on this blizzardy afternoon they are after nothing less than the place itself – maybe with a fence around it!

Yes, Bacalhao knows. He knows, in fact, that that is precisely what they are after. Carlos, his dorymate, has told him they were coming. Carlos has warned him that they are having "another spell of the historics." And Bacalhao knows that while these ladies are thus afflicted nothing will

Chapter I: Bacalhao

hold them back in their warm white homes down at the east end of town, where they belong. Bacalhao has foreseen that, with the blood of hardy Pilgrim ancestors quickening appropriately in their veins, they would brave the snow and headwinds of a February nor'wester, they would march upstreet clear to the west end, they would even enter a Portuguese fish store – when they were moved by what Carlos called "the historics." Realizing all this, Bacalhao has begged Carlos to stand by him; but Carlos, a *fedorenta!* – the polecat! – has ducked out.

Now, in this tense moment, let us leave the three ladies while they are trimming ballast to the irregularities of Bacalhao's furniture, whisking off snow, and otherwise stalling before they start to tell him what he already knows. Until they begin working on him, there is still a chance to get a word in edgewise about Bacalhao himself.

Bacalhao – if you say "buckle" and add "yow," you will come pretty close – is the Portuguese for "codfish." The tall, square-shouldered fisherman who answers to this name when he is hailed along the wharves of Province-town doesn't look like a codfish. (And if you don't know just what a live codfish does look like, I've run across a description in *The Fisherman*, a Gloucester magazine of 1895 that may help: "Codfish are wholly unaware that they are not beautiful, rather priding themselves on the strong likeness said to exist between them and some of our leading opera singers in the act of vocalizing.")

No, Bacalhao doesn't look like that. His shoulders might disqualify him for ballet duty, and yet, massive as they are, they have a strange mobility, a curious roll-and-pitch as he gets up way, in which there is something of rhythm, something of grace.

His face, square-cut, is one of the few in this world that successfully carry off a gray stubble; and in his eyes – blue because his mother prayed very hard and under very favorable conditions – is a twinkle which was there in his childhood, faded in the nooning of his life, and has returned of these late years.

Painters of the art colony in Provincetown call Bacalhao's fish store "Motif Number One." It is the first structure alongshore that one would choose to paint. But they think Bacalhao himself a very handsome subject too – a big bargain at the fifty cents an hour for which he will pose when it's too rough to go fishing – and for him the artists pay cash. What more could one say?

Once Bacalhao had another name. That was a long time ago, when he was a little boy in far Fayal, one of the Azores, or Western Islands, as those tiny possessions of Portugal are sometimes called. He remembers, of course – it was Antoine Brava then – but that was beyond the ocean, beyond many, many oceans as Bacalhao looks backward; it has a strange sound to him now, that name! – what these Cape Cod Yankees would call "furrin."

Bacalhao, or Codfish, is a nickname, and yet something more than a nickname; and later on I shall have more to say about the wonderful nicknames of Portuguese fishermen. The night when Antoine Brava ran away from his home on the island of Fayal to ship on the whaling bark *Cicero*, four weeks out of New Bedford – that night was the beginning of Bacalhao.

As a Western Islander of sixteen, Antoine was facing conscription and the prisonlike army life in barracks of far-off Portugal; or, to escape it, the adventure of a whaling voyage and, after that, the great unknown, the New World. Young Antoine chose to write his future with a question mark rather than parentheses. He would a-whaling go – to America.

And so one day he went to Horta, to the office of the agent for a New Bedford whaling firm. There they said things, Antoine nodded, and then they wrote down things, and showed him where to mark a cross. And one night shortly thereafter, carrying out instructions they had given him, he stole away to the beach, kindled a little signal fire, and waited. He prayed, too, until he heard the creak of tholepins and the splash of oars.

When they took him aboard the whaleship that night, they didn't ask his name; they gave him one. The second mate of the *Cicero*, himself a Portuguese, looked Antoine over, asked about his home, what business his father was in. Antoine said his father was in the *lugres bacalhoeiros* – the Grand Banks codfishing fleet. The second mate nodded and said, "*Mais uma vez, Bacalhao!*" (Once and for all, Codfish!) and moved on to the next greeny in the line-up on deck.

And from that day forth, Antoine Brava remained in the New World – *mais uma vez, Bacalhao.*

By this time, the three Cape Cod ladies who are calling on Bacalhao in his little fish shed have sniffed back their composure. They are ready for the attack. By prearrangement, Mrs. Nickerson is to "do the talking," but by force of habit Mrs. Cook takes over rather early in the game.

"Naturally we are interested," Mrs. Cook explains, "because, you see, we ourselves are descendants of the *Mayflower* company. On both sides, Mr. Bacalhao, *direct descendants!*"

And because the lady has paused, and is looking at him, Bacalhao smiles.

"Is very nice," he murmurs.

"Do you – do you know what the *Mayflower* was, Mr. Bacalhao?" asks Mrs. Nickerson.

Yes, Bacalhao knows. Many times, he himself has been out in the very breakers of Pollock Rip where the *Mayflower* nearly foundered three centuries ago. He knows, perhaps a shade better than his callers, why the little ship wore about, there on Chatham Shoals, and made her run for Provincetown Harbor in that wild November storm. If these ladies could understand Portuguese, he could tell them something more, perhaps, than their history books did about the "deangerous shoulds and roring breakers" out there; he might even add that it was too bad he wasn't on deck himself to lend the *Mayflower*'s skipper a hand when "one of the maine beames in the midd shipps was bowed and craked," for he, Bacalhao, knows even better than the *Mayflower*'s people did, what to do in a case like that.

"Well, Mr. Bacalhao," Mrs. Cook goes on, "then you realize what a historic event it was, when the Pilgrim fathers came off the *Mayflower*, and stepped ashore here in Provincetown. In our own very town, they put foot on land for the first time in the New World!" She is warming to her work now. Again Bacalhao smiles, and tries to appear delighted. "Is *very* nice!" says he.

"And so, for the past year our little group has been making a study. We wanted to find the *exact spot* where the Pilgrims came ashore, where they washed their clothes, where they found their little spring of water. And think of it, Mr. Bacalhao! – we have just met with success!"

"You – you find water?" asks the breathless Bacalhao.

"Not yet. But we *have* found the exact spot where they came ashore!" At this point Mrs. Cook pauses. Her tone flattens out abruptly. "Unfortunately, the spot is where this fish store stands."

Bacalhao shakes his head, clicks his tongue, and exclaims, "Now, look at that!"

"Well, Mr. Bacalhao, all we can do now is to put the matter up to you.

We've made our plans, and we've subscribed the money to place a marker on this – this sacred spot. A boulder – a big rock, or something."

"A beeg rock, here in thees store?" Bacalhao stares dubiously at the high-piled bights of fish net, the strings of net corks, the buoys, anchors, tubs of trawl, and other gear with which the place is cluttered.

"No, no! I don't think you understand," Mrs. Cook says. "Not *in* the store. You see, this place would have to come down."

Bacalhao, who has known all along that this was coming, nevertheless looks stunned.

"Come down? But me and Carlos, my dorymate, we got to feesh! We got all our gear here! Thees gear, he's got no place to go!"

Mrs. Cook nods. "I was coming to that. As I say, we've raised a fund – a little fund, Mr. Bacalhao – and we wouldn't expect you to *give* the place."

This, too, he has heard. But he is quite sure the offer will be far below what his hard-won spot on the waterfront is worth; and Bacalhao has dealt with Yankee fish buyers long enough to know that there will be no improvement on that first price. That is one thing about these Yankees, they do not stoop to haggle; from the first prices they offer, nobody could stoop.

But the little speeches about "our" forefathers and about history and all – well, Bacalhao has been too polite to do anything but hear them out, and now they bother him. That is why he wanted Carlos to stand by. For you see, Bacalhao's own sense of fitness demands not only that he convince these ladies that their price is not fair, but also that he answer, somehow, that emotional plea in the name of history, that he give some good and sufficient reason, on historical grounds, why he, personally, should not be called upon to make this sacrifice.

They talk a long time. In desperation Bacalhao mentions the chance that Tony Souza might be willing to sell *his* fish store, but Mrs. Cook stiffly reminds him that the Pilgrim fathers didn't land there. And when she falls back on "our duty to that heroic little band," Bacalhao ponders and silently curses the heroic little band, and Mrs. Cook, and most of all Carlos, for walking out on him. In the silence, Mrs. Cook lashes out again:

"And *you*, Mr. Bacalhao! Isn't it your duty, too, to help us write their names in solid rock? Think of those names, the first great names in American history! Bradford, and Carver, and Brewster, and – "

Chapter I: Bacalhao

"Names?" Suddenly Bacalhao straightens his huge shoulders and towers over his visitors. Mrs. Cook trembles and suspects that somehow she has stuck her neck out. "The feerst great names, you say, in thees country? Ladies, men call me Bacalhao. You know what thees name mean?"

The ladies do not know.

"Codfeesh, ladies, codfeesh! And when the *Mayflower* come to thees shore, long time ago, what you think the crew have for supper? What you think they find here, so they don't starve to death?"

The ladies are silent.

"Codfeesh, ladies, codfeesh!"

That was nearly thirty years ago. Since then, another group has studied the matter of the Pilgrims' landing, and guided by the map in *Mourt's Relation*, has located another spot where the *Mayflower* company first set foot ashore in America. A marker has been placed there, and if you go to Provincetown today, you will find it by the roadside – a tablet of bronze set in hewn rock, and inscribed, "Place of the First Landing of the Pilgrims."

The little shanty on the waterfront that saved Cape Cod from a grave historical error is gone now; but if this present marker is really in the right place, then Bacalhao's fish store has served society in general as well as Bacalhao in particular; and my friend Bacalhao, to the time of his death a few years ago, was very glad indeed that the forefathers finally got their marker.

But in his claim for the priority and greater historical significance of the codfish, as against the Pilgrim Fathers, Bacalhao stuck to his guns. And to back up that claim there is a little story that old Bacalhao himself probably had never heard, an item of recorded history which, it seems to me, has not often been given the space it deserves in the work of our country's historians.

We shall have to go back now, not to the arrival of the *Mayflower*, but beyond that by more than a century, to the period just after Christopher Columbus sailed to America. In the year 1497 an English ship, under command of John Cabot of Venice, sailed from Bristol to find the shore across the sea. This vessel took the northern route and reached Labrador. Then, doing what almost anyone would do after finding Labrador, Cabot turned around and sailed home. Nevertheless, this discovery of North America caused great excitement back in Bristol, and the next year John

Cabot sailed westward again, taking with him his son Sebastian. This time the Cabots landed at Newfoundland.

Even the Lowells were not there, and some of the contemporary writings hint that neither was God. The people lived "like heardes of beastes" in that cold country, "whose inhabitantes are Idolatours and praye to the sonne and moone and dyuers Idoles." Yes, and they ate "flesshe and fysshe and all other things rawe. Sumtymes also they eate man's flesshe."

But "man's flesshe" did not rank among the staple groceries. The chief item was fish. On those vast shoals which later came to be known as the Grand Banks of Newfoundland, there were "multitudes" of fish. And when the Cabots had returned to England, Sebastian explained that they had named the new land after that fish. *Using the word of the native inhabitants*, he said, they had called it "Land of the Baccalaos!" And so it appears on many early maps – the first land name given to the northern part of America.

For centuries before the Cabots went to Newfoundland, men of Brittany and the Iberian Peninsula had been bringing home codfish which was split, salted, and stretched for curing on a stick (*baculum*). In Portugal it was *bacalhao*; in Spain, *baccalao*. It is scarcely likely that these people of southwestern Europe and the natives of distant Newfoundland had hit on the same word by coincidence. But assuming that the Newfoundlanders must, somehow, somewhere, have heard the word from Europeans – from fishermen who had been venturing farther and farther from home in their search for rich shoals – how long are we to suppose it would take those natives to drop the most important food name in their language and replace it with another? Or, if they still had their own word, how long would they be in learning another term for the same thing, well enough to use it interchangeably?

Is this a process that takes place within, say, six years – which would mean that bold Portuguese and Basque fishermen were actually crossing the Atlantic on business while Columbus was sailing on his voyage of discovery? Or within a decade, or a generation? I do not pretend to know. But if you care to make your own guess, and then subtract that number of years or decades or generations from 1498, then you may be able to determine when the forebears of Antoine Brava first were in America.

Chapter II
Admirals in Shirt Sleeves

THE TALE MAY BEGIN ANYWHERE – except at the beginning.

If Columbus had sailed the northern route across the Atlantic, he might have run across some of these men who were going westward to do business in great waters, and asked them then and there, "How long have you fellows been out here?"

Poor Christopher Columbus! They have even taken the egg away! They have made it known, those relentless, killjoy historians, that that little story of the upended egg "belongs to the class of migratory myths, having already been told of Brunelleschi, the great architect who built the dome of the cathedral at Florence," long before Columbus was born! Well, for the poor old Admiral's barrel-clad ghost, there remains at least one bitter-sweet reflection: These delvers, these Peeping Toms at the keyholes of history, who have so thoroughly discovered that he was not the real discoverer of America, have all been wasting their time; for each must learn in turn that somebody else has pointed out that fact before him, and now nobody can claim the credit for saying it first!

The question whether Columbus really ought to get the credit for discovering America flares and flickers as the fashion in hero worship waxes and wanes in this country, or alternates with the fashion of "debunking." But as a bone of contention it has been pretty well gnawed over, and I have no hankering to lay tooth to it.

Interested romancers and local chambers-of-commerce have placed, among the before-Columbus corners, Chinese missionaries in Mexico, Japanese junks in Oregon, Irish anchorites in Iceland, Portuguese explorers in Newfoundland, and those busy Norsemen at the end of every town landing from the Chesapeake through all points north. Yes, all before Columbus! Yet of only a few such callers is there anything remotely like proof, and to the world that sent them their visits proved nothing.

To Columbus, egg or no egg, one would think a little credit might be surreptitiously slipped for finding something worth having, even if he didn't know what it was. And in mentioning the chance that he might have run into a bunch of the boys out there on the Grand Banks, had he been going their way, my purpose is no more damaging than to point out that in the ventures of many men which led to the Great Discovery by one, the lowly fisherman did have a hand. And it was true of much other discovery, in the record of which he is seldom included. For our concept of exploration, as shaped for us by conventionally written history, only the climax is preserved; the galaxy of glorious names and significant dates shines on, and what might have been discerned in the shadows is left to lose itself there.

Fishing has ever been a dangerous business. Grand Banks fishermen, who lived by the hardest labor ever laid out for the hand of man, were not ones to give a thought to such matters as having their names set down in school textbooks. They were at sea to make a living, and they lived if they caught fish. Therefore they looked for fish, and for nothing else; and shores they may have seen many times were left for others to "discover." Time and again the matter-of-factness of these crews to all else than the haul in hand has mystified landlubbers. The incredible distances they went for their fish, the uncharted seas they combed, the storms they weathered – in a landsman's perspective, these are things that do not sit comfortably under the heading of "incidentals."

All men who go down to the sea for a living – not by discovering worlds, but by everyday business with the trawl, the hook, or the harpoon – have shown something of this trait. In the summer of 1820, two Russian warships ventured deep into the Antarctic on a voyage of exploration. Through floe-ridden seas they snaked their perilous route to the southward – south and still south – seeking a continent to claim for the Tsar. For if land were to be found, the first to see it could claim it for his country.

At last, from one of the ships a great cheer went up. Down near the bottom of the world, land – a new continent – had been sighted! But while it still showed only as a faint blue-penciling across the white of polar seas, a fog shut in over the Russians.

Rejoicing as they went, the battleships edged along in the direction of the land. But when the fog lifted, to their amazement, there near the shore, peacefully squatting at anchor, bobbed a little Yankee sloop!

CHAPTER II: ADMIRALS IN SHIRTSLEEVES

She was on no voyage of exploration. She had merely made a jaunt down that way after seals. And for some weeks she had been cruising in the vicinity – just "sealing." Disgusted, the Russians went home.

Two years later, James Weddell, English navigator, "discovered" Graham Land in the Antarctic. By this feat, he was set up as a minor success in the discovery business, and England mildly applauded. For it was construed to mean that the whole continent of Antarctica – for what it might be worth – was England's. At the time, England didn't really feel that the whole of Antarctica would cut much ice in world affairs, but it required nothing in the way of coast defenses and that sort of thing, so she accepted it as one accepts a birthday necktie.

Since that time, airplanes have been developed, science has knuckled along, and the world has shrunk accordingly. It has occurred to the great powers that an extra continent almost anywhere may come in right handy some day. And it remained for America to point out, in 1938, that a Yankee sealer – the same troublesome fellow who had sent two Russian battleships about other business – had been to Graham Land before Weddell. For the sloop's skipper, Captain Nathaniel B. Palmer of Stonington, Connecticut, had made maps of the place as he cruised about; and the maps used by Discoverer Weddell were those made by Sealing Master Palmer!

Shortly before finding that she was eligible to argue for the bottom of the world, the United States had learned there was also a continent at the top. In the summer of 1937, three Soviet aviators came around North Pole way, with the surprising report that where geographers had supposed only an ocean of ice ringed the Pole, there was land four hundred miles north of Point Barrow, last outpost of Alaska.

The American government got busy. As reported in the *New York Times*, early in 1938:

> The State Department was reticent in discussing the case, but it was learned that the Administration apparently acted quickly in attempts to verify the report, and if verified, may claim the land for the United States.

To "verify" such a report, for purposes of establishing claim, the United States must either send somebody up there or show that somebody has already been there. And if the State Department has any difficulty finding applicants for a mush over the frozen North, first to Point Barrow and then to the new-found land, it might be worth while to go back to our prosaic old seafarers again, and thumb through a few whalers' logbooks.

I don't know offhand whether any of the Americans or Portuguese who together carried on the Arctic whale fishery in its later years ever saw that continent near the North Pole. I do know that almost until the World War, the American fleet of bowhead whalers had its base at Point Barrow and sometimes spent two winters at a stretch in the surrounding ice; and that several of these vessels ventured even farther north, among them the *Grampus*, for example, which grubbed around from Point Barrow to Banksland in 1896. Banksland, seven hundred miles east of Point Barrow, is also two hundred miles farther north.

If I were the State Department, before I asked an explorer, however intrepid, to risk his skin on this uncomfortable mission, I should want to make quite sure no old New Bedford blubber boiler hadn't raised that continent years ago – just a-whaling.

Whalemen have been particularly annoying to great explorers. They were like the stagehand who misses cue and carries off the strong man's weights before the curtain has been rung down. Peary himself, after he reached the North Pole, was said to have been disturbed by the suspicion that a whaleman might have been there first, and just hadn't bothered about the place because he saw no whales. Roald Amundsen felt a little warmer towards them – and perhaps because of them – for when the Norwegian in 1905 ended the search of four centuries for a northwest passage American whaleships at work along the way cheered him on and gave him a handout when he needed it.

They were not only troublesome birds in the explorers' otherwise clear sky; they were early ones. Whalemen were poking alongshore in New England before 1660, and it was not many years later when they were making for the deep water. In 1727 the *Boston News Letter* reported many vessels fitting out on Cape Cod "to go a-whaling." Before 1750 they had worked through Davis Strait and learned their way around Baffin Bay. While the celebrated Captain Cook was making history for his country in the Pacific, men from the little Cape Cod village of Truro were catching whales for theirs in half a dozen seas. They had gone to the coast of Guinea in 1763; a few years later, they whaled off Brazil; and in 1774

Chapter II: Admirals in Shirtsleeves

they were taking a fling at the Falkland Islands. From Nantucket, as soon as the wars were out of the way, they rounded the Horn for the South Pacific. Setting down in their logbooks, without comment, the same distances that had made a world hero of Captain Cook, they crisscrossed the surface that he had only scratched – all incidentally to bringing back "the ile." The English, settling in Australia, huddled in a spot near where Sydney is now, and there they stayed. During the same period, Yankee whalemen settled Australia too – only they settled rings around the English, at innumerable spots alongshore.

It is only within the recent past that the United States government has shown an active interest in the comings and goings of these maritime trail blazers. Impressed now with the importance of the hundreds of islands in the great "Kingsmill Whaling Grounds" and in other vast reaches of the Pacific, and wanting very much to claim good locations for airplane bases, the American government has lately been curling up with musty old whalers' logbooks borrowed from the museums of Nantucket, New Bedford, and Salem. And it has found them very profitable reading indeed.

As a beginning, on March 5, 1938, an order was filed in the archives at Washington:

> By virtue of and pursuant to the authority vested in me as President of the United States, it is ordered that Canton Island, an atoll of coral formation, 50 to 600 yards wide and surrounding a lagoon about nine miles long . . . also Enderbury Island, 2.5 miles long and one mile wide . . . are hereby reserved, set aside and placed under the control and jurisdiction of the Secretary of the Interior for administration purposes.
>
> FRANKLIN D. ROOSEVELT.

Nobody knows when Canton Island was first found, or by whom. Whalers in the 1820's called it Mary Island, and Mary Balcout Island. But on March 4, 1854, the New Bedford whaleship *Canton* (Andrew J. Wing, master) ran on the reef during a gale, ground herself to pieces that night, and left her crew marooned on the barren atoll, where the heat "in the best procurable shade" was 135 degrees.

Captain Wing, who was a well built man of nearly two hundred pounds, arrived home some months afterwards, weighing just ninety. While he was recovering, his little daughter Annie made him tell over and over the story of that shipwreck. She was only four years old at the time, but it was a story that Mrs. Annie Wing White, past her eightieth birthday when the government claimed Canton Island, was not likely ever to forget.

The captain and his crew of thirty-three men spent a couple of days on the island. It was drier there than it was in the water, but that was the sole advantage it offered. The ship's stores, except the little they had been able to take out in a boat, were gone. But they patched up three boats; and limiting the rations to half a biscuit and half a pint of water to each man daily, they set out on a 3,800-mile trip to the Ladrone Islands. You may recall that Captain Bligh and the men who were set adrift by the *Bounty* mutineers traveled in their open boat 3,618 miles, and endured forty-six days of it. It was all set forth in the books and the motion pictures. On this longer voyage from Canton Island, the Yankee whaler and his crew were forty-nine days.

One part of the skipper's story that Annie Wing liked to hear was about Jake Johnson, a New Bedford Brava who was in the crew. "Bravas," part Portuguese and part African negro, were men from the Cape Verde Islands off the west coast of Africa which include the island of Brava. These Cape Verders were able sailors, and good whalemen, and they were also uncomplaining, satisfied with practically nothing at all. This was exactly the kind of men the Yankee skippers wanted, and Yankee vessels by the dozens put in at the Cape Verdes to recruit their crews.

Jake Johnson was obedient, so obedient that he "made a damned nuisance of himself." The Canton had a few pigs on board and, whaling voyages being what they were, there was ample time for replenishment of the supply without going ashore for more. But one day in a gale the old sow lost footing, rolled over on her litter, and crushed all but one little pig. If any were to be crushed, that particular little pig should have been one of them; for he took the run of the ship thereafter and, preferring the quarterdeck, improved his time mainly in getting between the captain's feet. The first time he was tripped up, Captain Wing passed it off. The second time, he swore. And the third time, he called Jake Johnson aft.

"From now on, it's your see-to-it that that damned pig don't get afoul of my feet again! I want you to watch him till the day he's butchered, and don't never let him out of your sight!"

"Yes, sir! No, sir! Yes, sir!" said Jake.

CHAPTER II: ADMIRALS IN SHIRTSLEEVES

In obeying orders to the letter, he was cursed by the third mate, cuffed by the second, and kicked by the first; but even when there was danger of crossing the skipper himself Jake kept his eye steadfast on the pig.

On the morning after the shipwreck, the little group stood helplessly on that barren beach, and scanned the waters for floating ship's stores. Unless they could find some of their own provisions, they would soon be desperate for food. Suddenly there was a squeal, a ripping and a popping of buttons, and then a cry from Jake Johnson. With his shirt-tail out, in panic he ran towards the skipper. He was chasing the little pig, and yelling as he went:

"Watch the feet, Captain, watch the feet!"

In its first researches, the government found about seventy-five islands which, like Canton and Enderbury, were definitely charted, named, or otherwise identified for the first time by American whalemen. In reporting the formal reservation of the first two, the *New York Times* said:

> Claims to other islands in the Pacific are in prospect in a broad move which, if carried through successfully, will mark the greatest overseas expansion in American history.

And "if carried through successfully," this expansion will be due not to the storied heroes who make advance contracts with radio broadcasters and follow them up with vast autobiographies, but to the putterings about of greasy little hookers in the Pacific, manned mostly by Portuguese, ships that whaled while the whaling was good, and then went into coal-barging and other such maritime small chores, until their seams started of old age and they were auctioned off as water-front junk.

This same tradition – the catch is the thing, let strange lands rise where they may – was probably old among fishermen on that undatable day when North American natives first heard the word *bacalhao*.

The Breton and Portuguese codfishers probably had no idea, years after they had been working in it, that this was a "new world." Columbus himself, after four voyages across the Atlantic, didn't know that; and when he died, in 1506, he still believed he had discovered a new route to Asia. These poor fellows, unlike Columbus, didn't even know enough to think they were going to Japan – and as long as they could catch enough fish to make a living out of it, I doubt if they very much cared!

On the wharves back home, therefore, such talk as may have been heard about new shores, strange people, far across the sea – any tales of this sort which they brought back may well have remained through the uncounted years as fishermen's yarns, tall stories for that ancient waterfront institution, the Liars' Bench. Governments of France, Spain, and Portugal were no more likely to consult their common seafarers on the lofty subject of geography than was our own government – before it had learned that it might profit from a study of those old whalers' logs. From their fishermen, rulers of fifteenth century Europe expected only fish and taxes.

One of the popular mental hazards which explorers of the flat-world era had to overcome in seeking support for their ventures was that "going-downhill" feeling one gets while watching a ship put out to sea. The vessel, hull-down beyond the horizon, does look as if she were out on a slant, and men were afraid that if they should slip too far, they would never be able to claw back: Ferdinand Columbus wrote that this was one of the reasons Portugal had refused to back his father's project of a voyage westward across the Atlantic. Wily King John II, after calling in his junto of cosmographers, turned Columbus down. But he had made notes from the sailing plans, and later he did send a ship out secretly to try it, starting from the Cape Verde Islands. The pilots, however, were scared out by this same prospect of sliding down so far they might never get back. Before they had left the islands very far behind, they wore ship and returned to Lisbon. Coasting voyages were all right, even when the vessel got out of sight of the land. But setting a course straight out to sea? Not for us!

Yet fishermen and whalers of Portugal had known their way offshore long before the era of exploration was launched by captains in the service of Prince Henry the Navigator, grand-uncle of this same John IL Whalemen had been working off the coast of Minho, Portugal, in the twelfth century, and probably earlier; and the codfishers, who had been in the business since no one knew when, had already found their way to Iceland – five hundred miles straight out to sea from the tip of Scotland!

Christopher Columbus would not turn back, because he had certain "modern" ideas about the shape of the earth, certain theories; but, more important for practical purposes, fifteen years before he sailed on his big voyage of discovery he had made a trip to Iceland. He embarked for that voyage at Bristol, which had been receiving cargoes of "stockfish" (cod)

Chapter II: Admirals in Shirtsleeves

from the Iceland fisheries, and though there is no record of the type of vessel that took him to the "island of Thule," it is not unlikely that she was a fisherman. The discoverer-to-be was only just out of his twenties then. If it was indeed a fishing vessel that took him, it is quite possible that he got in the way at times, and that he asked a great many questions. But that is no reflection on him; everyone who goes out with fishermen does that!

To those who care to read, books have made it clear that behind the shouting and the bell-ringing, the discovery of America had really been a long process, an evolution begun before Columbus was born, and that the voyage which ended triumphantly at Palos on March 15, 1493, was really an already written drama with the leading role left blank – waiting for the actor worthy of it.

But books have not made it sufficiently clear that there was an untheatrical, trumpetless first act of this drama, in which not even the secondary leads, the lesser lights of exploration, took part, an act which had for its props the fo'c's'les of humble little fishermen, and the homely craft of men whose only concern was to keep black try-pots aboil with the blubber of the whale.

Too often, I think, those who write history slip into the convention, time-honored in Shakespeare's day, of associating the great with the world of the great, and of dissociating them – retroactively if need be – from all else. If the man of humble origin do great deeds, he is made knight or admiral, to bring him into scale with his achievements. And once this correction is made, those who sing his praises also sing of his humble origin, for song is so much the better for that. But the fact that those who remain lowly and unnamed may still have had something to do with the great deed is disturbing, a note out of the harmony, and therefore stricken from the score.

Chapter III
Ghost Town

AT THE RIVER'S EDGE in Berkley, Massachusetts, stands a strange rock which is partly submerged at high tide. It is strange because, on a flat face which rises five feet and spreads eleven feet across, there are inscriptions which have kept Harvard University professors in doubt for more than two hundred years; and anything which can keep Harvard University professors in doubt for half that long is strange indeed.

Townsfolk and old-timers in neighboring Taunton used to call it the Dighton Wishing Rock, because originally the limits of the town of Dighton included it, and because the limits of Yankee credulity did not exclude the chance that wishes made over such mysterious markings might come true. When the town of Dighton changed its borders in 1799, the rock still kept that part of its name; but after some years in which it had failed to make good, people gave up their wishing pilgrimages, and now it is just the Dighton Rock.

About those strange markings, however, the archaeologists are still arguing. Some have said they are Phoenician; others say Icelandic, and think they recognize the old Norse touch. Still others, because they make out the numerals "1511," suggest that the carving was done by Miguel Cortereal, a Portuguese voyager, one of several known to have sailed for parts west almost on the heels of Columbus – though it seems to me that inasmuch as this Cortereal embarked from Portugal in 1502, the date on the rock would do about as much to count him out as in. Nine years, in the wilds of America of that time, would have been a long stay indeed for anyone who had not come equipped to settle.

At any rate, a President of the United States once saw a copy of the Dighton Rock inscription in Harvard's museum, and when he was told all the things it might be, he smiled and said, "No, those marks were just another sample of the scratch-pad drawing done by our own American

41

Indians." He had often seen the same sort of thing in the Virginia woods. He was quite sure it was only this and nothing more. And if what that President said wasn't the truth, then all the grade-school history books in America will have to be revised, which would be very hard on the taxpayers. Let us leave the rock to the Indians.

The luckless Cortereals – there were three early voyagers of this family who sailed, one by one, for America – definitely had a part in the opening up of the western world, but most of the story has been lost to us.

Just when the historians, in one of their more conciliatory moods, were approaching some working agreement on the question of exactly what Columbus had done and, whatever it was, whether he was the first to do it, a scribe of Lisbon suddenly threatened their paper world with a brand-new bonfire. Luciano Cordeiro, writing in 1717, and basing his argument on the record of an earlier chronicler of the Azores, stated pretty flatly that in 1463, a generation before Columbus, a Portuguese explorer had made the voyage to Newfoundland, had found the "land of the codfish," and then had returned to the Azorian island of Terceira, where he became governor. This man was João Vaz Costa Cortereal.

The transfer of the governorship of Terceira in 1464 is on record; but whether João Cortereal had really sailed to Newfoundland just before that event, we have no way of knowing now, and neither did the eighteenth century historians. The then weary pros and cons in the Columbus debate simply dismissed the whole story of Cortereal's voyage as based on insufficient evidence; and, so as to be spared their troubled speculations any further, by all means let us do likewise.

But the work of João Cortereal was carried on by his sons, and an important voyage was made by Gaspar Cortereal in 1500 – important because he lived to tell the tale, and because he had come back with fifty-seven natives as evidence. He had sailed to Newfoundland; then to Terra Verde, or Greenland; then to Rio Nevado, or Snow River, as he called what is now Hudson Strait; and then home.

The following year he tried it again, taking three ships. His own vessel failed to return, and the two that did reported that Gaspar Cortereal had stayed across to explore. Another year passed. Then Miguel Cortereal, his younger brother, took three ships and sailed to find Gaspar. Again two ships returned. Miguel was lost, too. Vasqueanes, eldest of the three brothers, wanted to go then, but the King would not give his permission.

Chapter III: Ghost Town

The fate of the brothers Cortereal was never learned, but the family retained a long-distance hold on the land they had sought to explore. A letter patent had been granted Gaspar, making him governor of "Terra Nova." In 1506 the King transferred this governorship to Vasqueanes, despite the fact that he had never been across the sea, and was not allowed to go thereafter. On the death of Vasqueanes, the right was passed on to his son Manuel, and then through later generations of Cortereals, until the temporary annexation of Portugal by Philip II of Spain in 1580.

Thus, before America was even a fond gleam in the paternal eyes of the French and British empires, the "New Land" was nominally under the rule, by royal grant, of a Portuguese family on a tiny island in the Azores!

Azorian sailors were shipped – whether they liked it or not – on many voyages of exploration. And, volunteers or conscripts, they made good sailors. When John Cabot undertook to cross the Atlantic in 1497, part of his crew had been recruited in the Azores – this despite the fact that there was no saltier town in England than "ould Bristow," Cabot's port of departure.

A reward had been posted, in the name of His Majesty the King of England, for the first who should raise land from Cabot's ship. And as the vessel neared the western shore, the first among her crew to cry the land was one of these men from the Azores. This fellow, like many who have followed him to the sea, had been a farmer. He knew a piece of land when he saw it, and when he saw it he yelled. After the welcome cry was given, the master of the vessel wished to present this lookout with the King's IOU. It was necessary to identify him; but Englishmen of that day were notoriously bad spellers, as the record shows; and when the master heard this Azorian name, doubtless he gave it up at once as a bad job.

Anyhow, the man was a farmer. In answer to inquiries, he had said "*Lavrador*," and he had made it clear that this was Portuguese for "farmer." And so, misspelled "Labrador," down it went on the record. And because the Cabots seem not to have been as insistent on naming things after themselves as some of our later explorers have been, they gave the land that name, too. On a map of the year 1534 appears the legend:

> Country of Labrador, which was discovered by the English of the port of Bristol, and because he who first gave notice of seeing it was a farmer from the Azores.

Although the farmer's name is forever lost, I think his spirit must rest content, for there remains this entry in the privy purse of King Henry VII of England:

August 10, 1497 – To Hym that found the New Isle, £10.

It is safe to say that he never earned £10 that quickly farming in the Azores.

The Cabots' *lavrador* was probably the only Azorian sailor to turn such a handsome profit in the discovering-America business, but he was not the only one engaged in it. Another entry in the royal account book, dated 1505, shows how the King settled up with some sailors from the Islands who had made a deal with him, and had gone to the "New-found-land":

To Portyngales that brought popyngais and catts of the mountaigne with other Stuf to the Kinges grace, 5 *l.*

But the fishermen in the rapidly growing Portuguese Grand Banks fleet were making much better money – without having to whip their weight in "catts of the mountaigne." Only a year later, in 1506, King Emanuel of Portugal detected pie in this business, and a pie well worth the royal finger. He therefore ordered "the fishermen of Portugal at their return from Newfoundland to pay a tenth of their profits" to the customs.

In spite of taxes, business on the Grand Banks went ahead by leaps and bounds. In 1500, a corporation had been formed by three towns, Vianna and Aveiro in Portugal, and Angra on the island of Terceira in the Azores. By 1550 the port of Aveiro alone, less than half the size of present-day Gloucester, was sending one hundred fifty vessels back and forth regularly over the two thousand miles of ocean to the Grand Banks; and from Oporto went a like number.

Thus offshore America was a busy place, a century before the much-marked travels of the *Mayflower* company on Cape Cod. On shore, the story dims and dangles tantalizing loose ends; but its beginnings, at least, can be retold here.

On the east coast of Cape Breton Island, near the northern tip of Nova Scotia, is the little village of Ingonish. Portuguese fishermen of Gloucester who today go "down to the east'ard" for cod and haddock often come

Chapter III: Ghost Town

ashore at that port. Four hundred years ago Portuguese fishermen from across the sea likewise made it their base.

In Vianna, one of the towns heavily interested in the old fishing fleet, a company was formed in 1521, was allotted a grant from the King, and sent two vessels to colonize the territory frequented by the fishermen. An account of this venture is given in a tract written in 1570. The tract was thought to have been lost in the earthquake that shook Lisbon into a pile of ruins in 1755, but it turned up again many years later. This is the *Tratado das Ilhas Novas* (Tract of the New Islands) by Francesco de Souza. After it was recovered, in 1877, it was published at St. Michaels, Azores. De Souza wrote:

> It will be 45 or 50 years since certain gentlemen of Vianna associated themselves together [that is, in 1525 or 1520] and according to information which they had of Terra Nova de Baccalaos, they determined to go to settle some part of it, as in fact they did go in one vessel and one caravel.
>
> But finding the country to which they were bound very cold, they sailed the coast from east to west. Then they sailed from northeast to southwest, and there settled. And having lost their vessels there, we have had no more news of them, except through the Biscayans, who are in the habit of going to that coast . . .
>
> These men give information that they had asked them to tell us at home how they were situated there, and that they desired priests to be sent to them – that the natives were mild, and the country fertile and good; as I have been informed otherwise, and as is known to those who sail thither. And this is Cape Breton, at the commencement of the coast which runs to the North . . .
>
> There were in the company some families from the Azores, whom they took on their way, as is well known.

But what happened to these people is not well known. When Champlain came to Cape Breton, he found "several harbors where they catch fish," among them Niganis (Ingonish). "The Portuguese at one time wished to inhabit this island," Champlain wrote, "and spent one winter there, but the severity of the season made them abandon their settlement."

There are a few other scattered references to that one-season stand, but more to the point are the hints as to where they might have gone, and what they did next. Richard Hakluyt, the geographer, wrote:

> This coast from Cape Breton CC leagues to the South West, was again discovered, at the chardges of the cardinall of Burbon, by my frende, Stephen Bellenger of Roan, the laste year 1583, whoe founde a towne of four score houses, covered with the barkes of trees, upon a river's side, about C leagues from the aforesaid Cape Breton.

When Sir Humphrey Gilbert crossed the Atlantic in that same year, he planned a stopover at Sable Island, a little more than a hundred miles southeast of the Nova Scotian coast. His reason for this was that he had been told "of a Portugal, who was himself present when the Portugals, above thirty years past [or some time before 1553] did put into the same island neat and swine to breed, which were since exceedingly multiplied. This seemed to us very happy tidings," he adds, "to have an island lying so neere the maine, which we intended to plant upon, such store of cattell, whereby we might at all times conveniently be relieved of victuall, and served of, store for breed."

Incidentally, while Sir Humphrey was at St. John's to claim Newfoundland for Queen Elizabeth, the Portuguese fishermen showed him kindnesses "above those of other nations." In a note on the "liberalities of the Portingalls," he tells how, upon his departure, they "put aboarde our provision, which was wines, bread or ruske, fish, wette and drie, sweet oyles, besides many other, as marmalades, figs, lymmons barrelled, and such like . . . In brief, wee were supplied of our wants commodiously, as if we had been in a countrey or some citie populous and plenty of all things." The incident, to one who knows the Portuguese fisherman of today, seems in character.

But of those early Portuguese and Azorian residents of America, we know only the bare facts:

That they came to settle in 1520 or thereabouts.

That after they removed from the uncomfortable settlement at Ingonish, where they had spent their first year, somewhere they built a town of eighty houses.

That they were still carrying on thirty years later, for at least some of them were busy at that time stocking Sable Island with cattle.

Chapter III: Ghost Town

The "towne of four score houses" was never found. In the little village of St. Peter's, however, on Cape Breton Island, there is a spot which the townsfolk have long called "The Pirate Fort," or just "The Old Fort;" and they have called it that only because they couldn't hit upon any likelier name. It was the remains of an earthwork, but neither the French nor the British had built it, and the people of St. Peter's knew of no others who had ever fortified those parts; hence the romantic but vague explanation – "pirates."

Acting on the notorious *non sequitur* that where there are pirates, there's buried treasure, a party went digging into the earthworks, about 1840. They didn't find any treasure, but they did come up with an ancient cannon. It was so corroded that it fell to pieces, but an examination was made of the fragments. According to the local keepers of records, it was a French cannon; and if it wasn't French, then it had no business being there, for the French were the only ones known to have built forts along that coast.

But the French didn't begin their forts on Cape Breton Island until after Nova Scotia proper had been ceded to England under the terms of the Treaty of Utrecht, which was not signed until 1713; and this ancient cannon, as described by those who saw it – hooped muzzle, breechloading – was of a type not used later than 1540. The only historical record that could reasonably explain its presence there is the reference to the vanished Portuguese town.

Dates are deceptive. Sometimes, in the march of the centuries, they need to be scaled alongside some mighty climax of the great continued story. Suffice it, then, to say that before the ship of Ferdinand Magellan had completed the first circumnavigation of the globe, a colony of his countrymen were making homes in America. The forebears of Antoine Brava, fisherman, were not only among the first to see the new land, after the Vikings; they were, as well, the first to try living in it.

Chapter IV
Land of the Free

London, January 9, 1898

DEAR FRIEND

Well, here I am in London, and am going to try to get a chance to come home on a steamer tomorrow. Myself and three other fellows ran away from the sch. [whaling schooner *Enola C.* of New Bedford] in St. Vincent and shipped on a cattle steamer, the *Horace*, for London.

The man that says anything to me about going on a whaling voyage again will get told to mind his own God damn business. No more for me.

Yours,

H. A. JACKSON

IN CHOOSING THE CAPE VERDE ISLAND OF SÃO VICENTE for his retirement from whaling, Mr. Jackson acted wisely. At that port, instead of sending an armed force after him and his companions, the skipper of the *Enola C.* would find it simple enough to fill their berths with Cape Verde Islanders; and in fact, because these "Bravas" made better whale-men than did the water-front floaters taken on in New Bedford, the skipper was likely to consider himself well rid of the deserters.

But the letter tells an old story. The four Americans were doing what thousands of others had done before them, often under less auspicious circumstances and sometimes at the risk of their skins. Desertions, in spite of guns and port police, were so frequent that recruiting was part of the routine duty of the whaling skipper, and calls at the Azores and the Cape Verdes were made regularly for that purpose.

Of all the hard-boiled industries man has created for the employment of his fellow man, only war and slaving have surpassed the pursuit of the whale. This hard-boiling point was fully attained by the New England fleet in the nineteenth century, and the man who could come through a whaling voyage with skin and bones all in their proper places was a man indeed. As the business grew, canny ship-owners of Nantucket and Cape Cod and uncanny ones of Boston and New Bedford perfected the profit technique, which combined slow starvation with brutality, and brought this treatment of foremast hands to a point that now seems fantastic.

It was not in terms of low wages or long hours that this technique soared into the realm of fantasy. There were no hours, no wages, in whaling, within the present meaning of those terms. Though the formal deck-watch system was followed, the crew was on call twenty-four hours a day, seven days a week. Working on a share or "lay" basis, the whaleman averaged earnings of from $3 to $8 a month; but because it was necessary to buy clothes and tobacco at outrageous prices from the slop chest – marine equivalent of the company store – few men saw cash at the end of a voyage.

Such trivialities as these would not have bothered the whaleman, certainly would not have driven him to run away in a penniless state, to wander through the streets of some foreign port, or through the jungles of some tropical island. Nor was he unwilling to assume the ordinary risks of faring to sea in a leaky old hooker, often too far gone to pass the insurance tests, or the extraordinary risks of the encounter ending in "a dead whale or a stove boat."

What did worry him, increasingly through the years 1830-1881, was an empty stomach or a stove skull. He was kept constantly hungry, and constantly in danger of having his head bashed in with a belaying pin. It is a side of the story that has not received much attention from armchair spinners of sea yarns who tell of the captain's lone-handed victory over plotting mutineers; even the nonfictionists generally fail to point out that, in all but a small fraction of mutinies on our whaling and merchant ships, there has been a single, unromantic issue – food.

An anonymous rhymester, having his fun with the old Yankee merchantmen, aims a shaft yet too frail to get under the skin of the whaleship owner:

> Old horse, old horse, how came you here,
> From Kennebec to Portland Pier?
> I've carted stones for many a year,
> Till warned by blows and sad abuse,
> I'm salted down for sailors' use.

In the case of the whaleman, it was not that he wearied, day after day, of eating "salt horse." He saw the salt, but where was the horse?

The legends built around "the Doctor," as the cook was known on board the whaleship, are too many for one chapter or one book. I choose to pass on one version of an old tale starring not the cook, but Captain Clothier Peirce, of the bark *Minnesota*.

They said in the countinghouses of Bedford port that Clothier Peirce was a pious soul – but that he should have been an "accommodation mourner," wailing for hire at lone folks' funerals. He had a face as long as a squally night off Cape Horn.

Alongshore in Bedford port, seafaring men gave his vessel, the bark *Minnesota*, a wide berth. She had just completed a "broken voyage" – no whales – and you wanted to look out for a vessel like that. A man might sign for a voyage on the *Commodore Morris*, say, and at least get molasses for his coffee, but all he could expect on the *Minnesota* was piety, blessed piety, and twice-blessed prunes. She was, in short, a "hungry ship."

But prunes, Captain Clothier Peirce had discovered, were a boon to the bowels. They were healthful; there had always been something peculiarly fine and moral about them; and good, God-fearing men ate them and were satisfied, gratified, and fortified. Perhaps that was why an openhanded Providence had seen to it that they were uncommonly cheap.

Nevertheless, able hands for the *Minnesota* were not to be had, for love or promises; and Captain Peirce sailed from New Bedford with a skeleton crew, calling at the Azores to make up the needed complement.

Providence had never been open-handed with the skipper in the matter of dispensing sperm whales, and so it happened again that the bark *Minnesota* rolled up long months of cruising without sighting a spout. More than ever, the captain spent his time in lamentation, in trying to wheedle Fate, in just daring his luck to break by producing one small whale; and in shouting to the gray Atlantic skies that he was quite sure it wouldn't.

The *Minnesota*, meanwhile, became a hungrier ship than ever. Her men were beginning to stare hollow-eyed at one another, and a Portuguese fo'mast hand kept seeing mirages and mumbling about *uma talhada de toucinho* – a rasher of bacon.

Although the keeping of the log was a job usually entrusted to the mate, Captain Peirce chose to perform this duty himself. In his doleful account of the voyage, these entries appear:

CHAPTER IV: LAND OF THE FREE

July 1 [1868] – No signs of LIFE here. Nothing for us. June has passed & we get Now wheir. No chance for us this season I fear, three seasons in the North Atlantic to get *One Whale* in this unfortunate Vessel – Barren Water. Nothing to be seen.

Men of the *Minnesota* that day were served one small portion of duff and prunes.

July 4 – Comes in with a Head Wind. Fresh breeze from E S E Heading about N E. Will the *Wind* ever change . . . This is the Fourth of July, a day of rejoicing with People at home: but a sad day with us. No Whales in the Ocean that we can find. (A Head Wind.) No chance to do anything or to ever get *One Whale*. The LORD'S HAND appears to be against the poor old *Minnesota* and all concerned in her. Will the Lord in his infinite Mercy ever ever suffer us to get *One Whale?*

Dinner that day on the *Minnesota* was limited to one cook's-spoon of lobscouse and prunes.

July 8 – Some lucky ship I fear has Boiled out the last Whale in the Atlantic. Captain Howland of the *Comm. Morris* I suppose.

Menu for July 8, one doughboy (dumpling made of flour and porpoise meat) and prunes.

July 16 – I am discouraged this voyage. The Hand of Providence is against us: I do not find any Whales. I do not expect to get *One Whale* this season. The Hand of Fortune is against us. Nothing for us I fear.

And nothing that day for the *Minnesota*'s people except one small slice of maggoty salt pork, and prunes.

October 28 – *I am about discouraged.* I think the ocean contains nothing that we can ever get. Not a Whale can I see.

On this day, only prunes.

November 14 – The Minnesota will not get even a Small Whale.

Prunes.

And thus things went from bad to worse, both for the poor old *Minnesota* and for her long-suffering crew, through Thanksgiving, Christmas, and to the end of the year. "Not one Whale," and prunes, prunes, prunes. Then, on January 1, 1869, the lookout suddenly rolled out the long, thrilling call from the masthead:

"Ah-h-h Blo-o-ow!"

The skipper's voice vaulted into falsetto as he shrieked orders at the mate. A boat was lowered, and Captain Clothier Peirce, afraid to follow her fortunes from aloft, waited and walked the quarterdeck. It was the first day of the new year. Did this mean that the Unfortunate Vessel was at last changing her luck? Ah, sweeter the thought than – than a Small Whale itself! But no, Providence was not going to suffer the poor old *Minnesota* to iron a whale. He was sure of it, the Hand of Fortune would cause the iron to draw . . . And then, from the masthead:

"Fast O!" (Boat has succeeded in getting an iron into the whale.)

"No!" gasped the skipper. "Look again, up there! It can't be so!" And he reached for his glass and scurried up the rigging to the foremasthead. "Well, bless my soul!" Not only fast, but there was the whale, already fin-out – dead! Turning towards the lookout on the mainmast, Captain Peirce cupped his hands and shouted:

"Fast she be, and blowed her last! The Lord in His goodness has seen fitten to forgive us our sins! Go down and tell the cook to put some prunes to soak!"

Next to being starved by the inch, the whaleman's pet dislike was being seized up by the yard. In that position a man froze or burned, depending on the latitude, and had his arms nearly rolled out of their sockets or benumbed to the point of paralysis, depending on the weather.

This and other punishments were meted out for any reason ranging from real misbehavior on the man's part to a pet grudge on the officer's. One skipper, having become enraged at a sick Portuguese cabin boy, is on the court record as having beaten the lad with a heavy rope until his face was unrecognizable. The boy's offense was that while he was at the helm, with a heavy sea running, he lacked the strength required to keep the vessel's head to the wind.

But bloody decks wash well in salt water. Cases were not often taken to court because the whaleman knew he couldn't win; and statistics left by the whaling industry lump all the figures that might have been of interest here under the simple heading, "Deaths."

To complain on these ships was to invite a "hazing." And the real terror of a hazing was not in the kicks and floggings a man got, but in his own well grounded fear that a little of this procedure would lead him, like a lamb to the slaughter, into "mutinous conduct."

Almost anything, from a whispered word to a scream of pain, could be interpreted as "inciting to mutiny," and that was dangerous business. "If any man in the crew of any American vessel on the high seas . . . endeavors to make a revolt . . . or conspires, or confederates with any other person . . . or solicits, incites or stirs up any other of the crew to disobey or resist the lawful orders of the master . . . or assembles with others in a tumultuous and mutinous manner . . . he shall be punished by a fine of not more than one thousand dollars, or by imprisonment of not more than five years, or by both such fine and imprisonment." Whalemen must have thought the framers of our admiralty law had a rare good sense of humor when they set the limit to that fine!

But a land of democracy clearly was poor training ground for fo'mast hands in New Bedford's whaling fleet. Sailors of the merchant marine bore their full share of ship's discipline in the old tradition, which could be traced back to the time of the galley slave; but the "bully captains" and "bucko mates" of the American whaling fleet hove tradition overboard and did their own pioneering in the field of human torture; and it was their achievements which in the end drove native New Englanders out of the whaler's fo'c's'le.

In the practice of their art on freeborn Americans, these officers had already mastered the fundamentals of slavery when circumstances opened up an opportunity for them in the actual slave trade. Using Medford [Massachusetts] rum for money, a man could buy negroes on the coast of Guinea at bargain prices, and sell them at tremendous profit to the South. It was a job these whaling masters were well fitted to handle, and many of them went into it permanently or took a flyer at it now and then. There is an old whaling chantey that goes:

    O Captain Ball was a Yankee slaver,
        Blow, boys, blow,

He traded in niggers and loved his Savior,
Blow, my bully boys, blow.

After the Civil War, Americans not only tried to desert the whaleships at the first port of call; they couldn't be induced in the first place to sign on for a voyage. It became difficult even to scrape up a skeleton crew in New Bedford, to take the vessel to the Azores or Cape Verde Islands for her complement. Owners therefore dropped persuasion for the shanghai system. And a fancy system it was. In its heyday, the waterfront had become a lively market for knockout drops, and the sailors' boarding houses were the sluiceways for a flow of "blood money." Men were put aboard the whaleships by "crimp gangs," whether they wanted to go or not; and the crimps were paid standard prices for doing the job. Bid and asked quotations generally met in a sale price of around $150; and years after the last black man had heard the gavel's rap in the South, white men were being bought and sold in Massachusetts, "cradle of American liberty."

But it was exclusively a market for "greenies" – men who had never been on a whaling voyage, and preferably men who had never been to sea at all. Able seamen were not wanted, and if by mistake the crimp gang should chance to include one of these fellows in a consignment, he was got rid of as quickly as possible. For experienced seamen knew too much. Some of them knew more about the technicalities of admiralty law than the whaling skipper did himself. They were aware, for example, not only that it was illegal to buy free men off to sea, but also that the law set certain limits after the ship had left port. There were certain kinds of murder that even ship's officers could not commit. Many of these experienced sailors, these "sea lawyers," knew such fine points of the law, and one of them could corrupt a whole crew. They were damned nuisances. And so, they were put ashore.

As for the greenies, once spirited away to sea, they were rushed through their education – or through the remainder of their existence.

The necessity for adopting the shanghai system in New Bedford merely to get men for a skeleton crew may suggest how far democratic America was from a Yankee whaling captain's idea of Utopia. He loved his country, he believed that men should be willing to die for its principles – as he interpreted them – and occasionally he saw to it that they did. But America

Chapter IV: Land of the Free

was not the place to find men who would work hard enough and eat little enough to suit the owners of these whaleships.

In time, it became apparent that there were places where such men could be found. There were places in the world where people were so oppressed that what they had heard about America made that country seem like heaven itself. There were distant colonies of European nations, places where imperialism was keeping alive the old traditions of serfdom and absentee ownership of the land. There were poor people who had been paying heavy taxes so long that they were used to starving. There were young men, among these provincials, who were destined for military conscription and discipline in far-off army barracks of the mother country, and who would be forced to fight the battles of a nation they could not look upon as their homeland. And it was for such men – the oppressed, the desperate, ready to take any avenue of escape from the life that lay before them – that American whaling captains had employment.

I do not mean to depict a New Bedford skipper, sitting before a map of the world and searching it for rotten spots. Doubtless he was unaware that these were what he needed. But when he chanced to drop anchor in such a port, recruiting was inevitable. And these captains were not long in discovering in the Portuguese island colonies a rich source of just the sort of labor they needed. For one thing, the islands were close to the whaling grounds in the east Atlantic where Cape Codders and Nantucketers had been at work through much of the eighteenth century; and more important, the people of those colonies had been living under precisely the conditions that would render them fit material.

In the Azores, every boy faced exile at the age of sixteen for a term of eight years of military service in Portugal – nine hundred miles across the sea. Every farmer's cash income, no matter how small, was taxed almost to the point of confiscation by the mother country. Even the tithe system, which other peoples had found burdensome, would have been welcomed here as a blessing from heaven. And finally, on these nine tiny islands which the Portuguese and Flemings had settled four hundred years before, there was now a need of living space. As against a population per square mile averaging about 88 in Europe, they were more than 300 and still increasing – which is not surprising when you know the Portuguese.

As early as 1820, American vessels were taking on men and boys from the Azores and Cape Verde Islands. Most of these early fugitives continued as whalemen, even after they had disembarked in America from their first voyage. This was especially true of the Cape Verders, who were superior sailors and quickly rose to the rank of "boat steerer" or higher.

But within another twenty years, escape from the Azores via American whaleship, now on a much larger scale, had a new objective. Instead of running away merely to spend the rest of his life on board the whaling vessel, the young Azorian saw his chance to settle in America, to make his home there. Some had already done that; and a few had even come back to the islands, with grand tales to tell of America. You could make a living as a fisherman, or in the mills of New England, or you could go out again on the whaleships. Fishing was hard work, but you got something for it – you could *eat!* And you could "get ahead," for the first time in your life; you could save your money, buy yourself a home, and send for your sweetheart, or your wife.

Still using the whaleships as their means of escape and transportation, they began coming over in scores during the 1840s, and in hundreds during the next few decades. Thus through a channel unique in the story of immigration to America, a route few other Europeans would have chosen or endured, was begun a major movement into this country.

Later there were packet and steamer lines from the Azores and the Cape Verdes to New England ports, and thousands came on those vessels. But it was back in the 1840s, when migration by whaleship had got under way in earnest, that the names of Silvas and Souzas, of Costas and Silveiras, began to show in numbers on the town records of New England ports – making homes in America; and straight through, from that time to the end of whaling as a New England industry in the 1920s, ships of New Bedford continued to bring these islanders in "before the mast."

New England has left to us a low opinion of the "furrin" crews that manned her whaleships in the industry's later days. Among writers of our maritime history, "dregs" seems to have been the favorite descriptive term for these men.

"As the better types of Americans forsook the fore-castles," one of these historians explains, "their bunks were filled by criminal or lascivious adventurers, by a motley collection of South Sea Islanders known as Kanakas, by cross-breed negroes and Portuguese from the Azores and the Cape Verdes, and by outcasts and renegades from all the merchant services of both the Old World and the New."

Chapter IV: Land of the Free

The information was not plucked out of thin air by this and other writers who have passed it along; on the contrary, they got it from a first-hand source – the voluminous writings of retired Yankee whaling skippers.

CHAPTER V

Ports of the Grand Bankers

NEXT MARCH, below the seven hills of Lisbon, a galaxy of sail will whiten the river Tagus. Crowds will line the waterfront of the sophisticated old capital, and the talk will be of such matters as the grace of a schooner, the tall perfection of a bark; sometimes it will be of tides and gales and Newfoundland fogs; and sometimes of the hardiness – and the foolhardiness – of men.

It is farewell to the *bacalhoeiros*. Farewell to the cod-fishers of the North Atlantic. And on this Sunday afternoon, a small boat weaves out from the cluster of steamers and everyday craft in the Tagus, to ride in view of the thirty or forty large sailing vessels which make up the fleet of the fishermen this season.

As the little boat loses way, there is silence over the water. A glittering figure in cloth-of-gold cape and golden miter rises, faces the fleet, stands with arms uplifted; and then, for the men on board these vessels which are going to spend the next six to eight months on the distant Grand Banks of Newfoundland, God's watchfulness is asked.

They are poor, the men in these crews. None but the poor would go out to what lies ahead for them. And they go knowing that some will not come back. Much is left to chance, but that much is certainty.

As the crowds witness this farewell across the water, as they watch the figure with arms raised, there is silence alongshore too. Afterwards, there will be those in the crowd who will remember that the whole proceeding is merely a studied pageantry. But they will speak of it so only when they have blown their noses and blinked the moist shine from their eyes.

From the hill topped by the old white-lace tower of the Belem Monastery – the hill where Vasco da Gama once prayed to God for his own safe return – Lisbon watches the fleet slipping down the nine miles of broad river, and out to sea, as she has watched her fishermen long ages before da Gama.

CHAPTER V: PORTS OF THE GRAND BANKERS

Time was when hundreds of tiny vessels – small fry beside Columbus's *Santa Maria* – were needed to supply the home market with *bacalhao*. But a season on the Grand Banks was a hazardous undertaking for such craft, and a steady demand was not enough to keep them steadily on the job. There were long periods when capital at home was too scarce for this speculation, and it was left to the big French fleet from Saint Malo, and sometimes to the Yankee schooners from Provincetown and Gloucester, to keep Portugal in salt cod.

The last such interruption ended in 1885. On resuming their voyages then, the Portuguese Grand Bankers fitted away in fewer but bigger vessels than they had ever sailed before – bigger, even, than the Yankee schooners and French square-riggers with which they would have to compete.

Until 1902, there were only twelve such craft in the Lisbon fleet, but their capacities ranged up to 7,000 quintals – 784,000 pounds. They operated under close supervision of the government; and then, as now, the owners constituted a fish trust, shielded by the government against all competition. On imports of codfish caught by others, a duty of $2 per quintal was imposed. The price was kept rather high, around $12 a quintal, or nearly 11 cents a pound. But rich and poor paid it, for the fifty-two Fridays were only the beginning of a meat-lover's troubles in Portugal. Gross profits in *bacalhao* were correspondingly large, but the shipowners were obliged to let the government share in them, as they had been since the year 1506.

To keep down competition, a peculiar rule was enforced, limiting the fleet to the twelve vessels then engaged, and further stipulating that should any of these be lost or scrapped, no new craft were to be admitted to the fishery in their stead. But alterations were allowed; and as the business grew, the owners merely increased the size of the ships they had. In time, they had worked out their own interpretation of this law, to the point where they were building practically new ships around little pieces of the old ones. When a vessel was wrecked, if a single plank or other fragment could be salvaged, that piece was "the vessel," and she was rebuilt around it! And that was all right with the government.

For the season of 1902 the ban on new craft was lifted, and from that time on the fleet has gradually been enlarged. In recent years, thirty-odd vessels have been sailing to the Grand Banks from Lisbon alone.

These vessels of today are larger and better found than the old-time craft. They are iron ships, three- and four-masters, costing more than $100,000 each, and they can carry fares of better than a million pounds. They are sticking to sail, but they can make the long voyage in three weeks or less, and some have crossed in less than ten days. Below, they have staterooms and baths – for their officers – which the skippers of our democratic little Gloucester schooners would regard as plain sinful.

But aside from these few trimmings, they are fitted out strictly for business. Each is equipped with a fathometer – the electric depth-finder that does away with the laborious business of lowering a sounding lead and hauling it back by hand dozens of times a day – and each has radio transmission.

Along with the *bacalhoeiros* is sent a government-supported hospital ship, with four doctors and all essential equipment on board. With more than two thousand men to look after, she is one of the busiest craft in the fleet. Both Portugal and France have supplied these hospital ships for many years – a safeguard which, it may be noted, our own government could not be prevailed upon to finance for its fishermen through nearly two centuries – despite the fact that on the Grand Banks these men were nine hundred miles from home.

Meeting the Lisbon fleet off the, coast of Newfoundland in March will be other vessels from, the homeland – from Aveiro, Figueira, and Oporto. And in each of these ports, the ancient ritual of the robed figure will take place as the home port bids them, *"Boa viagem, boa pesca! Que Deos va convosco!"* (Good voyage, good fishing! And may God be with you!)

Coming "home" to New Bedford on a whaleship, the young greenhorn from the Azores, who had never seen New Bedford or any other American port before, found himself standing at still another great crossroads of life. There new paths met – landways and seaways – and from there they spread again to the far corners of this new world. Having broken away from the home of his childhood, and from everything which that life had meant, he was now faced with another big choice. It was, a little bewildering.

From here, he might follow his shipmates from the Cape Verde Islands, back to sea on the whaler. Or he might go, as thousands from his own Azores were doing, to California to hunt for gold; or, as other thousands, to Lawrence, Lowell, or Fall River, to work in the mills. Or he might go

Chapter V: Ports of the Grand Bankers

back to the work of his forefathers, the fishermen, men of the ancient *lugres bacalhoeiros*. He might go, as they did, to the Grand Banks of Newfoundland.

Long before the revival of the Lisbon fleet in 1885, Portuguese fishermen had been working the Grand Banks from this side of the Atlantic. Provincetown and Gloucester were both lively ports for salt fish, and during this interval cargo after cargo went out from Gloucester, the curing center, for Bilbao and Lisbon – cod to the country of the codfishers!

The sixty big Grand Bankers in the Provincetown fleet – "high liners" of the New England fishery of that day – were manned largely by Portuguese, men from the Azores, who had come to Cape Cod as whalemen and then had shifted into banks fishing. When Portugal decided to send a fleet of her own to the Grand Banks as of old, she had neither schooners nor men to sail them. And so, curiously enough, she had to go shopping around in Cape Cod ports for both!

Most of the dozen vessels that were bought for this new phase of the Old World fishery were former Yankee schooners. Of three owned by a firm in Figueira, two were ex-Yankees. The *Julia II* had been the old *Carrie D. Allen* of Wellfleet, Cape Cod; and the *Julia III* had been the *B. F. Sparks* of Provincetown. In command were several men from the Azores, who had trained in America; and Captain Manuel Rogers, one of these islanders who had been taking out Grand Bankers from Provincetown for years, went to Lisbon to serve as "fleet-master of the *bacalhoeiros*."

So thoroughly "rebuilt" that they were not even recognizable as former Yankee schooners, these big Portuguese three-masters would run up the coast occasionally to put in at American ports for repairs. A correspondent for the *New York Journal* was in Provincetown in July, 1901, when the *Julia II* sailed into the harbor.

There she was – a storybook ship in Cape Cod's storybook harbor! An old Yankee fisherman turned Portuguese, there among Portuguese fishermen who had turned Yankee!

> With blue and white national ensign pulling at her mizzen pennant halyards, and thirty swarthy wearers of sash and skullcap on deck, the big deep-sea schooner was a sight to draw a crowd to Railroad Wharf in this little village today.
>
> And from the west end of the little village came many an onlooker in

that crowd who could exchange greetings with those "wearers of sash and skullcap," and who went aboard to swap yarns of the Grand Banks.

At about this same time, while Provincetown was still sending its own big schooners to the Grand Banks, a newspaperman from remote Chicago stopped there for three days. He was on his vacation, but so mightily had the town impressed him that he had to let himself go in a piece for the paper, which was the *Tribune* of that city, and from which I quote:

> The people wear quaint and primeval garbs, and the whole town is begirt by flakeyards [for sun-curing codfish] which "sweeten" the air for leagues around. The mighty power that gives life to everything and pushes the wheels of industry along is fish . . .
>
> The main business street is paved with rock cod. The women use the hind fin of the giant halibut for brooms; they are secured to poles, and sweep as clean as the best corn brooms in the market. Awnings shading the store fronts are made from the skin of the sportive porpoise, skillfully tacked across light scantlings . . .
>
> Sunday I sought respite from the everlasting display of fish by going into the little gray church on the village sandlot. As I entered, I was struck by the peculiar appearance of the bell-rope swinging in the entry. I examined it. It was made of eels, cunningly knotted by some old sailor. Over the altar was a picture of a whale, under which was the legend of Jonah's sea voyage . . .
>
> At the close of the session a collection was gathered, and the receptacle passed around was the top shell of a turtle, with a whalebone handle. After the choir had sung "Pull for the Shore," the church crew passed down the port aisle, into the street . . .
>
> Provincetown ladies trim their hats with the red gills of the mackerel, and confine their long tresses with small sculpins. Minims are used in place of clothespins. These dwarf fishes are smoked and cured like herring, and their mouths are snapped around the clothesline supporting the week's washing and secured in place by the sharp claw of a crab.
>
> Flying fish are as plentiful around the village as English sparrows on Boston Common. They roost in the branches of trees and caw like crows. Dogfishes often lie around on the shore at low tide and bark and howl in a frightful manner . . .
>
> Lobsters make intermittent incursions through the lanes of the

town. Some of them are intelligent, and learn to follow children along the dusty roads to school . . .

And so on, down the columns, for the consumption of Chicago's freshwater populace. This piece came to my attention because an irate old Provincetowner had clipped it, pasted it in his scrapbook, and headed it himself: "A Damned Liar's Description of Provincetown."

But the inlander was exaggerating less than he thought. In those days, when a hundred schooners, Grand Bankers and others, could be counted riding at anchor in the harbor, fish was indeed a "mighty power."

Provincetown was referred to as "Cape Cod" by her neighbor towns on the peninsula, and boys and girls of the villages of Truro and Wellfleet used to sing out this taunt at the Cape-enders:

> The Cape Cod girls they have no combs,
> They comb their hair with codfish bones;
> The Cape Cod boys they have no sleds,
> They slide downhill on codfish heads.

I don't know how well the combs and the sleds performed, but I do know that Provincetown youngsters used to carry around bits of a delicacy known as "skully-jo," which was a kind of dried fish, cured until it was very hard, and that they munched on this as children of other places ate candy – only it was said of skully-jo that the longer you chewed on it, the more you had. And if you ever lost or mislaid it, you could buy a new piece almost anywhere in town – including the hardware store.

The old town hall, which stood on Provincetown's only big hill, had a cupola which could "berth six lookouts." Until 1877, when it burned down, this cupola was a fine vantage point for those who were anxiously awaiting the return of the Grand Bankers. From there one could look far out to sea off the Back Shore. The cupola was kept locked, but citizens could rent keys at an annual fee.

In mentioning the fish flakes that sweetened the air for miles around, and in letting it go at that, our Chicago satirist was bearing down very gently indeed on Provincetown. Times have changed, and so has the air; but back in those old days the smell of fish in that village was no joking matter.

But the inland scribe was a little ungracious, I think, when he took refuge in the fishermen's church and then proceeded to make fun of it –

not because of what he chose to say about it, but because he omitted to mention the fact that this church was built out of the hard-won earnings of Portuguese fishermen who wanted a place of worship and who volunteered a percentage of the receipts from each voyage they made to the Grand Banks. Starting in 1870, one of the first duties of every Portuguese skipper on his return from the Banks was to go up the winding hill on Prince Street, bearing the donation from himself and his crew. For three years, until the little church was built, none failed in this.

Forty-eight "captains courageous" were commanding Grand Bankers out of Provincetown in 1877. Of these, six were Yankees, thirty-three Nova Scotians, nine Portuguese. There had been a large influx of Nova Scotians earlier in the century. They had their own salt-cod fleets out of Halifax, Lunenburg, and Cape Breton ports, but they flocked to Gloucester and Provincetown because the American vessels were paying off in gold during periods of currency inflation, when greenbacks went as low as 72 cents.

By 1885, when a dozen more Grand Bankers had been brought into Provincetown's fleet and the industry was in its heyday, most of the skippers were men from the Azores, and their countrymen kept coming over to fill up the crew lists.

"This was a great town then," one old Nova Scotian, commander of eleven vessels in his time, told me. "There was a sailmaker and blacksmith on every wharf, and calkers, painters, and riggers galore. You wouldn't be here six months when the townspeople would have your weight and measure. If they found you were a right man, they didn't care where you hailed from, and they'd kick you to the front as fast as they could."

Apparently the Portuguese were "right men," for within a few years they had gained command not only of the dwindling Grand Banks fleet, but also of the town's up-and-coming fresh-fishermen. Of their career the local newspaper in 1894 remarks:

> In model, rig and fishing methods, our fleet conforms to the fleets of other fishing ports, but in the matter of crews it is strikingly different. Other fleets are sailed by men of all nations, no one race predominating largely, but the Provincetown fleet is manned almost exclusively by Portuguese.
>
> A great and marvelous change from former conditions in this respect is apparent. In former years, men of American birth,

principally, formed the crews, but the sons of the Azores, coming here on whaleships, sent tidings home that induced others of their people to embark for the "land of the free," and today men of Portuguese birth or extraction have superseded men of our own nationality in the business.

Captains and crews are all, or nearly all, Azorean, and from a mere handful in 1840, the Portuguese population has increased to upward of 2,000 souls in 1894. Not all of these are natives of the Western Islands; a large portion were born here. But born in America or the Azores, they take kindly to the sea, and make excellent fishermen.

The article, written by a Provincetowner with the good old Yankee name of Swift, goes on to say that by nature, the Azorian fisherman "is not quarrelsome, though he is, by habit formed on his own wine-bearing islands, a lover of the cup that cheers. Wines and spirituous liquors do not dispose him to brawl and riot, but seem to make his sunny disposition more mirthful and merry." And while such generalizations are not always safe, to one who has gone to sea with these men and lived among them ashore, this seems fair enough.

The Grand Bankers of Provincetown always fitted out for four or five months and always hoped the trip would take them two. The season began in April or early May, and as soon as the vessel had "wet her salt" (used up the 150 barrels she had brought along for salting down the fish on board) she would go home. Then if there was time enough, she would make another trip. At the end of the season she would haul up for painting and repairs and then set out on other chores until the following spring, sometimes shipping oysters to New York, other times chartering out to New York or Boston people for the West Indies trade.

Unlike the fresh-fishing fleet, the Grand Bankers paid their men fixed sums per trip. There was no share system in this branch. The skipper sized up his man and told him what his pay would be on that voyage; and good voyage or bad, the owners settled in that amount. Good men, veterans in the salt-cod business – or reputedly lucky ones – sometimes drew the top wage of $300 a trip; the majority went for $150 and up, and occasionally down.

A vessel flying Old Glory, signal that she was coming home with a full fare of salt cod, would gross anywhere from $9,000 to $16,000, of which the crew received between $3,000 and $4,000. As against this prospect, there were the rather large risks of a "broken voyage," or even of a lost vessel; but for the man in the crew, as against his top wage of $300, there was the equally large chance of a lost life.

So much for Provincetown as a port of the Grand Bankers, where our young Azorians might go and find men speaking the language of his homeland, toiling in the way of his people. In Gloucester, the scene was different. There the fleet, although dominated by "old-stock Yankees," and generously salted with Nova Scotians, was indeed "sailed by men of all nations." Until the big mechanized beam trawlers captured the industry for Boston, this Cape Ann town held its place as the leading fishing port in America; yet the Portuguese community of Cape Ann was never as large as that of Cape Cod.

Even so, that steep rise of ground overlooking Gloucester Harbor which on old maps was designated "Lookout Hill" came to be known before 1870 as "Portygee Hill." Men from the Azores, coming to New Bedford, were moving on to take their places among the Gloucester fishermen. By 1880, rows of homes owned almost exclusively by Portuguese fishermen lined the streets newly laid out on Portygee Hill. And before 1900, men from the isands were commanding schooners out of Gloucester for the Grand Banks.

There have been nights in Gloucester, so the old-timers say, when a man could "walk across the harbor to Rocky Neck on the decks of fishermen at anchor there." Older than the Boston & Maine Railroad which spurs down on Cape Ann is the assurance given the traveler that he will recognize Manchester-by-the-Sea and Gloucester-by-the-Smell.

The Gloucester fleet in the eighties varied between four hundred and five hundred sail. They went for mackerel, cod, haddock, and halibut, and they went amazing distances for them. In the spring, the seiners sailed south to meet the great schools of mackerel as they showed up annually off the Jersey shore, and to tag along as these fish did their regular "coasting," all the way to the Gulf of St. Lawrence in the fall. For haddock they went to Georges, La Have, and Western Banks, and for cod to all those places and the Grand Banks.

The halibuters, who brought home "fletches" (salted strips of the fish, ready for smoking), worked a great deal on the Grand Banks. They went to Greenland too, where they were nineteen hundred miles from home; and for a number of years Gloucester also had its "Iceland fleet" of halibuters, working twenty-seven hundred miles away! Twenty miles offshore there, and disconcertingly near the polar ice pack, they would mingle with the Danish, British, and Norwegian codfishers, and with the two hundred to three hundred fishing smacks from Brittany which made two trips each season to those grounds.

In August, 1895, the local fleet wasn't doing so well off the Iceland shore, and most of the vessels turned back for the eight-hundred-mile jaunt to the Greenland grounds. Their activities were reported in *The Fisherman*, a Gloucester publication of the day:

> Fishing on the coast of Greenland has proved very unsatisfactory the past season. Halibut were very scarce, none of the vessels having obtained a full trip. The presence of a Danish man-of-war, destroying a large part of the provisions of two American schooners, the *General Cogswell* and the *Mary E*, without warning after permission had been given by the governor to land, has made it harder still, and seems unwarranted. There is no doubt but that the coming of the American fishermen to that coast brings many luxuries, and that they are gladly welcomed by the natives.

Judging from what is said to have gone on in Greenland, I have no doubt that the Americans were welcomed by the natives, but there are serious doubts as to whether all the things they brought to that coast were luxuries.

Not only was the Greenland fishery highly speculative as a moneymaker, but those who tried it ran into the added danger of getting iced in for the long winter. The bark *Serene*, arriving in 1895 at Philadelphia from Ivigtut, reported discovery, in a small cave on the southwest coast of Greenland, of the bodies of eighteen fishermen. A year before, the schooner *Ambrose H. Knight* had left Gloucester for the Greenland fishery with a crew of eighteen men, and had not been heard from.

"Home" for the men who worked off the Jersey shore, and for those who went to Cash's Bank and the Bay of Fundy, or to Georges and the Western Banks, or on "down to the east'ard," to "Queero and the Grand," or to Greenland and Iceland – "home" for all these was the thronged wharves of Gloucester Harbor. "Home" was inside the "Dog Bar," where it wanted a sharp skipper to thread his way without collision even in broad day, and where by night the deck lights for crews who were dressing their fish looked like a torch procession all the way to Eastern Point.

A motley town it was. There was a time, not so long ago, when the unblushing local historians of New England regarded a "foreign element" at best as something useful in rounding out the progress of the Yankee population. Squeamish pens have touched only lightly on the Nova Scotians, and still more lightly on the Portuguese, of Gloucester.

With these Nova Scotians, who were themselves a line of many odd strands; and with its Portuguese, Irish, Newfoundlanders, Icelanders, Swedes, Norwegians, Finns, and later its Italians; with its generous sprinklings of half a dozen other nationalities that were constantly finding their way to those wharves from one fishery or another, the waterfront in that period was one of the most cosmopolitan spots in the world. And Gloucester's waterfront was Gloucester.

When the fleet was lying over and the work was finished on board, the men came ashore. Most of those who had homes went there; but on nights when two or three hundred vessels were in port, several times that many "floaters" and boarding-house customers were ashore, improving the precious hours in ways that kept an unsympathetic police force in a grim whirl, and an equally unsympathetic clergy in a pious dither. The Gloucester lockup after the Civil War embraced schools of fishermen rivaling the mackerel in Cape Cod Bay – though the offenses that had landed them there were mostly against the dignity of the police force rather than against that of the law.

Looking back through the newspapers of the time – dead serious though all such chronicles were – one suspects that the fishermen crowded into those cells were really not much more sinister than a bunch of youngsters suddenly let out of some overlong confinement. But the forces of law and order in Gloucester, if they suffered from a swollen sense of dignity, were not overburdened with other sensibilities. Almost anything was jailworthy if a fisherman did it.

For many years the town was "dry;" but this dryness appears to have served mainly as a blotter to soak up the wash of a smudgy political machine. A bartender quoted in a Boston newspaper remembered "those palmy prohibition days in old Gloucester," when he was kept hopping in a Front Street "recreation parlor" from six A.M. until midnight.

CHAPTER V: PORTS OF THE GRAND BANKERS

But many of the crimes that sent fishermen to jail were less heinous, less sophisticated, than drinking. It appears that when the return of any large part of the fleet was in prospect, "owners of fruit trees looked to this event with great apprehension."

When these men came ashore from their trips to the banks, they were hungry for fresh fruit. Some were even sick from the lack of it for months at a stretch. But mysteriously, as the fleet arrived, fruit prices in all the town's stores would go skyrocketing. Gloucester, fattening on the fish these men caught, held back its apples and said there wasn't going to be any core!

Night marauders, home from the Grand Banks or the Greenland or Iceland fisheries, began taking apples where they could find them. They frittered away their earnings on tobacco and liquor and women (tobacco was an evil one quite properly mentioned in the same breath with liquor and "women") instead of buying good, wholesome fruit. Then they went out and stole; and thus Crime flourished in the fair city of Gloucester, until the *Cape Ann Advertiser* warned: "The citizens have rigged spring-guns under the fruit trees on their land."

The conglomeration which the banks fishery was unloading on Gloucester wharves led to some odd encounters. There is the little story, for example, of the Frenchman who, many years ago, was brought home by the schooner *Clara Friend*.

The vessel was returning from a Grand Banks voyage. Cape Ann looked pretty good after three months off the bleak shores of Newfoundland; and as the green hills of Gloucester hove in sight, you could have set down the heavenly gates, opened wide for the vessel just outside the "Dog Bar," and her skipper would have passed them by.

As soon as the *Clara Friend* was made fast to the wharf, the men jumped ashore and hurried their several ways home, forgetting all about the "Frenchie" they had on board.

From one of the big square-riggers of Brittany that was fishing on the Grand Banks, the fellow had jumped overboard, swum to the *Clara Friend*, and by signs made it known to the skipper that he would like to go along with him to Gloucester. There were probably good reasons why the poor devil wanted to get away, and the skipper nodded assent.

En route they had treated him as fishermen traditionally treat guests – with the simple kindness and generosity that so often takes landlubbers

aback and makes them feel a little ashamed of their own hard-boiled world. But to a fellow seafarer they were as informal as they were hospitable; and when the *Clara Friend* made port, in the excitement of getting home they had left him on the vessel – penniless, friendless, speechless.

The Grand Bankers, unless they had made quick trips, were not likely to be well provisioned on their return. Therefore when a market boat came into the harbor and tied up alongside the *Clara Friend* next day, her crew was a bit puzzled by the smell of something wonderful a-cooking on board this schooner just back from the Grand Banks. Half a dozen big Irishmen from the market boat came aboard and met the Frenchman down in the fo'c's'le. He had a stew on the galley stove – and what a stew!

With much bowing and gesturing, the stranger managed to convey his invitation to the men to join him at his table. They fell to at once.

"Tis a grand bit o' pot work, Larry me boy!" one of them sighed as he finished up and sat back to light his dudeen. "Sure it's the Frenchies that's hoigh loin when it comes to puttin' the sauce to a bird!"

"So do they, Pat," Larry agreed as he mopped up the last of his stew and swallowed his pusher. "But divil a bit kin I tell what kind of a bird it was! Do yer know, now?"

None among them recognized this bird from the taste. Then Pat turned to his host, talked much, motioned more, and at last made him understand the question before the house. The Frenchman smiled amiably, but unable to tell the company in words, went to the forehold and brought back what was left of "the bird."

"Howly Mither!" yelled Larry.

"Dear Jasus!" Pat groaned, as he made a dash for the deck.

They had partaken of Gineral Grant – most popular wharf cat on the Gloucester waterfront.

The Portuguese among those fishermen of old Gloucester were as sinful as any others. But because they had always been a marrying lot, and were generally happier among their children than among somebody else's apple trees, there were fewer of them loose on the streets.

In the year 1898, for which figures* are available, 9,896 Western Islanders were living in Massachusetts, and during the twelve months only four persons represented that group in the jails of the state. Statistics like these don't show how many ought to have been there, but the arm of the

American Statistical Association Records, Vol. VI, p. 327.

law in Gloucester seldom relaxed for anything except cash, and the same was true of Provincetown and New Bedford. As the fishermen seldom had cash, the statistics are likely to be fairly indicative. This ratio, of fewer than 5 per 10,000, was lowest for any ethnic group of any consequence in the state; but I shall not carry on through comparisons which might be distressing to the more race-conscious Yankees.

Chapter VI
Success Story

TONY MELÃO KNEW AMERICA. He knew it by heart. Long before he sailed for this country, the mighty little plowman of São Miguel knew all about it.

In the poverty-ridden valley of the Furnas, on the island of São Miguel, people had nothing, were nothing. Men worked from dawn to sundown for *dois tostões* – twenty-one cents – a day. The field a man plowed was not his own; neither was the corn he harvested. The house was not his, nor the cart, nor the ox. All he could call his own were his wife, his children, and the pig; yes, and sometimes he could be sure of only the pig.

Tony, stocky, stubby, and starry-eyed, didn't have a wife. But he expected to have one, and he could congratulate Clara on the uncommon good sense she displayed in being willing to wait for him. After he had gone to America and had done well – which should not take Tony Melão very long – he would send for Clara and marry her over there. Meanwhile, there was dreaming to be done; and to share a dream, one must put it into words. Almost every evening Tony would go for a stroll with Clara; he would seat her under an orange tree, and then gravely he would consent to tell her more about America.

America! It was a *big* place, this America, for *big* men – like himself. (To Clara, one did not have to stop and explain that a man's height was not the real measure of his bigness.)

But the land over there in America was *big!* In the fields, a man didn't waste half his day turning the ox at the corners. There was room, the farms spread out for miles. America was ten, *fifteen*, maybe even TWENTY times as big as all the Azores Islands thrown together! And with all that the people had over there, a man didn't have to think about such things as making too little money, or living in a house that was too little. No, there was *big* money, there were *big* houses, and while a man had these things and raised a *big* family, he could turn his thoughts to other things,

things these people of São Miguel were not even permitted to dream of! He could even own a clock.

Sometimes Clara would laugh when Tony talked of America, and sometimes she would pat him on the head, as if he were a small boy. But these were only little habits she had; Clara laughed at many things; and really, for a woman, she was surprisingly smart! She always listened; she wanted to hear about America as often – or almost as often – as Tony was willing to tell her about it. God knew, she was better than those others, the girls of the neighborhood, who were deaf and blind – like so many stones! – when it came to sharing a dream!

The neighbors were all, in fact, pretty much like that in the valley of the Furnas. When Tony Melão tried to tell folks about America, they had a way of shaking their heads and repeating to Tony Melão an old saying: *Quem conta um conto acrescenta um ponto* (Who tells a tale adds on a little).

They would agree that America was the best place. Many men of São Miguel had gone there already, and had sent for their wives and children; and a few had come back to visit the old folks, and to tell them how wonderful the new country was. But there was a limit to the things a man could expect, in America or anywhere else in this world. Not everyone could become a big landowner, or a great sea captain, living in a fine house and marching through the streets like an *heroe bravo*. Tony Melão's father was a poor man, like the rest of the people in the valley; Tony himself was a *trabalhador*, a laborer; and it was irritating to hear a poor man, son of a poor man, talk the way Tony Melão talked – yes, even of America!

The sunny-natured folk of São Miguel had a droll custom of attaching nicknames to their neighbors, odd nicknames which replaced surnames, and then of persisting forever after in the use of them. Once a family was thus nicknamed, the new name outlived generations, and in time the real name was all but forgotten.

Tony Melão's real name was Antoine Joaquim Souza. But once at a gay harvest-time gathering of long ago, Tony's grandfather was on hand for the pig-killing and the feast that went with it. It had been a good year. People were happy; and when people were happy they liked to talk of simple things. So it was, that evening at the long board piled high with the season's blessings; and so it happened that during the feast, someone

CHAPTER VI: SUCCESS STORY

pointed out the striking resemblance of Senhor Souza's head to the cantaloupes that were then gracing the table. Senhor Souza at once became Senhor Melão – Mr. Cantaloupe – and he lived to be Grandfather Cantaloupe to a houseful of little Cantaloupes – among them Tony Cantaloupe.

It would have taken heaven and earth to remove the name of Tony Melão in São Miguel. Many islanders had been unable to escape their nicknames even when they had crossed the ocean, and some were resigned to the probability that their immortal souls would have to carry these same names through the heavenly gates!

Not so the soul of Antoine Joaquim Souza. He was determined that the broad waters of the Atlantic should wash away forever this smear across his dignity, that Melão should never become Cantaloupe! When he came before the English-speaking agent for the whaling ships, he was ready with a deep-laid plot. He would not give the name, Tony Melão; and to cover up further, he would not even give his first name; he would use his middle name instead.

And so, when the question came, "*Que nome?*" Tony Melão braced himself and answered:

"Joaquim."

The agent studied a moment, and then, as he had done many times before, wrote down what he thought to be the nearest English equivalent:

"Joe King."

Tony asked for a copy of the name as it stood on the record. Later he learned that "King" was a fine name, the English for "*Rei.*" A very observant fellow that agent! Why, he was almost prophetic! Informed that no further personal attribute was implied in the name "Joe," Tony decided to drop that part, and go into the New World as Tony King.

When the day came at last to say good-by to Clara, Tony told her he had learned how to say his nickname in English – the new nickname, which he was taking to America – and he informed her gravely what it signified.

Clara told him again she would wait for him, and promised always to believe him when he said it wouldn't take him long. Then she laughed – a little – and said:

"*Boa viagem, Senhor — Keeng!*"

On June 12, 1887, whales were sighted by the schooner *Rising Sun*

75

(Thomas S. Taylor, master) of Provincetown, Massachusetts, cruising on the Charleston Grounds. She had been to Ponta Delgada, St. Michael's (São Miguel) for new hands; she had spent a few days at sea in drilling the greenies; and now she was on the whaling grounds, ready for business.

When sperm whale spouts were raised by the *Rising Sun*'s lookout for the first time on the cruise, the hearts of half a dozen young Azorian farmers collectively skipped a beat; they had already learned that whaling was risky business in which the most trivial mistake might draw a bone breaking blow with a belaying pin, so that now, with the big prize actually at stake, there was plenty of reason for taut nerves, shaky knees. The corn fields of São Miguel suddenly rose in retrospect, sweeter, than they had ever been before.

The youths stood silent at the rail, waiting for the commands they had learned to carry out in rehearsal, and hoping to acquit themselves at least well enough to get by without any more of those fearful beatings. But one among them, more eager than afraid, boldly climbed a few ratlines on the fore-rigging and scanned the horizon. It was wonderful, this whaling, thought Tony King! The Americans were wonderful! Even when they gave you a kick, they gave you a big one!

Look! The whale! Only a flash, Tony King got of him, and then the creature sounded, went under. But what a monster! *É possivel?* Could any living thing be so huge? And was it to be expected that men in tiny boats could row out to kill such giants? Ah! These Americans!

A few seconds later, orders came. The *Rising Sun* put over two boats, and Tony King was in the captain's. Some of the boys had to be reminded to grunt while they rowed – a practice they had been taught because it was conducive to hard rowing – but not Tony King. The way he was pulling on his oar, the grunts came naturally.

When the whale broke water again, not more than a hundred yards away, he was not only bigger than Tony King could have imagined any living thing; he was also the biggest "sparm" bull that Captain Taylor himself had ever seen!

While the whale lay placidly at the surface, the skipper's boat pulled up almost alongside. The skipper fired his bomb-gun. Down the big fellow went, with an iron deep in his in'ards. He took out a hundred fathoms of line. In a few minutes he came back, and lay dead-ahead of the boat, as if pausing to think over his next move. Meanwhile the mate's boat had

Chapter VI: Success Story

pulled up to help make the kill. When he was only about ten feet from the whale's side, the mate rose, bomb-lance in hand, and as the chance offered, drove the lance in, at the same time yelling:

"Starn all! Starn fer yer lives, boys!" And both boats raced to get out of reach of the deadly flukes.

But the whale made no last wild "flurry," as was to be expected at this stage of the game. This whale was different. Instead of lashing out at them with his tail, kicking up a great lather, and finally blowing out his life blood, he let himself down by the stern, until his body stood nearly perpendicular in the water. Then, in one mighty breach, he shot up, towered above the captain's boat, and fell backwards at it, as if he meant to crush it that way.

He missed his mark, but came down like thunder, sending clouds of spray around him and showering all hands. Both boats were nearly swamped in the wash.

Now, Captain Taylor had dealt with some wicked whales in his day, but never had he known a natural-born creature to carry on in this fashion. Never had he had any personal dealings with the Devil or any of his emissaries. The best thing was to row away like everything; and this he ordered his men to do.

But the whale wasn't through. On he came, in a fury, after the skipper's boat. And then, to quote Captain Taylor himself, "then was beheld the strangest sight ever granted to whalemen's eyes!"

The whale opened his mouth. The men, seeing him make for the boat directly amidships, crowded towards bow and stern. On came the gaping jaws. They slipped over and under the craft; and grasping it thus, as a trained dog carries a package, this brunette Moby Dick lifted boat, men and all, "to a height of twelve feet above the sea," and started jogging off! For the men, this was enough. They dived out. And a moment later the jaws slowly crunched on the boat, coming together as if there were not so much as a toothpick between them.

The second boat, standing by, took the men out of the water. But no sooner were all hands picked up than the whale started rolling back for another of his flying tackles. With what the skipper described as "sinister care," he placed himself, sank tail-first, and once more launched his body half out of water. As he crashed down, he missed again, but this time it was all the men could do to keep their crowded craft from capsizing.

While they were bailing out, the mate, who had kept a cool head, took aim with his bomb-gun; and just as the whale was about to try a third splash, he was finished off with a shot from that weapon.

"So ends," as whalemen used to say. And so, too, ends the strain, both on Captain Taylor's terrified men and on our own credulity. But here, in defense, I fly to the record:

Provincetown, Mass.

On this twenty-first day of May, in the year of our Lord one thousand nine hundred and three, before me, the subscriber, a notary public of and for the Commonwealth of Massachusetts, personally appeared Thomas S. Taylor, to me known to be a reputable and upright citizen of recognized veracity, who made oath in due form of law to the following statement, viz:

That this tale of the whale . . . is a true and accurately described account of one of my battles with fighting sperm whales

THOMAS S. TAYLOR

Sworn to and subscribed before me,

WILLIAM H. YOUNG, Notary Public.

[Seal]

But for Tony King, wonders did not cease here. At home, when a man came through anything like this with the breath of life still in his body, he hurried off to sell his pig and buy some candles for the church. But here – here these fellows thought nothing of it! Anyone who might have come back on board ship with ideas for holding a little celebration over the miracle of his escape would have had such notions booted out of him quickly enough. In fact, that very thing happened to Rodrigo, one of Tony's shipmates. Rodrigo, poor fellow, had paused on deck long enough to get down on his knees and breathe a prayer of thanks. That was a very unlucky position to be caught in.

For there was still work to be done on this whale – cutting in, mincing, boiling, stowing down, and the good God know what else! From one thing to another they went, these Americans, from danger to drudgery, from death on the water to toil on the deck, all in stride, part of the day's work! And Tony King, for all his haste to obey orders that were being barked about now, had to pause long enough to grin, and shake his head, and to murmur:

Chapter VI: Success Story

"Ai! Estes americanos!"

If a man had money, he might own a piece of some whaleship. But if he had brains, he let the other fellow take her out to sea.

Young Tony King, of course, was the brainiest man in America. But his "lay" from that first whaling voyage amounted to exactly $21.25 – not enough to buy a piece of some whaleship and let the other fellow take her out to sea. And so, when the schooner *Rising Sun* at last dropped anchor in Provincetown Harbor, and Tony came ashore to America, he decided to become a fisherman. He was prepared to be satisfied – temporarily – with the distinction of being high-line fisherman of America.

Also being, to his knowledge, the strongest man anywhere, he knew he could do the work; and suspecting that he was at the same time the toughest, he was confident that he could stand the gaff. There was one other major requirement – Luck. But upon the settling-up of the whaling voyage, Tony was convinced that he must be the luckiest as well. Had any other man ever come to America with $21.25 cash in his pocket?

Fishing came easily to Tony. In almost no time at all, he had found his place in Provincetown's big Grand Banks fleet. "To the east'ard for cod by the grace of God" he sailed, with his fellow countrymen, hundreds of them, in the great schooners of that day. And his strength, his toughness, and his luck stood by him.

On the Grand Banks, Tony King did some hard and heavy hauling on the hand line; and more and more often, as time went on, his dory came back to the vessel "high-line for the set." There was only one trouble. As a fisherman, Tony King discovered that it would take high and mighty hauling indeed to set this America on its ears!

It was even bigger than he had told Clara, this America! It might have been better, he reflected, if he had not given her quite so much "information."

There were Portuguese here, fishermen who had come over from the Azores before Tony King, and they were bigger fishermen than he. Captains, they were, and some of them were commanding crack schooners of the Grand Banks fleet. There, were men like Captain Joseph Swazer (Silva) of the great *I. J. Merritt*, which had earned her entire cost more than twice over in her first season on the Banks; and like Captain George Brier (Silva) of the *Joseph P. Johnson*, one of the fastest sailers of her time; and there were Captain Manuel Caton, of the *Sea Fox*; Captain Manuel

Enos (Inacio), of the *Gertie Winsor*; young Captain Marion Perry (Perreira), of the *Mary Cabral*; and a long list of others, Western Islanders all, and many of them from Tony King's own São Miguel.

In this America there were other ports, too, places on Cape Cod and on Cape Ann, ports like Gloucester and Rockport, and towns still farther down the coast, whence men of the Azores were going to the banks.

Provincetown, little city at the tip end of Cape Cod, was still the home of the captains, the big men who commanded big schooners and lived in big houses – each with a clock – and raised big families; but Tony had heard that the Portuguese of Gloucester were doing some big fishing too, that some day there would be great Portuguese captains there, among the great Yankee captains, the great Nova Scotians, great Italians, and great Unknowns, of Gloucester town. And in New Bedford, too, commanding square-riggers in the whaling fleet, there were captains of his race, men from São Jorge, from Terceira, from São Miguel, as well as those others, those dark fellows from the Cape Verde Islands.

Ai! Big men, these Americans!

In those days, no self-respecting codfish got very far in the world without salt. People who lived inland had to eat salt cod and like it, or stick to their beef, pork or other meat. Fresh sea food was a shore-line luxury. Even New Englanders were not eating enough fresh fish to justify the envy of the inlanders. They couldn't get it at certain times of the year, and they couldn't get much of it at any time.

In 1876 fresh-fishing was still an infant industry, and as such, was very much in need of a change. Though the market possibilities were large, the vessels that engaged in it were not, and they worked at it only in the winter months. But in that year, Joseph Manta, venturesome shipowner and mogul of the Provincetown Portuguese fleet, decided to take a flyer. He bought the *Waldron Holmes*, a fine 150-ton schooner, and fitted her out for year-round trawling for fresh fish.

She was to do her fishing anywhere from the grounds known as the "South Channel," off Nantucket, on down to Cape Sable, Nova Scotia. Except for a couple of weeks around Christmas time, when she would be refitting and repainting, she was to carry on steadily, summer and winter, on Georges Bank, Brown's Bank, and the Western Banks; and her trips were to be of about two weeks each, or less when she was lucky.

Lucky she was indeed. Within a year, she had done so well that Captain

Chapter VI: Success Story

Manta decided to fit out another schooner, the *Fred and Elmer*, for the same kind of work. Other owners followed. And although the Grand Banks salt-cod fishery continued to grow, peaking around 1885, the all-season fresh-fishing fleet that had its beginnings in a single schooner was destined to take the lead a few years later, and eventually to win for the port of Boston the place it now holds as hub of the entire Atlantic fishery.

I have brought all this in because it was still busily happening while Tony King was hauling on the hand line, away down on the Grand Banks in the salt-cod fleet. For him, things were going well enough. On the schooner *Bucephalus*, he had been making $150 a voyage, and there were two voyages each summer. Where else in the world could a man go and earn $300 for six months' work – and sometimes only five months!

But in the summer of 1891, the luck of the Grand Bankers was not so good. Luck came and went, but whenever it went, people shook their heads, and Cape Cod newspapers saw the end of the fishery – if not the end of all things:

> The Grand Banks fishery has proved to be a grave for all our hopes. The vessels are now dropping in from long voyages of five and six months, with less than one-half fare each, and this too from fishing grounds where, but a half-dozen years ago, three, two and a half, and even two months was sufficient time in which to secure a solid fare of fish.
>
> But not only do we lament the great scarcity of fish and a consequent lack of funds wherewith to meet the bills incurred in prosecuting the voyage, but we deplore the blackness of the outlook for the coming years. Men who have for many years fitted at great expense and sent their fleets out upon the sea in search of the finny fruit shrink from the thought of fitting again for the coming season, to pursue a calling so uncertain, and in which the risks are mighty and the profits nil.

The Grand Banks fleet did go out the next season in search of the "finny fruit," quite as eagerly as ever, but Tony King didn't go with it. Insight into the mysteries of Yankee psychology comes only with the years. Tony King had taken it all to heart, had supposed these Cape Codders meant it when they turned their wharves into wailing walls. He was convinced there would never be another salt-fish voyage to the Grand Banks.

81

For him, that was a lucky mistake. He learned how to bait and set a trawl, the long line used by the fresh-fishermen; and because he was known as an able doryman, a hard plugger, and above all because he was known to be lucky, he had no trouble getting a "site" on one of the vessels in Joseph Manta's fresh-fishing fleet.

On the schooner *Frank Foster*, men went share and share alike. No matter how lucky you were, how many fish you brought back to the vessel, in your own dory, from your own trawl, your fish were pooled with the rest, and your shipmates shared equally with you in the "stock."

That was all right with Tony King. Probably there would be a few in the crew who weren't big fishermen, and some who were down on their luck; but he, Tony King, would take care of that. If such fellows brought the average down, he, Tony King, would bring it back up. In the end, it would work out well enough.

And so it did. In her next two trips, of ten days each, the *Frank Foster* settled with her crew at $38 a man and $46 a man, respectively – phenomenal earnings for banks fishermen of those days – and Tony King rushed a cable to São Miguel, instructing Clara that she was to take the next Azores packet clearing for New Bedford. Via New Bedford, she would reach Provincetown.

The house was ready for her – and it had a clock.

Tony King's luck held good on the afternoon of November 26, 1898. That day the skipper of his vessel decided not to sail, to lie over in Provincetown until the weather looked better. That day, Tony King stayed ashore. And next morning a hurricane – Cape Cod's worst in the two hundred and fifty years of its history since the "Bradford Gale" of 1635 – was roaring over Provincetown Harbor.

Snow had come first, then a freeze, and with it the dread, spiraling wind of the hurricane, which was registering ninety miles an hour in Nantucket. Some time during the night the excursion steamer *Portland* went down – no one has ever learned just where – with a holiday crowd of two hundred and seventy persons on board. A score of smaller vessels were lost, but New England remembers that storm as the "Portland Gale."

"If any man is out there now," Tony King told his wife Clara, as he stared over the harbor from an upstairs window on the morning of November 27, "God help him!"

Chapter VI: Success Story

Clara shuddered. But for the chance decision of one man yesterday afternoon – not to take his vessel out because he "didn't like the looks of the weather" – but for this . . .

Tony drew on his seaboots, slipped into oilskins and sou'wester, and went down to the waterfront to find out what all fishermen wanted to know on that wild morning – whether there were any poor devils caught out there in the harbor and, if so, whether it was possible to do anything for them.

The beach was a misty mangle of sleet and flying sand. There Tony ran into Captain Robert Lavender, grizzled Yankee skipper of the "furrin trade," and one of the grandest old men in the business. Huddled around him in the lee of a beach bulkhead were several others, fishermen whom Tony knew.

Yes, there were some poor devils caught out there! Beyond the surf that was breaking as if it wanted to carry away the whole of the Cape, there were vessels in distress, there were men, and the frozen bodies of men.

'Cross-harbor, on the beach at Wood End, half a dozen small craft had been wrecked, and offshore the two-hundred-fifty-ton schooner *Lester A. Lewis*, of Bangor, was pounding on the bar. Men of the Wood End Life-Saving (now Coast Guard) Station had been working all night, taking all kinds of crazy risks, and they had more than a hundred rescued seamen over there in the station now. But they had not been able to reach the *Lester A. Lewis*. Even for those veteran boatmen, an attempt to launch in such a surf would have been plain suicide. The schooner's men had climbed into the rigging to escape seas that were breaking over her. Four of them were last seen, still up there – four frozen corpses.

Captain Lavender had come down to the beach to see if there were any way of saving them. He saw that there was no longer any reason for trying it. But he had also sighted another vessel, the fishing schooner *F. H. Smith*, stranded in shallow water, with one man clinging to her rigging. And in a temporary thinning of the sleet, Captain Lavender had seen that man waving his arms.

A seine boat – large, open craft used in the mackerel fishery – lay beached alongside the bulkhead. The old skipper looked her over. She had been hauled up for repairs, and she wasn't very tight. Nevertheless, he decided she would have to do. He picked up the long steering oar, reserving that for himself. Knowing what was coming next, a couple of men in the huddle on the beach turned and, without a word, walked off. Then, solemnly, from those still gathered around him, the old man counted off ten. There was no asking for volunteers. There was only a separating of ten men from the others. If anyone decided against it, he had only to step back; but until the skipper gave his order to launch the boat, no man moved.

They were driving their oars into the sand, trying to pole the craft afloat, when a big sea swung her about, catching her broadside. The unwieldy steering oar shot up at Captain Lavender's jaw, knocking him overboard. He fell between the boat and the bulkhead. Rolling back clumsily on the next sea, the heavy boat would have crushed him before the men could check her, but for the fact that he was jerked bodily inboard at that instant by Tony King.

Tony took over the steering oar. It knocked him down three times in further attempts to launch, but at last the boat was cleared. Then, fighting to keep her head to the breakers, the men drove and pitched their way out.

They rowed for more than an hour, and half a dozen times they came within an inch of capsizing, in the wickedest water ever seen off that shore. When they had reached a position to windward of the stranded fishing schooner, they dropped an anchor; and while one of the men paid out two hundred feet of line, the others worked the boat around, into the schooner's lee. Maneuvering on that side, they were better able to keep their own craft afloat while they took the man off the wreck.

The spot where the *F. H. Smith* had stranded was only half a mile from the beach; yet to make shore again in that sea, the seine boat had to run a sidelong course, going more than a mile to the westward, and finally landing in an inlet beyond the end of the village. Captain Lavender, soaked in his fall overboard, was nearly dead of cold. The round trip took more than three hours. But a life had been saved.

In October, 1899, Congress voted to award medals to Captain Lavender and the ten fishermen who had rowed out in the thick of the Portland Gale to save the life of William Forrest, a fellow fisherman. And a few months later, at the town hall in Provincetown, the medals were publicly tendered in a grand ceremony, with Congressmen and other trimmings.

"But, Tony," Clara said next day, as she glanced down the columns of the Boston newspapers, "they didn't put your name!"

Chapter VI: Success Story

Tony, with the medal still dangling where Clara had switched it to his blue dungaree jacket, just "to see once more how it looked," glanced over her shoulder and then pointed:

"... Joseph Brown, Jr., Joseph H. Settes, Antoine Joaquim Souza..."

"Ah!" Clara breathed again. "I don't get used to it any more, Tony! This Antoine Joaquim Souza! No more Tony King – no?"

Tony grinned. With deliberate show, he took off his jacket, unfastened the medal, laid it in the velvet-lined box, and clapped the lid to.

"Now," he said, getting back into his faded blue jacket, "now you call me Tony King!"

Like most medals that are awarded for true heroism, Tony King's was spared undue wear and tear as the years passed. Medals were nice to look at, but you couldn't feed 'em to the kids. But as doryman in the fresh-fishing fleet, Tony continued to do some high and mighty hauling on the trawl line. And through those same years, he had come to be known "up and down-along" the Cape as a high-liner.

When Joseph Manta, the shipowner, needed a skipper for his new little fresh-fishing schooner, the *Philip P. Mama*, he picked Tony King.

In 1911, Captain Tony King was placed in command of schooner *Jessie Costa*, then queen of the Provincetown fleet. The *Boston Herald*, reviewing the captain's record in the modest little *Philip P. Mama*, considered it worthy of note that he had never "stocked" less than $20,000 in a season.

In 1911 Captain Tony King of the *Jessie Costa*, biggest fisherman of the port of Provincetown, owned the biggest house on Court Street. He needed it. There were fourteen children – and a clock.

Chapter VII
'Tis Men's Lives

Granny Howland* is taking comfort – too much comfort for a January afternoon – ten miles off the Back Shore of Cape Cod. Granny Howland is still a-napping, but she wishes and whimpers of troubled dreams, and lifts white fingers in her tossing. Then up jumps Old Man Corisco,** and kicks her out of bed. Up jumps Old Man Corisco, and *ZOOMBA!* – like a tiger, he springs at the sun and lays it out cold. *ZOOMBA!* – like a drunken Newfoundlander in a water-front bar, he takes one swing at the January sky and blackens it up with a hundred-mile shiner. With a hop, skip, and jump, Granny Howland is back in the no'theast corner of everywhere, getting down to business at her washtub.

JANUARY. Ten miles off the Back Shore. And a no'theaster breezing up, fit to blast the dead out of 'Tarnity Acre!

João Pes-Grandes – John Big-Feet – passes the trawl to Joe Gasoline and trades places with him in the dory. It is Joe's trick at hauling back trawl. But as he sits at the tub, ready to coil the line while Joe dries it in over the roller, John Big-Feet looks at the sky and shakes his head.

"I think is better we cut the gear and go home, Joe," says John Big-Feet.

"Cut the gear? Why you think is better we cut the gear, John?" asks Joe Gasoline.

---

* Granny Howland's washtub made the suds for the fierce Atlantic northeasters, worst of winter gales. Granny Howland was chief kicker-up of these commotions, but the identity of her earthly counterpart, if any, has been lost to us. The term originated with the New Bedford whalemen, and it is possible that the lady was some particularly testy member of the Howland family of that city, famous as owners of one of the greatest whaling fleets in history. Isaac Howland was the great-great-grandfather of Hetty Green, and the Howland firm's profits formed the base from which the Green fortune mushroomed out.

** Demon of thunder and lightning, pronounced in the Azores *ko-r-r-reeshk* (accent on the second syllable and a good long roll of the *r*).

Chapter VII: 'Tis Men's Lives

"She's breezing up. She is came around to the no'theast, Joe," says John Big-Feet.

"Let 'er came, John!" says Joe Gasoline.

"By 'm by, we like to be home, when she's came up a livin' gale o' wind, Joe," says John Big-Feet.

"*Se me faz favor*, you cut the talk and coil the gear, we got plenty time, John," says Joe Gasoline.

"Them other fellers, they all cut their gear and go home, Joe," says John Big-Feet.

"Mmph! Sail, John! They got sail, we got the machine. Why you think we put in the machine, John?" says Joe Gasoline.

But John Big-Feet knows that the Atlantic Ocean, ten miles off the Back Shore of Cape Cod, is no place for a dory fisherman to be caught in a January northeaster, machine or no machine. And as he coils the gear into the tub, though he says no more, he shakes his head – which irritates Joe Gasoline even more than his talking.

For Joe Gasoline knows, too. But Joe is very proud of "the machine." It is the year 1901, and of the 150 dories in the Provincetown shore-fishing fleet, theirs is the only one as yet with power.

Years ago, Joe Gasoline played with the notion of power, fooled with it a little, and got fooled a little in return. But last year, when he induced John Big-Feet to "mate up" with him in buying one of those new five-horsepower engines, which were already being installed in small pleasure craft, it worked like a charm.

John Big-Feet is older than Joe Gasoline. He knows the ways of sail, has been all but swaddled in sailcloth; and he was not easily convinced that any other work of the hand of man could take its place. It occurred to him that there might even be something sinful in this new put-put idea. The parish priest was a man of God, yet the fact remained that he didn't know a foresail from a jib; and even a consultation with Father Terra ended indecisively for John Big-Feet.

But at length Joe Gasoline succeeded in talking him into it, and late last season, before a head-shaking, tongue-clicking crowd at the wharf, they put-putted away on their first trip. Since then, they have been doing some big fishing together – Joe Gasoline, John Big-Feet, and the machine. For, as Joe Gasoline has said, over and over, when you got the machine, you should get out to the grounds quick; you should get home quick; you shouldn't have to cut your gear and run for the harbor when it starts to breeze up; you should show 'em a feller with a machine can take more chances.

Meanwhile I should pause to point out that the man who went "shore-fishing" in a sailing dory was in a different sort of business from that of the schoonerman. Both used the trawl – the long line with "gangin's" attached at five-foot intervals, each "gangin'" carrying a baited hook – and both laid their trawls along the bottom for cod and haddock. But the schooners, carrying their dories nested on the deck, went afar for their fish, spent weeks or months on their trips to the banks, and were built to take punishment accordingly; whereas the shore fisherman, working in waters that were often quite as rugged, had only his dory to see him home. He went out and came back the same day, and fifteen miles was about the limit he could risk.

But at any distance out, it was risky enough. In these parts, near the shore, the cod and haddock were winter visitors. They came each year from November to April – bad months to be sailing in "outside waters" with a little open boat. To make the harbor that was nearly landlocked by the final crooked finger at the end of Cape Cod, a man had first to "round the Race" – the northwest knuckle of that finger – and the water off "the Race" was a crowded graveyard for ships, a hazard in winter for dory and schooner alike

In the shore fishery of Cape Ann, of the down-east ports, and of Nova Scotia, the danger was much the same. The protected waters of Gloucester, of Rockport, or of Annisquam were close at hand; but for cod and haddock, one had to go "outside;" and many a dory crew, in their fight to claw back from the open ocean in such tiny craft, ran into odds that proved too great.

This dory-from-the-shore method of fishing, oldest in America, has always been fraught with more assorted perils than any other. That is why, now, poor John Big-Feet, in spite of the machine, is shaking his head while his huge hands go on mechanically laying in the rounds of trawl, and why Joe Gasoline is irritated.

Old Man Corisco comes doubling up the stairs of hell. He is puffing like a porpoise and there is blood in his eye. Zoomba! – he whacks the black clouds out of the northeast horizon; O Diabo! – he yanks the tail feathers out of Mother Carey's Chickens; Aiee! – he goes after Granny Howland 'with a

Chapter VII: 'Tis Men's Lives

marlin-spike. And the old lady screams and curses all the sinners of the earth, and works like fury at her washtub.

"What's a matter you fool with the machine, Joe?"

"I don' know what's a matter, the machine don' go, John!" Kneeling over the engine, Joe Gasoline tinkers with the fuel line and gives the fly another spin. But there is only a tinny wheeze – deadest sound in the world at such a time! – and then silence.

John Big-Feet, who knows nothing about engines but much about January northeasters, stares over his dory-mate's shoulder. For half an hour, while the wind keeps rising and Joe Gasoline agonizes in vain over the mysteries of the machine, the little craft drifts helplessly – drifts towards the hidden bars on the Back Shore of Cape Cod, where many a stouter vessel has pounded herself to pieces in just such a gale. Here, off the lee shore in a northeaster, no anchor can hold them at sea, no rescuing hand reach them from the land.

John Big-Feet keeps the dory head-on to the seas, while he lets his mind swing broadside to a dreaded conviction, and his thoughts go wildly capsizing. At last he moves aft and touches Joe Gasoline's shoulder. He points off to leeward, where they both know the deadly bars lie submerged in the tide. There is need only to point.

"Joe," John Big-Feet sobs, "you take the oars. You better row. Me – I pray, little bit."

"The hell you pray!" says Joe Gasoline, as he gives up the devilish puzzle at last. "We both row, John."

"Only one minute, Joe! I pray just little bit, one minute. I got something, Joe, what I promise God. Then I row too." And John Big-Feet, at the risk of being pitched overboard, kneels in the madly heaving dory and prays, in part as follows:

"God, you give one chance, no? You make the machine go – once more. Just once, God, you start her up, you make her go, and by 'm by, when we get ashore, I mash her up with the axe. I know you make the machine stop for because she is no good, the son-of-a-whore, no good like sail. But one time, God, one more time you make her go push-push-push, and when we get ashore I mash her up so no fishermans can use her no more!"

John goes back to the machine. He gives the fly one last spin, hears that dead, tinny wheeze again – and then turns away and takes up his oars.

Slowly they beat back. They gasp and pull for every inch of way they make. It is back-breaking business, but Joe Gasoline and John Big-Feet are dorymen to their freezing fingertips; and little by little they edge around "the Race," miracle by miracle they climb and plunge and survive – until at fall of night they are working at last into the safe waters of Provincetown Harbor.

Now they are rowing for the wharf – a last few racking pulls – but suddenly, when they are only a couple of lengths from the spiling –

Push-push-push . . .

The machine!

Push-push-push . . .

All of a sudden, and running like a mooncusser bound for a wreck! Joe Gasoline jumps up and shuts her off just in time to avert a crash.

Dropping his oars, John Big-Feet gives a loud groan. Slowly he rises, walks aft, and picks up the axe. And while Joe Gasoline stares like a man in a trance, John Big-Feet goes back to the machine, raises the axe, and keeps his promise to God.

Despite this untimely fate of Joe Gasoline's beloved machine, mechanization of the shore-fishing fleet spread as an almost overnight miracle. A boat suited to carrying power – white-oak-framed, with hardwood timbers, galvanized fastenings, inside ceiling and fore-and-aft decking – was quickly perfected, and anyone who could raise the $375 for one of these twenty-five-foot wonders promptly found that his earnings were doubled, his risk halved.

Yes, the "gasoliners" were the thing. And they were followed in 1905 by the first fishing schooners to install engines, mainly for speed to market.

But an engine powerful enough to scud a small schooner should also be powerful enough to do heavy hauling on the fishing-gear as well. A machine like that should be able to haul up a dragnet, like the big "beam-trawls" used by fishermen back in the Old Country. Those great bags of net were slow coming up by hand, sometimes three hours or more for a single haul. But an engine ought to pull one up in a fraction of the time.

So it was argued, and almost simultaneously the highly efficient "flounder dragger" evolved – a small vessel powered by a gasoline engine which could also be harnessed to a dragnet. A few hand-worked dragnets had been used by earlier fishermen in this country, but the Portuguese who adapted the dragging gear to power also proved expert with it. Nearly the

Chapter VII: 'Tis Men's Lives

whole of New Bedford's fishing fleet today, of more than fifty vessels, is of this type, manned mostly by Portuguese.

When the flounder dragger had shown what it could do, bigger dragnets were fashioned, for bringing up cod and haddock. Bigger vessels were rigged for this kind of "ground fishing" (cod, haddock, and flounder are all caught on or near the bottom, where the dragnet, or "otter trawl" as it is sometimes called, is drawn through the water). Then, in 1910, Boston stepped in with two steam-powered vessels equipped to "drag" on a bigger scale than ever; and from that beginning grew the great Boston fleet of "beam-trawlers," steam and Diesel, which bring in most of New England's fish today.

The story of dory fishing, as it goes backward from the day of Joe Gasoline's power dory to the beginnings of shore fishing in America, is a long one, an old one – about as long and as old, indeed, as the story of America itself. The "Swampscott dory," a sailer with deep centerboard and huge spread of canvas, was the immediate predecessor; before that was the flat-bottomed, file-sided "Grand Banks dory;" before that, the sturdy little two-masted "Chebacco boat" of old Cape Ann, built by the dozens at Chebacco, the town of boatyards later to become famous under the name of Essex; and before that, the shallops of Salem, of varying rig.

The dory parade, with many intermediate floats which I have not catalogued, will carry you back through all the stages of our country's history, and finally to those "cockling flyboats, wherein an English man can scarce sit without a fearfull tottering" – the birch-bark canoes which the Pilgrims bought from the Indians at Plymouth. For the English came here expecting to fish for a good part of their living, and fish they did, before anything else. They ate fish, fought over fish, farmed with fish, traded fish, and wrote verses about fish:

> The luscious lobster, with the crab fish raw,
> The brinish oister, muscle, periwigge,
> And tortoise sought for by the Indian squaw
> Which to the flats dance many a winter's jigge
> To dive for cockles, and to digge for clams,
> Whereby her lazie husband's guts shee cramms.*

For tracing mechanical evolutions, one may let paragraphs suffice; but

*William Wood, *New England's Prospect*, 1634.

for tracing the life story behind them, the covers of a book are close quarters. A single Boston beam trawler of the most advanced type today costs more than a quarter-million dollars, and in a ten-day trip can land more fish than the entire Provincetown dory fleet of one hundred and fifty craft could have brought back in twice that time forty years ago. Yet in the tale of life and death and struggle for a living on the sea, the great beam trawler as seen in its best light is only a happy ending; the battle was fought, the climax enacted, in the dory.

If I were scene maker for a reenactment of this drama, I should put in much of my effort on the strange little Cape Cod community that once existed across the dunes from Provincetown, back in the seventies, eighties, and nineties – the community known as Helltown.

Where Helltown once stood, on the Atlantic shore three-quarters of a mile south of Race Point, there is only bare beach now, fringed with poverty grass that shades back to the salt marshes of Herring Cove. Race Point Light, and farther alongshore the Coast Guard station with its huddle of summer shanties, are the only structures in the near vicinity. In July and August, cars of the summer people thread out on a state highway to watch the daily havoc when the Atlantic swallows the sun; but in January and February there is nothing out there, of movement none but the roaring surf, spray on the tide line, white mist racing over the beach.

In Provincetown, three miles across the sands of the "Province Land," the name of Helltown is still mentioned now and then; but local colorists have splashed it with nickel-magazine romance. Dirty doings, as hinted by the name, were the principal business of Helltown, one hears now. Beachcombing, a word which on Cape Cod can mean anything from scientific research to grand larceny, went the limit there; and men lived by wrecking, and mooncussing, and no one knows what else.

There is plenty of reason to suspect that on Cape Cod all these things have happened, in one spot and another alongshore; but Helltown itself had business of a wholly different sort. The twenty-odd little huts that squatted there, half a century ago, were simply winter quarters for Portuguese fishermen of Provincetown, men who had their homes and families in the village, who went to the banks on trawling schooners through the summer and fall, and who came out here to Helltown just after Christmas each year, to live in the shacks until the April following. By that time, the schooners again were fitted out to go to the banks.

CHAPTER VII: 'TIS MEN'S LIVES

The men bunked eight or ten to a shack. They called it Helltown because it was just plain hell to live there; they lived there because from that beach they could sail their dories to the winter fishing grounds off Race Point early each morning and get back by night; and they fished in the winter because what was left of the $300 to $600 which they had earned on the schooners earlier in the year would not carry a big family through four idle months.

All New England fishing ports of that day had their Helltowns, or their men who had to work at the Helltowners' hazardous calling until the banks season began. Boats and gear came high, but life was cheap enough in Helltown; and gale, ice, and fog drove many a one-sided bargain. Maggie's eloquent retort to Monkbarns – "It's no fish ye're buying; it's men's lives" – held good on both sides of the Atlantic.

Yarns of the smugglers, wreckers, and pirates of a place like Helltown are easy to listen to – and easy to spin. The tale of sacrifice, hardship, and death in the everyday fight for bread is elusive, and often left untold.

Minha maçã vermelhinha,
Picada do rouxinol...

Above the yaw and seethe of the surf outside, Senhor Miguel Bicho-Couve (Mike Cabbage-Bug) twangs at the six brass strings of his *guitarra* and lifts his baritone plaint:

My little apple of rosy hue,
The nightingale has sampled you...

The cigarette smoke rises, hovers above the "ram-cat" stove, and all at once vanishes into dark corners when a gust comes slapping through the east wall. Balancing on a keg-buoy near the stove, old 'Bastiao Dente-Ouro (Sebastian Gold-Tooth) is overhauling his gear. With skein of new gangin's draped on his shoulder and hook setter in hand, he goes over the coiled trawl round by round and, as he does so, sways on his keg to Mike Cabbage-Bug's lament over the state of his rosy little apple:

Quem te picou que te coma
Que te picou no melhor!

Let him who pecks devour you too,
For he has taken the best of you!

Chapter VII: 'Tis Men's Lives

Captain Domingos Sou'west snores on a pallet of old sailcloth under the window, and draws his peacoat up closer under his chin. Captain Sou'west has turned in early, and has curtly ordered his sixteen-year-old son, Man'el, to do the same. With the market offering no better than $2 a hundredweight for day-old cod, a man has got to turn in early!

Figure it out for yourself. There is 50 cents a barrel haulage to be paid to the fellows who take your fish in their dumpcarts the three miles across the dunes to the depot. There's 25 cents for the sugar barrel in which they pack your fish, and which holds two hundred pounds. There's 10 cents for heading, 10 cents for ice; and the bait you need to catch a barrel of fish stands you an average of 70 cents. Well, there's $1.65 gone, before your fish is on the train! Add a dollar for freight, and you see what you've got for yourself at $2 the hundredweight – $4 less the $2.65 it costs you, or $1.35 for yourself. And if you can catch an average fare of three barrels a day, week in and week out, you're a damn big fisherman!

The lad Man'el turned in when his father told him to. All Sou'west's kids do as he commands. But now that the captain has settled down to log a good steady run – dreaming, most likely, of four-cent cod – Man'el has taken up his perch by the stove again, to listen to the singing.

Dark-eyed, round-faced, Man'el is spoken of by the men of Helltown as "a fine boy when he wants to be." His father, gruff as a steam tug, has been making a real fisherman out of Man'el, ever since he lost his older boy at sea. But that Man'el, he still likes to play tricks, like painting black monkey-faces on a man's brand-new yellow sou'wester, or slipping a live lobster under a man's blanket and leaving it there. Most of the tricks he plays on the old man himself, though; and, so long as he does, the men of Helltown continue to speak of him as "a fine boy when he wants to be."

Ah, but if you want to hear all about Man'el, go listen to his mother! Then you'll hear something! You'll think he's a saint. And the old man – well, the old man is really just as bad when Man'el isn't on deck to hear him. At that, you have to admit it isn't every kid his age who's willing to spend a winter at Helltown. Some you couldn't hold if you made 'em fast to a killick! But Man'el came out with his *Pai* the day after Christmas, and a week's already gone by, and he isn't saying a word about going back.

"Mike, sing the one about the light again," Man'el says, as he pours himself a mug-up from the tall copper pot which is always kept on the stove. "You know, the one you sang last night."

"Light? Ah!" Mike Cabbage-Bug grins and nods and winks at the others. "You like thees song, eh? But you don't tell me for play thees song while *Pai* is up – no?" And Mike laughs and sings:

Candeia que não da luz
Não se espeta na parede . . .

Candle which gives no light
Never is hung from the wall . . .

As he strums the intervening chords, Mike goes through a couple of steps of the old *chamarita* and pauses to give Man'el a pat on the head.

O amor que não e firme
Não se faz mais caso d'elle.

The love which is not passionate
Never is noticed at all.

Through many stanzas, the song goes on. But not until Mike Cabbage-Bug has sung his last, and with a weary, "Ai, ai, ai!" has stowed his guitar safely behind a small forest of oars, masts, and gobsticks, does Man'el turn in for the night.

Tonight, out there in the sea, there is what fishermen call an "easterly rote" – uneven breaking and tumbling and backwashing, which trained old ears along the waterfront do not like to hear at night. But the ears of Man'el Sou'west are young, and in that broken whisper of the sea, that makes other men of Helltown fidget and roll even in their sleep, for Man'el there is only the laughing of Mike Cabbage-Bug, and the insistence of a stubborn little tune:

O amor que não e firme . . .

The night of the 2nd and the morning of the 3rd [of January, 1878] were terrible for those unlucky mariners who found themselves in a snowstorm, being driven on the treacherous sands of Cape Cod. Five vessels were lost. From the largest two not a soul was saved; every man, from the captains down to the deck boys, was buried beneath the cold waters. A few bodies were recovered, but the majority sleep in watery graves.

– *Fishermen's Own Book*, Gloucester, 1882.

Chapter VII: 'Tis Men's Lives

"All right, boy?"

Steering with one hand, Captain Sou'west holds the mainsheet of his careening little craft with the other, ready to let go the instant she heels too far. Close-reefed mainsail and storm jib are all the dory can carry, the way it's come up to blow this afternoon. Off the Race, and with home a twelve-mile beat dead to windward, this little boat has a piece of work cut out for her! Spray hurls itself clear over the slender gaff, white water buries the "washboard" and comes in sheets across the weather rail. Ice gathers out of nowhere to drape rigging, sails, and the men themselves, ice that is like a death-sheet being spun for them by slow, invisible hands.

"All right, boy?"

Tack by tack, Sou'west thrashes her into it, makes her fight for her life. Sou'west knows the way home; but before a sign of home is given, before there is a hint of winning or losing, the snow ends all signs. Gale and the wicked tide of the Race – and now the snow.

"All right, boy?"

Man'el doesn't answer, but Man'el is all right. Under his oilskins, his clothes are drenched. Even with the work, he is chilled to the bone. But so is the Captain, and Man'el knows that. The old man thinks his monotonous query is making Man'el feel that *he* is all right; but Man'el can see *Pai's* frozen hands.

So Man'el works on, and doesn't stop to answer now. With the bailer he works unceasingly, except when the boat goes in stays. Then he has to tend the jib sheets and jump back to the thwarts to shift the ballast bags to the other side. A man has to work fast, trimming ballast on one of these craft. The bags of sand are carried on the thwarts, not on the bottom where they ought to be, and they must be shifted at the exact moment of heading the gale; otherwise, over she goes – *zit!* – like that.

Through the dusk, Sou'west keeps her bowling along, and remembers every now and then that he must also keep offering some word of encouragement to the boy.

"I think we make it in a few more hours, boy, we keep up this way." And Man'el, his arms aching, fingers numb, looks at the old man and wonders if perhaps, after all, there is something more in the words than well-meaning show. For the old man does know these waters. He knows where he is with his eyes: closed. And then Man'el looks at those hands again – and marvels at him.

With the hours, the wind rises, then abates a little and begins to look as if it might be blowing itself out, only to come back fiercer than ever. It is from one of these spells of easement, long after nightfall, while Man'el is chipping ice from the rigging, that the worst of it comes. Suddenly Sou'west calls Man'el to the tiller. Then, working frantically, using his wrists and his teeth when the blued, stiffened fingers fail him, he tries to get the mainsail in. But before he can manage it, a great sea bears down on the dory and "falls her off" in spite of all Man'el can do.

Into the trough go boat and crew, while the weight of unnumbered tons rolls over to snap a stick, sweep away a bit of rag, and swamp the pitiful little shell that was built for sea.

And yet, rocking sluggishly now down the long after-slope, it is not finished, this shell. Bottom-up, it is still something to cling to, still a hollowed hull that can be righted, bailed out, handled somehow, and yes, ridden at sea! Sou'west, his arms over the gunwale, hangs on and gasps and tries to get the water out of his eyes. Slowly, timing his movements with the rolling of the hull, he works himself back into the dory.

There is darkness, there is heaving water, there is the silent slant of snow – only these to hear the cry of Captain Sou'west:

"Man'el! Man'el!"

Chapter VIII
The Ghosts of Georges Bank

HER DECKS AND SPARS aglitter in the moonlight, the new schooner *Charles Haskell* was like a queen enthroned as she sat chocked on the ways at Essex. At that time – December, 1869 – Story's boatyard was already more than a hundred years old; and all the miracles which that institution could perform with white oak and tall spruce had been lavished on the new craft. Yes, like a queen she was, and the moon over the bay that night was giving her a train of pure gold – and none too good for her!

The boatyard was through with her now. Everything those magicians could do for her had been done. Rigging and a suit of sails, ground tackle and gear – give her these, with an able crew, and she was ready for sea. Give her as she deserved, of these, and she would be the match of any sea she met, of any gale that blew. Yes, even of Georges Bank in the winter!

A worker walked through the deserted boatyard that night down to the ways, and climbed aboard the new schooner for one last look. He inspected the deck and then started down the forecastle companion. His foot slipped. Next morning, they found a man aboard the *Charles Haskell*, a man lying at the foot of the companion ladder – dead of a broken neck.

The skipper for whom the *Charles Haskell* was built refused her. She was perfect, he said. She was a beauty. She was everything they said she was. But no contract on earth could make him take her; because for his business, he said, she was now disqualified.

His business was winter-fishing on Georges Bank.

> Thus far this season there have been forty men lost who were engaged in the Georges fishery; of this list, quite a number are married and leave families, some of them in destitute circumstances . . . In view of these losses, we earnestly hope that those engaged in the fishing business will take into consideration the entire abandonment of Georges winter fishing. It has been pur-

sued at altogether too great a risk, and human life is worth altogether too much to be thus sacrificed.
— *Cape Ann Advertiser,* March 15, 1861.

The regular February appearance of large schools of codfish on Georges Bank, which is used by the fish for their spawning grounds, insures a large catch for the early fleet, and the temptation of big trips, and the consequent realization of good returns, cannot be resisted by men who have been lying idle and whose funds have run low, or to express it as they do, more emphatically, "We haven't a shot in the locker; the fish are there and we're just going for 'em!" And who can blame them? It is their business. They know its excitements and its dangers . . . Georges may be their grave; but this thought does not deter them from going.
— *Fishermen's Own Book,* Gloucester, 1882.

While the *Charles Haskell* is idling high and dry at Story's boatyard through the next twelvemonth, there is time here for a word about that weird expanse of shoal water — Georges Bank — one of the greatest fishing grounds in the world, and of all the most dangerous.

Father Neptune sets this vast submarine table with finest cod and haddock every winter, and tells the fishermen to come and get it. But, starting from a point about eighty miles due east of Nantucket, the table spreads out one hundred and twenty-five miles to sea and about seventy-five miles north and south, and the stretch of water that overlies it is the wickedest, the most treacherous in the Atlantic Ocean.

Fog, gale, and a whipsaw current do their worst here. The bottom is irregular, at some places more than fifty fathoms down, at others six fathoms or less. When we think of going a hundred miles out to sea, we ordinarily think of getting into deep water; but on what is known as Georges North Shoal, near the northwest edge of the bank, there is a spot which at low tide is covered by only three feet. The rip tides have a circular movement on the whole bank, the currents have the pull of a loosed flood in them; and in any sort of blow, the man in the little fishing schooner would rather be on the Grand Banks, on Quereau, on any other spot you care to name.

But Georges, from the time men first ventured there for winter fishing, a little over a hundred years ago, has been something more than a spot

Chapter VIII: The Ghosts of Georges Bank

of rugged water. The tales of Georges Bank are strange tales. Fishermen have strange dreams on that bank, and things stranger than dreams happen to them. Men go and are never heard from. Vessels are lost and their stories never known. It happened so often in the old days that fisher people soon learned to count that vessel lost forever which was overdue by only a few days from Georges Bank.

Only once, and in a few pitiful words, has the story come back from an unsighted Georges man. The schooner *Falcon* had long been given up for lost in Gloucester after the gale of December 11, 1895, when a mackerelman cruising the bank picked up a bottle hung with long strands of sea grass. The note inside read:

> On Georges Bank with our cable gone our rudder gone and leaking, two men have been swept away and all hands have been given up as our cable is gone and our rudder gone. The one that picks this up let it be known. God have mercy on us.
> *Schooner Falcon.*

There have been in this fishery any number of forebodings, premonitions of tragedy, placed on record by virtue of their weird fulfillment. What part of such a "premonition" is really afterthought I do not know; nor do I care, for what interests me is not whether these things actually took place as related, but the fact that they were *said* to have taken place.

One such instance was set down in the journal of Captain J. Wenzell of the Gloucester schooner *Sachem*. She had been fishing on Brown's Bank, but on September 7, 1871, ran up to cruise Georges. That night John Nelson, cook, went aft and begged the skipper to "get off Georges Bank." Making no bones about it, he explained that he had just waked from a dream. He had seen "women, dressed all in white, and standing in the rain." Twice before, cook said, he had this same dream, and each time he had been shipwrecked. "For God's sake, skipper, get off Georges Bank!"

A little later it breezed up. At one-thirty A.M. the *Sachem* was hove to under close-reefed foresail. Then, from the forecastle, one of the men yelled that the vessel was filling. Captain Wenzell went below and found six inches of water. Pumps were manned, bucket bailing was got under way, and cook was ordered to provision a boat. Believing the leak was under the port bow, the captain wore around and hove to on the other tack, in the hope that this might bring the leak out of water.

But nothing was effective against cook's "women dressed all in white." With a strong breeze blowing, the *Sachem* signaled the Gloucester schooner *Pescador*, and shortly afterward, at great risk to both crews, the men were got off the leaking vessel.

At two o'clock the *Sachem* rolled on her side, settled by the bow, and went down.

Perhaps it is simply danger, the constant nearness of death, that draws men's minds out of their workaday track and results in stories of the kind that have collected so thickly in the Georges fishery. Perhaps it is only this, but I should not like the assignment of proving that there is nothing more to the story of Georges Bank.

I do not mean to dust off the sermons, the facile allegories that were popular a few generations ago, when our Yankee clergy was constantly making moralistic capital out of the disasters that befell their seagoing parishioners. Nor do I mean to ask you to believe in ghosts, with or without morals. In forgiving the fishermen their superstitions – and especially the Portuguese, whose store of them was endless – I can only say that the waters themselves were much to blame. On Georges Bank, for example, what a man sees is more than the mere surface of water playing foil to the whims of an Atlantic sky. On a calm summer day, I have watched our vessel plowing through eerie patches there, patches as sharply limned, as highly colored, as the squares in a section of Iowa farmland. Yes, and I have seen meadows and canyons and high ridges and treacherous bogs – all of them, all in the flat of a summer slick on Georges Bank – and I have been in other waters reflecting patchy skies, and these scenes did not set themselves. Then they were only patches of color, without meaning.

In the unbelievably long September swell on Georges, caused by some gale perhaps fifty or a hundred miles away, your vessel is not merely making her way over an agitated sea; she is running from something, she is racing up one great slope and plunging down the next, climbing crazily a range of crazy hills. From something, perhaps fifty or a hundred miles off, perhaps nearly at her heels, she is running, trying to escape. In a February gale on Georges, where there are no bending slopes and all is breakage – rush and rigidity and then collapse – in such an hour you may be too busy watching your footing on deck to see what Georges is like; and until you are called above deck for duty, you choose your bunk and the easier plausibility of dreams.

Chapter VIII: The Ghosts of Georges Bank

Although tragedy on Georges Bank has been a continued story, even beyond the motorization of the fleet and into the present, with its wireless, Coast Guard cutters, planes, and other aids to mariners, the dread of a winter's gale on those grounds today is nothing like what it was in the days of sail. Then disaster lay in "going adrift" – parting the cable and running, wholly out of hand, to almost certain collision, and in that case, certain death.

The Georges fleet was a large one. Fishing ports from Cape Cod down to Newfoundland were represented among the craft there, and frequently from the rigging a man could count between two and three hundred sail. Where one vessel had good luck, others flocked to be "on the fish." And the result was that the fleet usually bunched itself over a few small spots on the bank.

In good weather this was well enough; but it multiplied the risks many times in a storm. For if the gale should overtake a schooner in those days, all her crew could do was to snug down, pay out a good string to the anchor, and hope for the best while they tried to ride it out. From then on, if anything less than the best happened, it happened first to that all-important part of their equipment, the ground tackle; the anchor would drag, or the cable part under the strain.

A single vessel, once set adrift in those crowded waters, was sure to spread destruction. If she struck another, both went down. But usually, before this happened, several vessels lying in her path had cut their own cables and gone adrift themselves, to get out of her way. Cutting cable was a last resort, but on each craft a man stood ready with the axe. And as each was forced to cut loose, by so much more were the others in the fleet endangered. Thus death went snowballing over Georges Bank on such a night.

Surviving the gale of February 24, 1862, when thirteen Gloucester schooners went down with 168 men on Georges Bank, a witness writes of that night in the old *Cape Ann Advertiser*:

> As midnight drew near, the gale increased fearfully. I had never experienced anything so terrific before, and the stories which were told on board the mackerel catcher now assumed a more truthful aspect.
>
> How the wind shrieked through the cordage and the waves

leaped! – seemingly impatient to add us to the many victims who have been swallowed up on this treacherous spot.

My shipmates showed no signs of fear. They were now all on deck, and the skipper was keeping a sharp lookout. Ben was also on the alert, and had placed a hatchet near the windlass to be in readiness should it be necessary to cut our cable. As he came near where I was standing, he very coolly remarked that if we did not break adrift ourselves, or some other vessel didn't run into us, he thought we might ride it out . . .

During the night a large vessel passed quite near us. We could see her lights, also her spars and sails, as she sped swiftly along on the wings of the storm. Glad enough were we to have her pass us, and I trembled at the thought of our fate had she struck our little craft. When I learned of the terrible disaster of the gale, I came to the conclusion that this vessel was the cause of at least some portion of it . . .

Somewhere about nine o'clock, the skipper sang out, "There's a vessel adrift right ahead of us! Stand by with your hatchet, but don't cut till you hear the word!" Ben was there at his post. He could be trusted at such a time, and would await orders. This all on board knew full well. All eyes were bent now on the drifting craft. On she came. It was a fearful moment to me, and it was evident that the men, some of whom had followed Georges fishing for ten seasons, thought there was danger now, but they were not afraid.

There they stood, determined to do their best for their lives. I knew I should share the same fate with them, and there was some consolation even in this.

The drifting vessel was coming directly for us. A moment more, and the signal to cut must be given. With the swiftness of a gull, she passed by, so near that I could have leaped aboard, just clearing us, and we were saved from that danger, thank God!

The hopeless, terror-stricken faces of the crew we saw but a moment, as they went on to certain death. We watched the doomed craft as she sped on her course. She struck one of the fleet a short distance astern, and we saw the waters close over both vessels almost instantly, and as we gazed they both disappeared . . .

Chapter VIII: The Ghosts of Georges Bank

Taking Georges Bank into account for what it was, and for what it meant to these men, it may be easier to understand the refusal of the skipper to accept that beautiful new schooner, the *Charles Haskell*. A man had died on board, while the craft was still on the ways. And that was an omen – a sure sign she was unfit for the Georges Bank winter fishery. But a year passed, and another Gloucester skipper did take her out. And now, let us go back to her story.

"Yes, sir, gentlemens," Joe Enos said in his remote, sing-song manner while he tossed the lead out after the snoods, "we get a breeze o' wind tonight, yes, sir, gentlemens!"

Hand-lining for cod forty miles west of Georges North Shoal, the *Haskell's* crew were doing some fast fishing at the moment. But, busy as they were, a couple of the boys paused to glance at "the Portygee." Joe, the only Portuguese on board, didn't have a great deal to say, but already on this first trip of the new schooner he had proved himself an able fisherman; when he did talk the others listened, and when he took the trouble to mention "a breeze o' wind" the chances were that it was going to be no ordinary weather.

"What makes you think so, Portygee?" George Scott asked.

"You see the way the fish bite now?" Joe shook his head. "Fish don't take the hook like this – only when we got a breeze o' wind by 'm by. Yes, sir, gentlemens, a breeze o' wind!"

Faster and faster, the fat cod were being hauled aboard. Within five or six miles of one another, more than a hundred vessels could be seen from the deck of the *Charles Haskell*, and on each the scene was the same.

Around noon the wind hauled to east-northeast, and from then on rose steadily. At three o'clock Captain Clifford Curtis ordered the *Haskell's* crew to haul in their lines.

"All right, boys! Heave in strads and give her cable!"

The crew took off the "strads" – pieces of rope bound around the cable to prevent chafing in the hawsepipe – gave her eighty more fathoms of the string, and stradded her up again. Then they took in the foresail, putting a double reef in it before they furled it, so as to have it ready for hoisting in case they should go adrift. The fishing vessel of that day carried no triangular storm trysail, such as is used for steadying the modern power-driven vessel; instead, for the same purpose, three reefs were taken in the mainsail, a rig that was termed "balanced-reefed mainsail."

By nine o'clock that night, Joe Enos's "breeze o' wind" had become a full-fledged hurricane. On Georges Bank, at the time, were 290 vessels; and with the wind continuing from the east-northeast, the deadly North Shoal lay under the lee of the fleet.

On board the *Charles Haskell,* as on other vessels, all hands were called on deck. Captain Curtis stationed himself at the cable, axe in hand. From his post he could see the lights of one unlucky schooner after another, passing by like a ghastly parade through the sleet – vessels that had already broken adrift.

Within an hour, the *Haskell* herself was dragging anchor, but before she had slipped far from her berth, the hook fouled something on the bottom and brought her up short. There she hung, giving and tautening by turns, when suddenly the men at the forward lookout yelled warning. Directly over the schooner's bowsprit, looking as if it were almost atop her, a light was riding.

Captain Curtis brought down his axe, the *Haskell* bounded off like a catapulted stick, and silently the stranger swept by.

"Up with the foresail! You, Portygee, keep her due west!"

Joe Enos nodded understanding. It was the skipper's idea to get to the leeward of the fleet if he could, and at the same time work beyond the North Shoal; for between collision and running aground on that shoal, there was precious little to choose.

After half an hour of running, they raised another light, this time on the weather bow. Captain Curtis, thinking the vessel was riding at her anchor, called out:

"Hard up the helm!"

But the other fellow, coming bow-on, also had his wheel hove up hard. Too late the skipper discovered that he, too, was running adrift. There was no chance then to pay off; and from a wave-crest the *Haskell* crashed into the other craft, cutting her down just abaft the port rigging. The stranger was split nearly to the mainmast.

As the figures of passers-by on a dark street are caught by a flash of lightning and "stopped" for the instant, so the crew of the unknown vessel appeared to those aboard the *Haskell.* One or two could have jumped aboard from where they stood, but none moved. And in the next instant, vessel and crew had vanished.

The *Haskell*'s main boom and main rigging on the starboard side had

Chapter VIII: The Ghosts of Georges Bank

carried away in the crash. The bowsprit had broken off, but was still hanging there, thudding against the planking and threatening to bash in the bow. The men cut this stick free, and in order to keep the mast from starting, made a line fast to the jibstay, passed it through the hawsepipe, and then under the windlass.

When the wreck was cleared, Joe Enos went below. No one aboard the *Haskell* expected her to stay afloat. No vessel stayed afloat when this happened. But down in the forecastle, Joe found George Winters, pointing and laughing hysterically, and screaming, "She's dry! She's dry! I tell you, there ain't a drop in her!"

Joe wouldn't believe it. He took up the trap in the forecastle floor. There was no water underneath! Then he ran to tell the skipper. Captain Curtis had the men try the pump. Below deck, the *Charles Haskell* was dry as a bone!

"*Graças a Deos!*" said Joe Enos. Then he turned to the skipper. "Those poor fellers! I see the faces, captain. – One, two mens. *Ai*, the faces!"

Captain Curtis nodded, and for a moment turned away and looked into the sleet. Then he asked Joe:

"Did you see what vessel she was?"

Joe didn't know. Neither did anyone else on board the *Charles Haskell*. When they had returned to Gloucester, they learned that nine vessels had gone down on Georges that night.

Wrecks of six had been witnessed by others standing by, or accounted for by the few survivors from among the crews. The craft which the *Charles Haskell* had rammed and sunk was one of the remaining three: schooners *A. E. Price* and *Martha Porter* of Gloucester, and the *Andrew Johnson* of Salem. Captain Curtis knew the skippers of all three; but which it was that his own vessel had wrecked, he supposed he would never learn.

The *Charles Haskell* was run up on the flats near her owner's wharf, repaired, and refitted. While she was there, thousands came to look at her. Old fishermen could scarcely believe the story that she had survived a collision on Georges Bank; yet there she was, and what she did no other vessel had ever done in the history of Georges; nor would any be likely to do it again!

So said the old fellows; but they also shook their heads and told Captain Curtis that if 'twas them a-skipperin' her, they'd go find another berth. After what *she'd* done, they wouldn't want none of *her*, by God! Ten good men of Gloucester – or was it Salem – walking the water somewhere out there on Georges Bank!

Captain Curtis didn't laugh at the old men; on the contrary, he turned upon them, excited, angry.

"We ain't got no blood on our hands!" he said.

Nevertheless, Miles Joyce and James Allen wouldn't ship on her for another trip, and the skipper had to find men for their places. Joe Enos, Scotty, and the rest stuck by him.

They were glad they did; for on her next trip out, she ran straight down to Georges, sailing it like a queen, and for the next few days, did some beautiful fishing.

There was nothing curious in the fact that all the men wanted the early watches. They always did that. And when it came to setting the watch, the skipper followed the custom of the time, calling the men around him to "thumb the hat." The crew stood in a circle, each man holding to the brim of the hat, thumb up. The skipper looked away, reached over, touched a thumb, and then counted ten from that one, going around the hat clockwise. The owner of the tenth thumb got first watch, and the business was repeated to determine who his watchmate should be, for the period from eight o'clock to ten. Then it was gone through again for the next two, and so on. There was nothing peculiar in the fact that Scotty and George Winters felt relieved when they were picked for first watch the night they arrived on Georges.

But the sixth day's work was over, fish stowed, crew long since asleep, when Harry Richardson and Joe Enos took their watch on deck. Shortly after twelve o'clock, while Joe was nodding over the wheelbox, he felt a frantic thumping at his side. He started, awoke, and faced his watchmate.

Shaking, unable at the moment to speak, young Harry Richardson pointed forward. Joe straightened up and stared over the wheel. In the starlit bow of the *Charles Haskell* he saw a little group of men.

"What's a matter them fellers?" Joe asked. "What's a matter they don't turn in?"

"Portygee," Harry Richardson softly croaked, "look at 'em again! Look at 'em! Them – *them ain't our boys!*"

Joe squinted, started forward, and after a couple of steps, stood still. The little knot of figures had grown! From somewhere, more had ap-

Chapter VIII: The Ghosts of Georges Bank

peared! He could see that. And then he could see a man climb in over the rail, coming up from the starboard side. And another. Out of the waters of Georges Bank, men – figures, shadows in the shape of men – were boarding the schooner. Things of the imagination, yes; mere apparitions seen there in the starlight – but seen, Joe suddenly realized, not by one pair of eyes, but two!

Joe Enos stood still and watched. Then he turned to Harry.

"I go wake the skipper," he whispered.

As he turned, the younger man clutched at his arm. "No, you don't! You don't leave this deck, Portygee! Not with me up here, you don't!"

It didn't matter to Joe *who* went for the skipper. Still staring at the bow, he was about to tell Harry to go when the men – the things up there in the bow – started to move.

"Look!" Joe said. "They come aft!"

Silently they were stationing themselves at the regular "berths" along the deck, baiting hooks, and heaving gossamer lines over the side. And as Joe watched, it became apparent that these beings, whatever they were, were paying no attention to himself and Harry Richardson. The waters from which they had arisen were calm tonight, peaceful, beneficent; in nothing was there harm.

"All right," Joe said at last to Harry Richardson. "We stay here. We don't say nothing, you and me. By 'm by, Scotty and O'Neil got the watch. We wait and see, no?"

And so the two men stayed at the wheelbox while fishermen fished for shadows, and out of the starshine, hauled up their subtile catch.

Three minutes after Joe Enos had called the new watch and settled himself in his bunk, there was a yell from the deck. He heard the thud of boots above him, pounding aft. Then all hands were called.

When Joe went up again, the crew of the *Charles Haskell* was gathered around the cabin companionway. The figures along the deck were still obviously tending their lines, still heaving over splashless leads and slatting airy shapes into the barrels.

"I see 'em!" Captain Curtis was saying to one of the men as Joe came near. "Ain't I got eyes? But I tell you, there's no blood on our hands!" Over and over he said it, and in his voice there was a strange mingling of anger and appeal.

"There's fair wind tonight for home, skipper," somebody said.

"Me, I ain't staying out here another night," another put in. "Not me – if I have to swim it back!"

Captain Curtis was for sticking it out, and in the argument voices rose – until one or another of the men glanced forward, and then all spoke in low tones again. For this there was no need. The *Charles Haskell*'s extra hands turned now and then to one another, and smiled as their lips moved soundlessly; but for all else that went on aboard the vessel, they seemed to have deaf ears, sightless eyes.

The skipper, alone in his stand, gave in at last.

"All right, boys. Get in the anchor. We're going home."

Gingerly the men went about their work. It was slow. There was much hesitating, much backing away, for now the strangers were hauling in their lines, their work finished. But when they had gone through the motions of leaving everything shipshape, one by one they filed to the bow, stepped over the rail, and walked into the darkness of Georges Bank.

Twenty-four hours later, during the same watch, the *Charles Haskell* again was manned with the silent fishermen. But she was homeward bound now. She had passed the twin lights of Thacher's Island, and under a good breeze, was bowling past the welcome glimmer of sidelights carried on vessels from the home port.

In the small watches of the morning, she brought Eastern Point Light nearly abreast. Then the captain gave the order to bear about for Gloucester Harbor, and took the wheel himself.

At that moment, each of the strangers turned, looked aft at Captain Curtis, and then went to join his shipmates up in the bow. While the *Haskell*'s men were trimming the sails, these others stood there, watching. Then from among them one stepped out, walked aft as far as the forerigging, and gazing intently at the helmsman, slowly shook his head. But the schooner was running fast for the mouth of Gloucester Harbor, and the skipper held her to her course. And so the lone figure mounted the rail, beckoned to his fellows, and was gone over the side. The others followed. And the last the *Haskell*'s crew saw of them, they were slowly marching through the dawn – *towards Salem!*

We may think what we will of the things men say they've seen. We may explain these nightly visitors of the *Charles Haskell* into being, or we may explain them away. Whatever we care to make of them will be of no more

Chapter VIII: The Ghosts of Georges Bank

substance than the ghost-fishes they themselves slatted into empty barrels.

But what men *do* because of the things they've "seen" – well, here is another matter. And the fact does remain that from the morning she arrived home from her second trip to Georges Bank, the schooner *Charles Haskell* was taboo in Gloucester. Captain Curtis could not find a crew for her. With good fishing in prospect, and not too many berths open for the men who gathered daily in Rogers Street, one might think that a dozen men could be found for the crew from among those hundreds who were looking for berths, crowd of motley temperament, men of many faiths and none.

Not a dozen, not five, not two, could be induced to ship on the *Charles Haskell*. But one – Joe Enos, the "Portygee" – did tell Captain Curtis he was willing to try it once more. And Joe was willing because, he said, now he understood. He knew what to do.

"Next time," Joe told the skipper, "we go to Georges, we fish, we set sail. But we don't take the vessel back to Gloucester, Cap'n! When we come back, we go to Salem. We take them fellers home first!"

But the captain, man of a colder, more practical race than Joe Enos's, did not understand; and for months the *Charles Haskell* lay idle at a Gloucester wharf. Finally, rather than keep her at a dead loss, her owners sold her off to a group in Digby, Nova Scotia.

Whether the wanderers of Georges Bank ever came on board the *Charles Haskell* again, I do not know. The next time I could find the schooner mentioned was in this little item in the ship-news column of the *Provincetom Beacon*, March 11, 1893:

> On Thursday last, sch. *W. B. Keene* was at Lewis Wharf, having on board a box belonging to a hand-horn of the type used by fishing vessels for giving fog warning. On the box, which had been newly split and but a few days in the water, was painted the name, "Charles Haskell." The *Keene* is fresh-haddocking this season on Georges Bank.

Chapter IX
Boreas Strains A Lung

THE OLD MAN knows where the school fish are. John Bananas doesn't know, Dominic Doryplug doesn't know, you and I don't know; but in some mysterious way the Old Man – he may be old in years or he may be younger than any of us – in some way beyond our ken or concern, he knows.

The codfish is a traveler, with a cruising range that would take in the moon if he had six fathoms of salt water to see him through. Just now, the codfish may be anywhere from the South Channel, off Nantucket, to Belle Isle Strait. Somewhere in those million-odd square miles of water, he is finding the feed which happens at the moment to suit him, and thither he is being followed by the fabulous circles of his acquaintance. To those few places under the million-odd square miles of shoal water off America, cod, haddock, halibut – the wealth of the Atlantic – are running; and to find them is the business of the fresh-fisherman – to "get on the fish," give himself a week or two to fill, and then go bowling off to market.

How the Old Man does it, the boys in the fo'c's'le neither understand nor care. There are charts of the banks; there are newspaper columns of water-front coverage, landings, arrivals, departures; there are government reports; and there is skipper-talk, that dignified swapping of shop gossip among the Old Men themselves, in which the fo'c's'le takes no part.

But there is something more to it than all these. As he takes his vessel out of harbor and then gives the helmsman the course – one hairline on a million miles of open water to the momentary hide-out of the school fish – the Old Man is giving orders inspired not by charts and reports, not by devices that merely mark the limit of the humanly possible, but by some higher salt-water wizardry, some strange gift denied to John Bananas and Dominic Doryplug, and to you and me. So John and Nick will inform us, in case we don't know.

To the code of the American fisherman, this is the one hangnail of class consciousness, the one tradition of rank that has survived. In no other respect is the skipper a man apart. He eats with the men, he shares his cabin with them. He may ask some fellow in the fo'c's'le how to make his wife behave. But he will not ask him where to go for fish. Nor will he tolerate advice.

The crew of the fresh-fisherman goes on shares. If the Old Man doesn't get on the fish, if somehow he has lost this mysterious magic, his men must suffer along with him, for what they earn depends upon what he finds. But instead of volunteering tips, they preserve the tradition, they suffer awhile in silence, knowing that if it keeps up, the Old Man won't be the Old Man much longer. On Cape Cod, he catches fish, or very soon finds himself working a turnip farm, or taking in summer boarders; on Cape Ann, the granite quarries may have a job open for him, or there may be a cemetery where the grass wants cutting.

Boston's volatile market, especially for fresh halibut, is even more uncertain than the weather; for weather itself is only one of many factors that may kick halibut through the ceiling or send the fish begging from wharf to wharf, all within a week.

Accordingly, as the fresh-fisherman works on shares, and as his share is figured out of the vessel's "stock," or proceeds from the sale of the fish, the price of halibut writes steep ups and downs into the lives of these men and their families.

By the fisherpeople, lean fares are soon forgotten, fat ones long remembered. There was the time, for instance, when Captain Manuel Caton, better known as "Captain Roll-Down," took the schooner *Carrie E. Phillips* into Boston on March 5, 1893, with 24,000 pounds of halibut and hit a market of 13 cents, resulting in a crew share of $75.68 a man for the two-week trip. Bigger shares have been made since, and, as the *Boston Globe* realistically editorialized, "twice that amount would be little enough reward for the hardships endured by these men on their winter cruises." Yet in those days, anything better than $30 a week was big money in a fisherman's pocket. Captain Roll-Down's stock was the highest that had been made in three years.

In midwinter of the year 1895, halibut were on certain "bank-clam spots" in the stretch off Nova Scotia, about midway between Georges and the

CHAPTER IX: BOREAS STRAINS A LUNG

Western Banks, known as La Have Bank. There the school fish were, and there the Old Men of the Provincetown fresh-fishing fleet had located them.

It was a wicked winter. There is an old saying of the housewives of Cape Cod, that "it's fixing to blow when the bean pot runs dry." I don't know what their bean pots were doing that winter, but they should have dried right up and burnt to a crisp. Wherever it shifted its operations, the fishing fleet was caught in gale after gale. There were several wrecks early in the season, and returning vessels crippled into the harbor looking like swollen white caricatures of themselves. Between Thanksgiving and Christmas, four schoonermen had frozen to death, six had drowned, nearly all had been left with marks of the ordeal. It was one of the seasons when wives of fishermen in all the little coast villages were doing their best for those left helpless, and wondering where it all was going to end.

And so, along in January, when the Old Men started talking of halibut on La Have Bank, women of Provincetown shuddered and asked God what strange and pointless law it was that decreed men must go to the sea for their living. But the Old Men knew halibut were on La Have; and the crews, though they were losing heart, said little and went to sea.

The *John F. Nickerson* (Simeon West, master) sailed for La Have on January 15, and soon afterward went two of the crack Portuguese schooners of the fleet, the *Governor Russell* on January 18, and the *Joseph P. Johnson* on January 28.

Mary, wife of Captain George Brier (Silva) of the *Johnson*, was afraid. Ordinarily, like many another captain's lady of that village, she would pack him off to sea with religion tucked carefully into his thoughts, as one sends off a schoolboy with the reminder to be sure to take along his lunch. Mary Brier had spent many hours making an elaborate frame of wax-flower ornaments, like those the women made back in the Azores, to fit around the painting of the Mother and Child that hung beside the skipper's bunk; and she had satisfied herself that Captain George knew at all times Who was bringing him home safe.

The skipper, like his colleagues in the fleet, approved of everything his wife said and did along these lines, and then went down to the vessel to look to her rigging; and if he found a fault anywhere, into the rigger's loft he would storm, to give "that swindler" the cursing-out of his life. Then he would go back to his wife for a last good-by, she would assure him once more that God would watch over him and keep him safe; and he was ready for sea.

But in January of 1895, Mary Brier didn't assure the captain. She was afraid. She begged him not to make the trip. In her argument there was nothing mystical; no strange premonition moved her. In that season, all men were being begged not to make trips. And when Mary timidly began to ask "foolish questions" about the condition of the vessel – inquiries that a woman had no business making – Captain George shrugged and repeated a thing Mary had often said to him, in times of fairer weather:

"*Não faça caso, Mary. A fé é que nos salva, e não o pao da barca!*" (Never mind, Mary. It's faith that saves us, not the wood of the vessel!)

Six days after the *Johnson* sailed, Provincetown knew there was to be a repetition, somewhere at sea, of the struggle for life – perhaps the bitterest of all. On Sunday morning the barometer dropped to 28.6, and "through the day half a dozen shipmasters asserted their glasses had registered the lowest ever known."

On Tuesday afternoon, the *John F. Nickerson* came home like a bedraggled ghost. Her trip of fish was still on board. She had not been able to make Boston to market it, and for more than twenty-four hours she had been banging around Cape Cod Bay.

The *Nickerson*'s men had a wild story to tell of gale, snow, and heavy seas on La Have Bank. While the schooner was anchored on the southwest part of that grounds, a sea came over the bow, sweeping the nested dories from the gripes, ripping the ringbolts from the deck, and carrying the cable tier clear into the stern. The *Nickerson*'s cable parted, and she was blown 50 miles to the northeast before the wind subsided. When she anchored in Provincetown Harbor, she was ice from deck to main truck.

But the *Nickerson*, battered though she had been, was safe in port. The families of those on board the *Governor Russell* and the *Joseph P. Johnson* listened to the story, and stood on the wharves and stared silently out at her ice and her twisted rigging.

Then Captain West of the *Nickerson* gave out his own report – about which the crew had said nothing. He had spoken the schooner *Fredonia* of Gloucester, the captain said, and that vessel informed him that another craft had been swept close by her during the worst of the blow. Men were clinging in the rigging of the stranger, and calling to the *Fredonia* for help as they were carried past. The disabled vessel was showing two

CHAPTER IX: BOREAS STRAINS A LUNG

red lights on her deck. Beyond this, all the *Fredonia* could say towards her identification was that she had a very short foretopmast. And from this, at Provincetown, "men united in a belief that the craft seen was the *Johnson*."

Two days later, on Thursday afternoon, the schooner *Sea Fox*, commanded by Captain Manuel Roll-Down (Caton) was towed into the harbor in a sinking condition. Trying to get home from Boston the day before, she had been blown miles off her course, and had struck on the bars off Billingsgate Island, in Cape Cod Bay. A steam tug that had come into Provincetown Harbor for shelter ran out to her assistance that night, saw that she couldn't get through the mass of suds over those shallows, and turned back. The next morning she tried it again, and this time she managed to get a line on board the *Sea Fox*, work her off the bars, and bring her in tow to Provincetown.

From the breakers, ice had made inboard on this schooner through the night, filling her almost level with the rail. Her bowsprit shrouds and bobstay had become encased in cylinders "as big around as a keg-buoy."

Billingsgate Island is thirteen miles from Provincetown, on the inside of the Cape. Yet the men of the *Sea Fox*, who knew the waters of Cape Cod Bay better than they knew the streets of their own village, had thought they were *outside* Cape Cod when they struck, and that they had run aground on the dreaded Peaked Hill Bar! Such was the gale, by this time, which had started the previous Monday night.

The *Governor Russell* and the *Joseph P. Johnson* were the stoutest craft in the Provincetown fleet. Children of the men who sailed those famous sea boats had learned to make that boast. Now they kept repeating it to their playmates – and to themselves.

> Friday, February 8. – Provincetown was visited by a full-fledged tornado. The violence of the wind will be remembered long by all who were buffeted by it. At 5 A.M. it shifted suddenly from east to southeast, coming with a terrific gust that shook the houses to their foundations. The harbor waters, sheltered though they are by the encircling arm of Long Point, were rolled in heavy surges upon the beach below the town. Tide was not due to reach its full height until 10 o'clock, but two hours before full, the surf was pounding at high water mark . . .

In the harbor, Schooner *Delia* sank at her moorings. Schooners *Frank Foster* and *William B. Keene* were in collision while riding at anchor, with a broken bowsprit resulting to the *Keene* . . .

On Sunday, February 10, schooner *David Sherman* arrived in Provincetown, dismasted, from La Have Bank. She had seen a vessel – "a fishing schooner, without any question" – sink in those waters. She had run to the assistance of the crew, but had found not a man. Her own men had seen the vessel go under; but all they could say about her was that she carried a short foretopmast.

People in Provincetown didn't believe the story. People were angry. And people were getting hysterical. Men came to blows with the *Sherman*'s crew.

The *Governor Russell* was at that time twenty-three days unreported; the *Joseph P. Johnson*, thirteen days. But the *Governor Russell*'s foretopmast was no shorter than the average; the *Johnson*'s was.

Day after day, Mary Brier crossed the Province Lands and climbed the high dunes "up-back," whence the rigging of a schooner could be raised miles out at sea. There she met other women of Provincetown. And from there she turned back with them at dusk, and forced herself, as they were doing, to talk of Halifax and Yarmouth, and other places where a vessel off the Nova Scotia coast might be waiting – yes, all this time – for the weather to clear.

Then, late in the afternoon of Saturday, February 16, from her vantage point at Peaked Hill, one of the women saw a sail, far beyond the Point. The group, shielding their faces from the stinging sand, stared to windward and waited for the sail to show more clearly. Someone shouted that she was the *Governor Russell*. A woman ran down the slope, laughing wildly. People followed her, back to town. The schooner rounded the Point, stood in for the harbor. Then others who had been watching there left, one by one, slowly trudging across the sand.

"It seemed too good to be true," the *Boston Globe* reported, "and many refused to believe the story." But there she was – the gallant *Governor Russell* – triumphantly berthed among her sister craft, safe in the harbor! Three dories were sent from shore to bring home her crew.

Alone on the dune, Mary Brier stared at the tall masts of the *Governor Russell*, heard the whistles blowing alongshore, and because of her

Chapter IX: Boreas Strains A Lung

thoughts, suddenly sobbed aloud:

"God forgive me!"

The *Governor Russell* had lived up to her name as a sea boat. From La Have Bank, she was running to the eastward for deeper water when the long series of gales overtook her. On the evening of February 4, she was hove to under double-reefed foresail to ride out the storm, but the wind proved too much for even that small canvas. She began to heel dangerously. When the men let go the halyards, in an attempt to take another reef in the sail, the freak gale kept it ballooned up. They couldn't budge it. At 4 A.M. it went to pieces. Several times the crew tried to get the trysail on her, but the ropes wouldn't stand the strain.

After fifty hours of rolling under bare poles, almost in the trough on the sea, the schooner became manageable enough for the men to get up a bobbed trysail and jumbo. Then, on February 8, the wind hauled suddenly to the southwest and rose to hurricane force. The crew, kept at work constantly up to this time pounding ice from the rigging, now had to give it up. They had never seen such seas. One of them broke over, smashed five dories, and wrecked the wheelbox. But below deck the *Governor Russell* held tight, shipping very little water. There was truth in the boast of the youngsters back home.

Through seven more days of gale, snow, and punishing seas, the schooner fought it out. In all but the worst of it, the men were on deck, pounding ice – an everlasting chore in such weather. Then, on the 15th, when the schooner had worked around to the northwest of Georges Bank, the storm abated. The *Governor Russell* was on her way home, with fair wind.

> Wednesday, February 20. – Schooner *J. J. Merritt* reached port, having sold a trip of fish at Boston. Five dollars was the amount cleared per man. The *Merritt* was out in the fearful storms of the past month and was blown into the Gulf Stream twice, but suffered no injury.
>
> Apropos of the scare story about Schooner *Joseph P. Johnson*, that craft is all right, as the *Merritt*'s men saw her making a set [setting trawls] on a day subsequent to that on which a craft resembling the *Johnson* in only one particular was sighted.

Again there was gladness in Provincetown. Later that same day, the growing crowd of watchers at Peaked Hill sent word into the village that a dismasted schooner was coming in, in tow of a steam tug. But within an hour the report was corrected; the tug was only bringing in a barge.

False hopes were raised, one upon another, in rumors from every village alongshore between the Cape-end and Boston. The fifteen women and their forty-five children who believed each new story because they had to believe something were already being taken care of as "folks left destitute by the disaster." And destitute they were indeed. Two days after the *J. J. Merritt* had come home with her cheering "news," a troupe of strolling players known as "Hartley's Minstrels" gave a benefit performance in Town Hall for "fifteen fishermen's families, left without means of support by the continued absence of the schooner *Joseph P. Johnson*." The hail was packed that night.

On March 2 – thirty-three days after the *Johnson* had sailed for La Have Bank, and ten days beyond the time when all hope for her had been abandoned – word from the schooner came to Provincetown – via cable from Fayal, Azores, two thousand miles away!

The message, from Captain Brier to his wife, stated that the vessel had made port at Fayal that day.

A few days later the *Boston Globe* reported that a cablegram had been received from Silveira, Edwards & Company, agents, Fayal, "listing injuries to the schooner *Joseph P. Johnson*, which arrived at Fayal Saturday last in distress, having been wrecked on La Have Bank during the gale of February 8." One man was lost. He was Manuel Barao, 23, of Provincetown and formerly of St. Michael's. The schooner's bulwarks were destroyed, decks and upper works badly strained, skylight stove in, six boats lost, one anchor and two hundred fathoms of cable gone, trysail and jumbo torn to pieces, and figurehead lost.

To the weary people of Provincetown, the cables "seemed like news from the dead, for as such the *Johnson*'s crew has been regarded these many days." The *Provincetown Beacon*'s editor did his best to say what those brief messages meant to his community:

> Good news! Good news! They are safe in port at last and mourning has been changed to rejoicing, while the whole populace breathes easier and considers it has good cause for congratulations.

After weeks of anxiety, news of the schooner *Joseph P. Johnson*

Chapter IX: Boreas Strains A Lung

and crew arrived on Saturday last from Fayal – the last place on earth one would have looked to for news of the missing craft – and in an hour after the tidings had been received, everyone knew and thanked God that the craft had reached port . . .

What caused the *Johnson* to sail across the Atlantic east, when the home port was hundreds of miles nearer, is a cause for conjecture. That she should reach the Azores – the native soil of nineteen of her crew – seems providential.

Two months later, on the night of Sunday April 28, the *Johnson* rounded Race Point and dropped anchor in Provincetown Harbor. After the sort of greetings that might be expected of these warm-hearted people on such a reunion, the story of her voyage came out.

The schooner was on La Have Bank after two days of bucking headwinds, and began at once to "set" for fish. From a journal kept by John Reynolds, cook, it appears that the men didn't have much luck on those grounds, and the skipper decided to continue on to the Western Banks:

> Jan. 31 we set four tubs to a dory, but did not get but 1,000 pounds of fish. Dories got aboard about 2:30 P.M.
>
> Feb. 1 got under way and set four tubs to a dory, got about same fish as on day before.
>
> Sunday, Feb. 3 anchored at 5:05 P.M. on Western Banks, hove a line over to try for fish and caught several dogfish. Captain said we were too far to south.
>
> Monday, 4th, got under way at 8 A.M. and steered E N E. At 3:30 P.M. we anchored with a good breeze going, and it grew stronger, until we had to give her all the cable before dark.

Cook's "good breeze," the men explained, turned out to be a hurricane. Shortly after ten o'clock that night, the vessel broke adrift, dragging her anchor along as she was batted to the southeast. The crew took three reefs in the foresail, hoisted it, saw at once she couldn't carry it, and took it back in.

Five hours later the anchor caught bottom, bringing the vessel up short in her banging race to leeward. She hung on for more than an hour. Then her cable parted, and she was off again to the southeast, now carried out faster than ever. All through the day following, with the same roaring nor'wester to broom her out, she scudded helplessly under bare poles.

> At A.M. Feb. 6 all hands on deck standing by. At 4:30 captain sent Frank to break the bulwarks on the port side. At 7 P.M. it calmed a little. Captain said we were southeast from Sable Island.
>
> Thursday, 7th, it started to blow heavy again at 12 midnight, as strong as before. At this time we were in the Gulf Stream, 4 men on watch. At 2 o'clock A.M. I was up to get breakfast ready. I could not stand up below for the rolling of the vessel. At 5:15 two of the men that were on watch came below to warm themselves, and João Victorino da Silveira and Manuel Barao stayed on deck. At 5:40 A.M. a big sea struck us, which laid the vessel broadside with masts in the water, started the planks off the side of the vessel on the starboard side, lost forestaysail boom, staysail box and staysail and six dories. Manuel Barao lost overboard.

Cook Reynolds' account, admirably condensed, was set down for those with some understanding of a fishing schooner and her crew, for those who would know what sort of gale it was when a sea cook "could not stand up below for the rolling of the vessel." As others in the crew explained further, when the two men of the deck watch went below, everything had been well snugged down, companionways closed, hatches battened; and it was this precaution that saved the *Johnson* when the "big sea" struck her. While she lay with her masts flat along the water, there wouldn't have been a chance for her otherwise, they said; and even so, she wavered for ten minutes with nothing of her lee side showing – ten minutes which none in that crew hoped to live over again – before she righted at last.

All hands were called on deck, but before they could make themselves of any use, following seas made inboard, scattering a raffle of broken boats and loose rigging.

> All hands were found on the port side when they came to. The rings that were on the deck, driven through the planks to hold the dories, were parted even with the deck. Part of the few livers we had in the barrels [halibut and cod livers are saved out as the fish are gutted] were found up in the cross-trees 3 days later. We also found a pair of nippers on the port rigging six feet above the sidelights. That afternoon wind moderated some.

Chapter IX: Boreas Strains a Lung

When this happened, the *Johnson*, according to cook's journal, was five hundred and fifty miles southeast of Highland Light, the lighthouse on the shore of Truro, near the tip of Cape Cod. And from that time on, the story is one of gale after gale, and of a vessel's losing fight to claw back towards home in the face of the never-ending nor'westers. They were not ordinary gales, for heaving-to and riding out an ordinary gale was routine business for a vessel like the *Johnson*. There were nor'westers in which even a fishing schooner couldn't lie to – which meant winds of hurricane force.

Feb. 8, Friday, at 2:45 A.M. called all hands on deck to reef the foresail, wind southeast with rain. At 11 A.M. wind came N W again, blowing heavy and snowing. At P.M. tried to lay her to on account of big cross-seas, but could not.

Saturday, Feb. 9, it calmed down again. It was so all the morning. At 1:35 P.M. the wind came from W S West . . . At 7 P.M. wind from the northwest with snow squalls and big seas.

Sunday, 10th, made sail at 8:30 A.M. Wind N E, steered N W until 4:15 P.M. Took in sail and hove her to, heavy breeze from northwest.

Monday, 11th, at 4:20 A.M. wind came from N W with bad sea and we were forced to run before it. Wind was too strong to lay her to.

Next day the weather moderated. The skipper ordered the reefs shaken out of the foresail, and once more hopefully wore her to the westward.

Wednesday, Feb. 13th, at 2:15 A.M. wind came from south, strong, and big lumping sea. At 2 P.M. crew made a drag with the big anchor and some boards with 50 fathoms of cable attached, and with this we laid all right. Next day we had to heave in the drag. Wind came from northwest with heavier sea than before and blowing very heavy. Then we started to run her before the wind again, for she would not lay to at all.

This went on pretty steadily until Saturday February 16, when cook made a significant entry – his first concerning the schooner's position since the reference to Highland Light.

According to the captain's reckoning, this day we were 700 miles from the Western Islands. The Captain made up his mind to go to Western Islands.

The course from the Western Banks to the Western or Azores Islands was about twenty-two hundred miles, east by south. Thus the nor'westers had already made up the captain's mind for him. Schooner *Joseph P Johnson* had been practically blown across the Atlantic! But her troubles were not over yet. To pick up cook:

> I told the crew that I could not give more than two meals per day, as I was afraid we would get out of provisions altogether. The men consented, willing to abide by my decision.
> Sunday, 17th, at 1:15 A.M. began to breeze up from southwest with a very heavy swell. At 6 A.M. a big sea struck us on the crippled side. Two dories broken. One man hurt. Last of the coffee was drank this morning.

More "breezes," until February 22, some of them fair for the Azores, some headwinds that blocked the schooner for hours at a time. Then:

> Between the 22nd and 28th fine weather was had. On the 23rd rations of two slices of bread twice a day were served to each man. This was caused by scarcity of flour, the only food we had left. The crew looked sorry enough when I told them we were almost out of flour and no signs of land ahead. The men were using ice from the fish pens for drinking purposes, but it made them sick. On Monday threw the fish overboard. They were rotten.
> Tuesday, 26th, at 10 A.M. sighted a sail to windward overhauling us. Got a dory over to board craft. Hoisted our flag at 11:35. The stranger hoisted French flag. The craft came in hailing distance at 12:45 noon. She was the French bark *Tourny* of Bordeaux. Captain went on board her and got latitude and longitude. We were 300 miles west of Fayal. The bark gave us 2½ barrels of hard tack, some coffee, vinegar, kerosine, sugar, 2 cans condensed milk and 1 bottle of brandy. The brandy and condensed milk are still on board.
> Friday, March 1st, sighted Fayal and Pico 30 miles off. Cleared ship at sunset, calm.

Chapter IX: Boreas Strains a Lung

Saturday, March 2nd, entered harbor of Fayal at 9:30 A.M. We remained there until April 3rd.

In the spring of 1895, the *Boston Herald* summed up its review of events of the preceding winter with this comment:

> It would seem that but little additional disaster would be needed to completely break the nerve of the fisherman and cause his retirement from a field that has grown steadily less fertile with the march of years.

On July 27 of the same year, this paragraph appeared in the *Provincetown Beacon*:

> The following vessels of the fresh-fishing fleet were in port the past week: *Marshall L. Adams*, crew share $17; *Nellie G. Adams*, $17; *Sea Fox*, $6; *Julia Costa*, $9; *Joseph P. Johnson*, $26; *Rosie Cabral*, $23; *Governor Russell*, $28.

125

Chapter X
Mist on the Western Banks

Pobre Antoine! De mao humor, eh?

Well, sit down, have one of my ready-made cigarettes, and tell me what's on your mind. Another argument with the boys, is it? Another wrangle – over nothing at all? Ah, Tony, Tony! All day long and half the night, the same old thing – the same old thing – argument, argument! They say there's one on every vessel, one poor fellow they all pick on – but I wonder whose fault that is! You'd think, if they just wanted to bait somebody, they'd pick a big fellow, like that José Ferro-Fundido (Joe Cast-Iron) – not the littlest man in the crew!

Is it because they know you can't take it, Tony? Or is it that, with all the miserable fog, the slow fishing we've been having this trip, they're like a bunch of kids, they've got to let it out on someone? Or maybe a little of both?

Here, I'll let you do the talking, and I'll turn it into English for the other fellow. Now, what's on your mind? Go ahead, Tony – it's all yours!

Talking! What's the good of talking? All I ask is peace! All I beg of them, all I cry aloud to heaven for – peace!

They don't like me, those fellows. I know that. I'm used to that. But I don't care what they think, or what they say behind my back (Oh, I catch 'em all the time, saying things behind my back!), if they'd only let me alone!

But no, they have to keep arguing with me, always arguing! That's no way to treat a man when he goes shipmates – fighting with him about his watch on deck, about the way he keeps his gear, the bait he takes, even his pitching fish, or ripping or gutting 'em!

Pick, pick, pick! It's enough to drive a man crazy! They don't like where I hang my oil clothes. They hide my boots. I take along my violin, they rub the bow with bearing-grease. They count the pork chops I take with

Chapter X: Mist on the Western Banks

my mug-up. They talk about my snoring in my bunk. *In my own bunk!* It's all right the way, Pete Sweet-Kees snores, or the way Gus Crapoo snores, but not the way *I* snore!

And when I go to eat supper – I tell you, they get a man so excited at the table, a man can't finish his meal! Pick, pick, pick! – till I have to get up and go on deck before I start a plank somewhere! Then, when I'm up on deck, I can hear 'em down there – the sons o' whores! – laughing, calmed down now, everything peaceful, everybody eating hearty!

Well, a man doesn't object when they call him Anão – Runt – and he doesn't have to listen to them when they laugh at him because he isn't as tall as some, or because he happens to have a voice that's pitched higher than some. A man was born that way. Those things aren't a man's fault. But when they keep after a man, day and night, playing tricks, bedeviling a man – Aiee! How does it go, the old saying? *Boa viagem faz quem em sua casa esta em paz* – He makes a good voyage who stays at home in peace!

> The fog comes
> on little cat feet.

Fog again! Wind sou'west on the Western Banks, and the soft quick treachery of fog! Fog with all the dories out on a "set!"

Here you have a blue sky, sun shining like a new nickel. You watch the skipper putting the boats out, one by one, to lay their trawls in a vast fan spreading from the vessel. The men go two to a boat – all except Tony. He goes "single-dory," because – well, just because he has no dory-mate, so they tell you. When the last boat is off, you go forward for a cup of coffee with cook.

Below, you chew the rag with cook for five minutes. Five minutes! – then you come on deck, and you pinch yourself, you rub your eyes! And you hear the skipper swearing and saying he wished he had a job ashore in the A&P.

"T'ick-a-fog!" Fog so bad a man at the wheel can't see the foremast. Is it the same world? Were you really here on deck, five minutes ago, lazing in the stern, gratefully letting the sun filter through your dungarees? Because this isn't even the translucent, sunlit sort of fog that comes in five minutes and then goes as quickly; this is *real* fog, raw, gray, cold fog, the kind that may hang on for days! In five minutes! Yes, that's how the fog shuts in over the Western Banks.

Through this pea soup the vessel goes chugging gingerly ahead at half-speed. You may remember that when you were a child, you sometimes closed your eyes while you walked along a road or street, testing yourself to see how many steps you could take before you had to open them. Within a few steps you had to look; you couldn't go on. There was no danger ahead, your eyes assured you; but the moment you closed them again, your mind began putting dangers there. How unbearable, you may have reflected, to be blind, to go on always without this assurance! And that feeling returns now as the schooner gropes ahead. But it doesn't last long, because you are watching the skipper working, and presently you are given to see what he can do.

By what strange assortment of extra senses he is finding his way around to those scattered dories, you will never know; but somehow, one by one, they are being picked up out of nowhere, and their men taken aboard. There is the foghorn to blow, there is the doryman's conch shell to listen for; there is the compass to figure by, and there is the tide-drift to count in. But for all these mechanical helps, it still looks like an uncanny piece of business. Boat after boat comes out of the mist, and you do not try too hard to understand. You do not even see these dories through the fog until long after the skipper has seen them.

"There!" he says. "There's Henrique – with another feller alongside."

You peer into the fog – and three minutes later you make out two shapes of faintest gray. The vessel chugs up, the gray shapes sharpen into dories, with men standing in them, calmly waiting to get aboard.

Out of the gray curtain they glide, until all are safe but one.

Pobre Antoine! Agora em paz? – in peace at last?

Around and around, the vessel spirals for the one man who has gone astray in the fog and has not been picked up. The boys grumble impatiently about Tony. If he'd been where he belonged, they would have found him by this time! If he'd listen for the foghorn, if he'd blow on his conch shell, if he'd time his answering blow correctly when they gave him the horn . . . But by this time Tony is probably so excited he doesn't know what he's doing! That feller, that Tony! He gets wild, you know, loses his head. It's the same way when he's ashore. His wife, poor woman, and the kids – from the day Tony gets home, they're nearly crazy in that house until he's off to sea again!

The skipper grimly widens the spiral course he is steering. Now and

Chapter X: Mist on the Western Banks

then he pulls the bell knob, signaling the engineer to shut off the power. As the vessel glides on, hushing her water line, the compressed-air foghorn gives two short sharp barks. The skipper listens. He tries it again, listens again. Nothing – nothing! He bangs his fist on the wheelbox.

"Son of a whore, why don't he blow that conch?"

Another yank on the bell, and on she goes, circling. The afternoon passes, and still the fog hangs on. Every few minutes now, the skipper shuts her off, blows the horn. And at last a thin answering cry comes dying on the wind! The horn again. And again the faint cry. To you and me, it might be coming from anywhere, but these fellows sing out as one man, "Nor'west!" No more is said, but while the vessel is running down that answer, it is plain to see that the tension on board is broken. Men who stopped cursing at Tony are at it again.

But Tony isn't there. The vessel finds two strangers in a dory – Nova Scotians – astray from their own vessel. They are out of Yarmouth; but night is settling over the Western Banks, and they, gratefully come aboard. They'll go to Gloucester, then take the steamer home.

Cook has had supper hot on the stove since three o'clock, the usual hour. Nobody has eaten, but now a few go below with the two fellows they have picked up. The skipper sticks at the wheel, ever circling, blowing the horn, listening.

After supper it starts to breeze up. The fog lifts, but the wind that clears it has hauled to the northward, and the glass is falling fast.

If there were any point in cruising longer in the search for Tony, the skipper would keep on. But now that is useless. It is coming up to blow hard. Either he has been picked up and is safe on some other craft by now, or tonight – tonight it is likely to be – for Tony – the "good voyage."

The two Nova Scotians are pardonably happy. In their shoes, men couldn't very well help feeling happy! But as night comes on, they understand. They drop their yarning, they are aware that "gamming" with these boys doesn't go now. In the face of the skipper, and of every man in the crew, there is a look that they have seen before, a look that they and all other fishermen have known at some time after the fogs that come and go on the Western Banks.

"Astray in the fog!"

Oft told tale in the banks fishery! And they dread it as much, these fellows of today, as men did when they had to rely on sail alone. When a man's adrift on the ocean in a tiny open boat, until they find him it's all one to him whether the mother-schooner has an engine, whether there are radios and Coast Guard planes that can be called out to look for him. His own boat is just what men had when they went astray on the banks forty and fifty years ago. He has a small jug of water, one little sail, a pair of oars, and his fishing gear. For some reason that nobody seems able to explain – least of all the fishermen themselves – they take along no food in case of such an emergency, and only a few carry compasses.

Yet the wind is as cold today, the sea as merciless, as in October, 1874, for example, when two dorymen of the Gloucester schooner *Marathon* were separated from their vessel on the Grand Banks and lived to hand down the following tale* of their seven days adrift:

> They could hear the shouts of their companions, but all efforts to reach them proved unavailing. It soon commenced raining, and the two men made up their minds to do the best they could through the night, in hopes to find their vessel in the morning. Fortunately there were three trawl tubs on board, and two of these were made fast to the painter of the dory, and did most excellent service as drogues, keeping her head to the sea.
>
> The night passed drearily, and they were glad enough when morning dawned; but the fog still continued to envelop them, and they concluded to row to the westward. It cleared up occasionally, but they saw no vessel, and night came on again.
>
> The next day was also foggy, and they laid to the drogue all day, drifting to the eastward. Took watch and watch this night, in hopes to catch a glimpse of some vessel's passing lights, but their hopes were disappointed. It rained during the night, and they caught a good supply of water in their remaining tub; of this they drank sparingly, and it served to appease the fearful pangs of thirst and hunger.
>
> On the third day they rowed to the northwest in hopes of getting into the track of the steamers. The fog still continued, no vessel was seen, and they passed another night in suspense. The men were by this time getting discouraged . . .
>
> The morning of the fourth day was clear, and it continued moderate through the day. This gave them courage, and although

Fishermen's Own Book, Gloucester, 1882.

Chapter X: Mist on the Western Banks

quite weak, they rowed to the westward, keeping an anxious lookout for some welcome sail, and doing their best to keep up each other's courage. A shark came along during the day, and they endeavored to catch him, as they would gladly have partaken of anything eatable, but they were unsuccessful. When the sun went down that night, the poor fellows felt their hearts sink within them, and they thought their chances of being picked up were rather slim.

Yet through more days and nights, each with some new agony inflicted by wind or sea, they kept their dory afloat and watched for a sail.

The sun went down for the eighth time, and still no signs of relief. They watched eagerly through the early evening hours, and knew they could not hold out a great while longer. They talked of their chances as men will talk in the face of a common danger, and both were of the opinion that they could not survive another twenty-four hours. Then they lay down, and in the depths of their hearts prayed that they might be picked up before morning.

That night a passing steamer sighted their boat, stopped, and took them aboard.

Others, astray on the banks, have suffered as much as these men, some even more. In July, 1898, Lucien Mintler and Jean Nichole, of the French fishing bark *Josephine Anna*, rowed their dory into the harbor at St. John's, Newfoundland, after having been adrift on the Grand Banks twenty-two days. Four lines in a newspaper is the only record of what they went through. On August 6, 1918, Charles Fernandez of the Gloucester schooner *Elsie G. Silva* went astray and was picked up by another vessel after he had spent ten days alone on the open sea. He managed to keep alive by building a little fire on some of his gear in the bottom of the dory and cooking the haddock he had caught. Raw fish or raw seaweed is useless at such times. It won't stay down.

Early in the afternoon of Tuesday March 2, 1897, the gay chores of making ready for a big *chamarita*, old-time Azorian square-dance, are going forward in a "Portygee hall" in Provincetown. Girls are busy setting out wine glasses and hanging bright streamers, and busier still in their chatter of what fun the evening will bring, of the costumes they have chosen for the masquerade, and of the persons they will be most especially wearing them for. Already there is laughter in the hall, and even in the kitchen, where very difficult little cakes are being baked by the older women, the experts who know how things are done in the Old Country.

Yes, a lively time is on the way, a good old-fashioned *festa*; for this is the *Dia dos Entrudos*, day for the prankish Shrove Tuesday carnival which even now – this very minute – is in full swing back in the Old Country. There will be tuneful strings of the viola and guitar, there will be castanets, and the whirl and skip and swing of the *chamarita* itself, with the singing and clapping that are part of it. Young and old will join in the turns of polka, balancing to partners, grand right and left, ladies' chain, with now and then a little waltz, and sometimes – because it is the *Dia dos Entrudos* – a sly kiss, and a not-very-discouraging slap. The music will get faster, the dance whirlier, wilder, until at last the prompter shouts "*Trilote!*" Then it will stop – for a while – and amid the ecstatic buzz of everybody talking and nobody listening, there will be time for wine and a glance at the masks and costumes of others. If any vessels make port at the last minute, there will be the fun of watching men in heavy seaboots and dungarees, mixing with the "port-hoggers" who have had time to dress ashore.

Over there is black-eyed Catherina Rose, already dressed in the outfit her mother brought over from Pico – dark blue skirt of heavy woolen *picote* with a border of scarlet; little blue hussar jacket with many seams in the back, and welted with red; and red kerchief about her head. Mary Santos is looking her over and weighing the question whether, tonight, Man'el is going to fancy Catherina's costume more than her own. One must say Catherina is gorgeous. But Man'el may take a fancy to the dress Mary will wear, and the other things that came from Horta, and the little sandals, the short full petticoat of gamboge hue with Roman stripe for the border; the white short gown with bright patchwork showing under it; red kerchief around her neck and square-topped, broad-brimmed straw hat. Yes, Catherina is gorgeous, but – well, wait and see!

In a corner by the tables set for cakes and wine is our old friend Senhor Miguel Bicho-Couve – Mike Cabbage-Bug – tuning up his guitar and polishing off a few of the numbers he will play tonight. As he strums on, now and then he breaks out with a baritone solo, which in English would go something like this:

Chapter X: Mist on the Western Banks

> I'd worship you, my darling,
> But one suspicion lingers;
> In the stoup of holy water
> Do all men dip their fingers?

Or like this

> Oh, I'd rather be on the deep sea,
> The sea so bitter and salt,
> Than on the lips of little snips
> Who are forever finding fault!

But in that excited forgathering there is one who sits over by the wall and stares dismally into a tumbler on the table before him, and now and then looks up and shakes his head.

Avô Panella (Grandpa Saucepan) was a fortune-teller in his day – one of the best known *bruxos* in all São Miguel – and when he came across the ocean he brought his claim to these powers with him. But alas, things are not the same with Grandpa Saucepan here in America. People don't take one seriously, no matter how famous one might have been as a *bruxo* in one's day. And the young folks – Well, one can scarcely blame the young when their own parents seem to have forgotten the old ways, or to care no more for them!

Here in America, for example, people call the doctor when they are ill – the doctor, who has to ask them all sorts of foolish questions first, and then sends them with a slip of paper to the drugstore! A good *bruxo* never has to ask folks what's ailing them! He already knows. That is his business. And knowing what ails folks, he knows what will cure them. Ah, but now – now things are different! People are different. The only time they seek out Grandpa Saucepan any more is on some day of merrymaking, like this *Dia dos Entrudos*, when they want him to tell their fortunes – yes, as a piece of entertainment!

Well, what can one do? It is bad luck to refuse. So, this afternoon, Grandpa Saucepan has arranged his own table in the hall. Everything has to be just so; for on the *Dia dos Entrudos* one looks into the future by a somewhat different device from those of ordinary times. One takes a raw egg and a tumbler of water. One breaks the egg, separates it, and drops the white into the water. Just so, it must be. Then one leaves it in a cool spot for a few minutes. When the white of the egg has settled, one finds that it has taken shape, some clearly defined form. And if one is a competent *bruxo*, one can read that shape, and from it interpret the future.

Grandpa Saucepan has broken an egg for practice this afternoon, and now he is shaking his head, again and again, but no one pauses to ask him, what the trouble is. No one notices.

Alas, these busy women, these happy youngsters! If that poor little Mary Santos, and Mrs. Cabral, and Mrs. Flores, and half a dozen other women out there in the kitchen – if they only knew that at this very moment, somewhere at sea, fathers and husbands are adrift – astray in the fog! – many hours in their dories, suffering with thirst and hunger, and waiting, still waiting for the sail they may never see! Alas, alas! – no one even looks!

From the *Provincetown Beacon*, Saturday March 6, 1897:

> The bonny 100-tonner *Joseph P. Johnson* came into the harbor early Tuesday evening with her flag at half-mast for the possible death of sixteen stalwart Portuguese members of her crew who left her side Friday morning to make a set of trawls on the Western Banks and went astray in a fog that shut in while they were at their work . . .
>
> At daybreak Wednesday an early riser saw a compact flotilla of small boats, gliding into the harbor, and a moment later the glad tidings of the safe arrival of the men of the *Johnson*, who had been lost 450 miles from home, was spreading like wildfire.

The two men who worked the *Johnson* into the harbor at Provincetown just at dinnertime on that Tuesday evening were Captain George Brier and the cook. As soon as the vessel was sighted, people began to gather alongshore and several men rowed out in dories. The hall, scene all set for the evening's *chamarita*, was silent now. One scared old man still sat at a table, his gaze fixed upon a tumbler of water with the white of an egg in it. All the others had gone down to the waterfront.

Captain Brier was taken to his home, but not before he had told his story to those who were waiting on the wharf.

The weather had been clear, he said, last Friday forenoon when the *Johnson* put out her dories on the western edge of the shoal. At about ten o'clock the fog banked up swiftly, drawing the visibility in to zero within a matter of minutes. The ship-keepers started at once to cruise back and

Chapter X: Mist on the Western Banks

forth for the dories. At noon, having failed to find a single boat, the skipper decided to drop anchor and take in sail, which would offer the dorymen a stationary goal in their search.

Through the afternoon, captain and cook kept grinding steadily at the foghorn. At dusk cook carried a lantern to the masthead and set other lights about the vessel. Then, all night long, they kept the horn going. At four in the morning the fog lifted. Captain Brier went aloft with his glass. He could see five miles, but no dory lay within that range.

The schooner was left at anchor until Monday morning, the two men keeping their vigil day and night. By that time the skipper knew it was useless to wait. That part of the bank was eighty miles from the coast of Nova Scotia. It would be a long row for the men, but the weather had been mild, sea smooth; and under those conditions, Captain Brier knew they would try to make the shore after their first few hours, or perhaps the first day, of searching for the schooner.

It was a big two-man job to work ship. Using the windlass, they took four hours getting the sails up. When they tried to bring in the anchor, they could get only ten fathoms of cable on board. Early in the afternoon they cut cable and stood away to the northward in one last effort to find the crew. They sailed twenty miles, then fifteen to the northwest; and then the skipper swung around for home, while cook got up the balloon gaff-topsail and staysail.

George Brier was sick, bodily as well as at heart, when he was brought ashore at Provincetown. He had had no sleep or food for forty-eight hours. He was like Captain Manuel Simmons, two years before, when the *Ruth Martin* reached Boston minus seventeen of her crew, who were missing under almost the same circumstances.

Captain Brier kept talking of the *Martin* crew's lucky return. All those men had been picked up by other vessels, and from one port or another, had eventually come home safe. There was a strong tide on Brown's Bank, where the *Martin* was fishing, and a rough sea, too. But out there on the Western Banks, where his own men had gone astray, there was no wind – no wind at all, the Captain kept saying to his friends, and it was only eighty miles offshore. But when the newspapermen came to the house, he broke down.

"I've been master twenty years," he told them, "and in all that time I've lost only one man. Now – now I wish I had never gone skipper!"

Out on the Western Banks, as soon as they saw the fog blanketing over them, the dorymen of the *Joseph P. Johnson* began to sound their conch-shells. Although the men on board the schooner couldn't hear them, the sixteen dory-men heard each other, and within an hour they were gathered at one spot, with their eight boats made fast, one to the next. At four o'clock that afternoon the fog lifted, but the vessel was nowhere to be seen. They decided to wait where they were, and hung at anchor there until daylight Saturday.

The wind was westerly that morning, weather clear. A few of the men had compasses. The little fleet set out for Nova Scotia with the dories arranged in two strings of four each, connected by the painters. The first three boats in each string set their sails.

But with the wind almost dead ahead, and with no food and only a little water on hand, the men saw those eighty miles stretching out rather like eight hundred. One of the groups got ahead, and to avoid being separated, they attached all the boats in one long string. A flat calm, coming a couple of hours later, suggested change; and the men began to row hard. Before noon it was breezing up fresh from the north, with a heavy sea making. One man in each dory had to bail, and keep bailing, while the other rowed. On Saturday evening they cast two of the boats adrift, taking the men into others.

Shortly after midnight they heard the creaking of the yards of a square-rigger. They set up a yell. When they raised her through the gloom, they managed to get her attention, and rowed near enough to speak her. She was the Norwegian bark *China* from West Bay – Yohs Andersen, master. Captain Andersen told them they were twenty-five miles from Nova Scotia. He said he would stand by for them; and when daylight came he took them aboard.

Next day the *China* spoke the Provincetown schooner *I. J. Merritt*, bound for Boston with a fare of fish. The *Johnson*'s men were transferred to her. On Wednesday morning the *Merritt*, coming to within ten miles of Race Point on her way across Cape Cod Bay, dropped the six boats off, and the men rowed on into Provincetown Harbor.

It was Ash Wednesday. Time for solemnity, for wearing a cross of ashes on one's forehead. And joyous fisherpeople of Provincetown dutifully kept the day, wore ashes and were silent.

But the gay streamers for a *chamarita* still hung in the hall, wineglass-

Chapter X: Mist on the Western Banks

es still were glistening, young eyes were going back furtively to corners where costumes were stowed away. Let the ashes be worn on Wednesday; let the six Sundays and the forty long weekdays of Lent go their subdued way; let the church call in her children on Holy Thursday; let the curtains be black, the altar stripped, and let the carpenters drive no nails on Good Friday; but there is still a Saturday, forty-six days later – Saturday afternoon for gayety, and Saturday night for a big Easter ball! Yes, Saturday would permit, masquerade and all!

On that Saturday afternoon Grandpa Saucepan broke another egg for practice and let the white settle in a tumbler of water. Out in the kitchen Mrs. Cabral was seeing that everything was ready, and here in the hall young Man'el Furtado was sprinkling the floor with cornmeal.

"Ai, ai, ai!" Grandpa Saucepan groaned. And when Man'el paused and asked him what the matter was, he shook his head and declared that it was breaking his heart – yes, breaking his poor, weak heart! *Ai, ai, ai, que pena!* – what a pity, what a pity! But there wasn't any use telling folks about it! They wouldn't believe it, they wouldn't listen! Nobody would bother about what an old man said. He, Grandpa Saucepan, really shouldn't have come at all. But what could he do? It was very bad luck for a *bruxo* to refuse! But these poor people – while they were laughing and dancing that very night – alas, if they only knew that somewhere at sea . . .

Young Man'el turned away and took the cornmeal back to the kitchen.

"Grandpa Saucepan's at it again," he told Mrs. Cabral. "Going on the same old way – *'Ai, ai, ai, que pena, que pena!'* – always the same! Why doesn't he stay home?"

Chapter XI
Big Wind on the Grand Banks

FOR THREE CENTURIES the Yankees have known it as the "West Injy Hurricane" – that dread unpredictable which comes screaming out of the south for a flying tackle at the Atlantic Ocean. But fishermen in the Yankee towns have a shorter name for it – the "Line Gale."

Some time in September, the old-timer alongshore will tell you, "sure as you're setting on that thwart, you're going to get a Line Gale in these waters. Here you'll be, minding your own business away up three thousand miles from the Line, but that won't make any difference; along in September, when the sun crosses the Line, you'll get it."

And if it's been easy sailing and good fishing up to September 21 – then look out! The sun is like a fisherman. Sometimes, when the whole world seems to be taking the windward beat, and luck is making low-liners of us all, a change is all right. But when things are going smoothly, and no one can kick, then naturally the sun doesn't like to swap berths. And that's when you're going to have a gale o' wind. If the weather's been *especially* smooth, you're in for a *livin'* gale o' wind. And if, on top of that, you've been making quick trips and the market has held up well, then you can just snug down for a West Injy Hurricane – a September Line Gale.

So say the old-timers from Cape Cod Bay to Fundy. What they mean by a Line Gale, meteorologists tell us, is not born on "the Line," or Equator, but a few degrees north, where the trade winds meet in the zone that sailors call the "Doldrums," and that scientists call the "Belt of Calms."

South of the Sargasso, the Atlantic Ocean wears this belt loosely across its middle, letting it slip down in the winter around the African Gold Coast, across to about Cape St. Roque, in South America; and hitching it up every summer as far north as the Cape Verde Islands on one side and Trinidad on the other.

Regularly this happens, year in and year out, and it is in September,

Chapter XI: Big Wind on the Grand Banks

when the Belt of Calms is hitched as high as it will go, that the world usually coughs up the West Indies hurricane.

This strange wheel of wind, the Atlantic's masterpiece of hell and high water, is turned loose to the northward, while it spins within itself; and ordinarily, with many bends and twists, it goes slowly screaming over the Caribbean, north perhaps to a latitude somewhere off the Carolinas, and finally out to sea.

That is what ordinarily happens. But anything may happen; and to say "freak West Indies hurricane" is poor English. All West Indies hurricanes are freaks; and of course, the more destructive they are to the works of man, the more freakish man is inclined to call them.

In 1935, after wearing several Atlantic charts through to the cloth, and making all other calculations it could think of, the newly organized hurricane division of the United States Weather Bureau set the boundaries of the "South Atlantic Hurricane Belt" for this country from Cape Hatteras to Brownsville, Texas. It was somewhere within those points on our own coast line that West Indies hurricanes were likely to strike when they didn't behave themselves and go out to sea.

Three years later, what was left of New England woke one morning to look out upon the work of a West Indies hurricane, the most devastating since the Galveston gale in 1900. The area hit on the night of September 21, 1938, lay hundreds of miles north of Hatteras. And the storm had been "freak" – that is, unpredictable – not only in its course, but in velocity of its main travel as well. Instead of moving its center up-coast at the usual rate of ten miles an hour, or even at the unusual rate of twenty, it had gone roaring through the night at sixty miles and more, taking half a dozen states in its stride before the people could be warned of their peril.

But for seasoned mariners, the September Line Gale usually releases advance publicity all over the sea and sky. They know as well as the wildly wheeling gulls when one is on the way. The long, unbroken swell that such a gale rolls before it has a different timing, crest to crest, from the ground swell of an ordinary breeze. Along with it, you're almost certain to get a stronger tide. You'll have a red sky, most likely, both morning and night, and you'll feel what the sky itself and the birds and your own shipmates are feeling in the fitfully changing weather that follows.

There's not much you can do about it, except to snug everything down good and taut. Then, out of what may be a dead calm, you get a slow-starting southeast breeze. Even while this is getting under way, the sea is breaking its vast swells into white water, and the vessel gets in more roll with her pitch. Rapidly then the breeze goes from light airs to gale force, to sixty, seventy, even eighty miles an hour.

You ride this out well enough. A few dories may be gone, some of the gurry kids and small gear ripped from the lashings; but if the watch on deck has looked sharp, you haven't lost any men. And suddenly, you find yourself in a calm! – but an eerie calm, with seas greater than ever, despite the fact that now there is no wind. You are, in fact, in the "wind's eye," the very center of the hurricane. This low-pressure hub of the wheel averages about fourteen miles across. It will take an hour, maybe two, for that to pass. While the lull endures, the air is warmer, drier. You can see the sun shining. Exhausted birds alight on the water, sometimes fall on the deck. And then the light begins to turn from yellow to gray.

The wind's eye has come and gone. And now you get the Line Gale at its worst. As you are caught up in the other side of the spinner, the wind hauls around to the northwest. As suddenly as it went calm, it comes back a-screaming. There is nothing more for you to do. Your life is to be saved by the timbers of the vessel, or by your faith – as you may choose between these – or given up to the sea no matter which you may have chosen. If you are washed overboard, your shipmates can do nothing for you. If the vessel starts a plank, or capsizes, they can do nothing for themselves. Until the final whirl, when the craft is riding it safely out or resting on the bottom, men will have to wait, disarmed of their one most precious weapon – their own initiative. And that is why your shipmates who may yarn or laugh or swear in other blows, pass the time in silence while they wait for the worst of a "Line Gale."

> The great demand now is for improved harbor facilities. The people of Texas and Galveston recognize this demand, and at their earnest instigation the government is now taking hold of the matter with vigor. An improved harbor is all that is required. Nature has done all that it is possible to do in furnishing shelter and protection and abundance of space.*

At eight o'clock on the night of Saturday September 8, 1900, the flooded, wind-racked city of Galveston pulled itself together and thanked God that the West Indies hurricane was over.

Encyclopaedia Britannica, 9th ed., 1891, article "Galveston."

Chapter XI: Big Wind on the Grand Banks

After driving the West Bay tide over the flood marks and then through the streets and into the first floors of the island city, after smashing windows, putting water and light plants out of service, and sweeping away all four bridges to the mainland, the seventy-mile gale had suddenly died down.

They were disheartened by the sight of hundreds of homes washed away; they were worn with the hours of terror; but Galveston's 38,000 thanked God that it had been no worse. For certainly, with the water where it then stood, it might have been worse! So said the people, when the big wind suddenly died down.

It took the deceptive calm-center of that hurricane less than an hour to pass over the city. Hauling around to the northwest, the wind struck again; and this time it was more terrible than before. The wind gauge on the roof of the United States Weather Bureau's office recorded a velocity of eighty-four miles an hour – then blew away, among the flying shingles, glass, and other wreckage.

In the three hours that followed, Galveston was laid low – homes, churches, schools, business section – and six thousand bodies floated through what had been the city streets.

Charlottetown, Prince Edward Island, September 15 [1900]. – The Texas hurricane swept over this province Wednesday night [September 12, four days after it had struck at Galveston] causing immense damage, full details of which are not obtainable as wires are broken down throughout the island. The fruit crop has been ruined. Bridges and wharves are destroyed. Thousands of lobster pots are lost. Boats arriving at Tignish report a terrible night. Ten craft belonging to the fleet are missing. [Prince Edward Island is situated north of Nova Scotia, in the Gulf of St. Lawrence, two thousand miles northeast by air line from Galveston.]

St. John's, Newfoundland, September 26 [1900]. – More than forty French vessels of the Grand Banks fleet of Saint-Pierre, Miquelon, are still missing as a result of the West Indies hurricane which swept over these grounds on September 13. Forty-two other vessels have gone ashore in the Strait of Belle Isle. Thirty of these are complete wrecks and the rest are almost certain to pound to pieces. The number of lives lost is unknown.

The British bark *Imogene*, arriving here yesterday, badly damaged, reported that she had passed through great quantities of wreckage. The French flagship *Isly* has been ordered from the treaty shore to cruise the fishing grounds for survivors who may still be afloat. Shipwrecked crews, aggregating 79, have been brought south by the mail steamer, and a special steamer will be sent for others. Immense stocks of codfish have been lost with the shipping.

The rescued crew of schooner *Willie A. McKay*, which foundered on the Grand Banks, left by steamer this week for their homes in Provincetown, Massachusetts. An unknown American fishing schooner also foundered on the Grand Banks in the same gale, and all of her crew, about 20, perished. The French bark *Thornly* sank and 14 of her crew were drowned. Reports of disaster continue to pour in from remote localities.

Schooner *Dreadnaught* of Gloucester – Joe Cusick, master – was a brand-new vessel with an old and tried crew, and when the Yankee port sent out such a combination, folks at home said: "Blow and be damned! She'll come back, that one, with no knots tied in her wake!"

The *Dreadnaught* came back from the Western Banks, dreading plenty. And before she saw Gloucester again, there were knots aplenty tied in her wake. The skipper, suffering with broken collarbone and shoulder blades, told his story in sick bay.

The schooner had reached the southeast part of the Western Banks on the afternoon of September 13. A little before five o'clock something happened there, without any warning, and "'twasn't a gale, t'wasn't a dry no'theaster, and no, 'twasn't even no ordinary hurricane! If you spliced a white squall with a whirlwind and threw in the devil on a seagoing plow, you'd get a little closer to it. Anyhow, me and my crew's been through just about everything that blows, but this was something new to all of us!"

The *Dreadnaught* had had her mainsail up when the devil appeared on his seagoing plow. As the men rushed to take the sail in, the peak block broke and the middle block jammed between the other two. "There we were, in the squall, the mainsail part way down and half overboard, and we couldn't get it up or down." The skipper went aloft and worked out on the gaff. Then "the block gave, there came a slat, and that's all I knew

Chapter XI: Big Wind on the Grand Banks

till I come to twelve hours later. The boys can tell you the rest."

"The boys" agreed that this gale had not been like others. Getting the skipper below after his thirty-foot fall to the deck, they took everything off the vessel except a three-reefed foresail, but the wind kept worsening until she couldn't carry even that. Then, through the night and the next day, while her crew expected every new deckload of white water to be her last, the brand-new schooner *Dreadnaught* shook and got down on her bulwarks at the bidding of the seas.

One of the moments which Captain Cusick said would stick longest in his memory came after he had recovered consciousness the next afternoon. Through the gloom he saw a big French fishing bark, driven before the gale, helpless, all her masts gone and only the stumps showing. She passed so near that above the wind he could hear the men calling, he could see them stretching out their hands towards him.

Next morning the *Dreadnaught* passed through "wreckage of dories, and timbers, spars, and other fragments which, from their nature, told that at least one French craft had gone to the bottom with all hands."

Vessel after vessel came back with pretty much the same story to tell. From Prince Edward Island, which it struck on the night of Wednesday September 12, the hurricane had moved to the Grand Banks that same night and then gone over the others in turn on its bend southwestward.

Schooner *Lottie Byrnes*, arriving in Provincetown from Banquereau – the shoals just west of the Grand Banks – after a wild night spent adrift with parted cable and with the watch on deck lashed to her masts, had counted more than a hundred vessels of the French fleet around her before the storm struck. "Her men fear that disaster has befallen some, as it seems impossible that all that host of craft could have escaped destruction in a storm of such tremendous power and fury." When the gale had subsided, they saw many square-riggers and schooners that had been driven scores of miles to the leeward, "and these appeared badly crippled in spars and rigging."

Ten days after the Galveston and Grand Banks hurricane, the twenty-four--man crew of schooner *Willie A. McKay* arrived home on the down-Cape train from Boston, and Provincetown heard how its big salt banker had been "literally battered to pieces" and sunk in the area of the Grand Banks known as Virgin Rocks.

Weather had been good – it was the first gale of the season – and fishing had been good, said the men of the *Willie A. McKay*. The schooner had three thousand quintals of cod in kench, and expected to go home at the end of the month with a full fare.

Fishing with her on "the Rocks" were a dozen vessels from the French and Portuguese fleets, and also the *Dido* and *Cora McKay* of Provincetown, the *Edith McIntyre* of Boothbay and the *Talisman* of Gloucester. The rest of the fleet was on Eastern Shoals, fifteen miles to the southeast.

When the swell under a southeast breeze suddenly rolled up Wednesday evening to set two hundred-ton schooners abob like so many peanut shells, John Marshall (Machados) was standing first watch on the *Willie A. McKay*. John, born in this country, was a big swashbuckler of three hundred pounds, with a heart of pure gold and a voice of leather and iron filings. That night he studied the weather a few minutes, then bellowed down to the skipper:

"Here goes our trip o' fish all to hell, Captain!"

Captain Johnson, a hard-bitten Nova Scotian who had fished with John for years, came up to ask him what he meant.

"I mean we ain't going to get home with no trip o' fish out o' this!" John said. "Look at it, Captain!"

Captain Johnson watched the sea making, and noticed the strange ribbon of deep scarlet that was all the daylight left on the western horizon.

"Does look dreadful squally, don't it! What do you make of it, John?"

John Marshall gravely shook his head.

"Captain, it ain't lucky to take a fish buyer on board a vessel. But I'm telling you, I wish there was a fish buyer on board right now!"

John meant that he wished they had a priest. Among Portuguese crews, "priest" was the one word tabooed at sea, on the ground that to say it brought bad luck, just as the word "pig" was absolutely forbidden among the Yankees and Nova Scotians. When they meant "pig," New Englanders and Bluenoses used the word "dentist;" and when the Portuguese meant "priest," they said "fish buyer." Now John looked at the skipper in dead earnest. "I wish there was a fish buyer on board right now – and that's what I make of it," he said.

Captain Johnson drew hard on his pipe. It was odd, very odd, to hear John Marshall talk like that. In a stiff blow, John usually got out on deck and cheered the more timid souls while he lent them a hand, and his fa-

Chapter XI: Big Wind on the Grand Banks

vorite remark to them was that such a breeze made "nice yachting weather." Aye, 'twas queer talk, dreadful queer, coming from John Marshall!

The *Willie A. McKay* had out a two-hundred-fifty-fathom string of cable. She held on to it through the night, when most other vessels on the Grand Banks had broken adrift. Around one o'clock, with the seas overgrown to heights that awed the skipper himself, the wind suddenly went dead.

The two men had remained on deck with the watch. Suddenly Captain Johnson straightened up. He looked aloft. The stars were out!

"Well, bless my soul!" he said. "It's clearing off! Now, John, what do you make o' that?"

"Go on and bless your soul, Captain, bless it good and taut! It'll need it. Me, I'm still wishing we had a fish buyer on board this vessel!"

In a little more than an hour, the light vanished as if a single switch had been pulled on all the stars in heaven. The wind, coming out of the northwest now, blew the schooner's trysail out to strings. And almost at the same time, John saw a sea coming.

"Look out!"

All on deck scurried up on the foregaff. The wave broke over the starboard side. It started the house from its deck-fastenings, and this opened the deck on both sides, letting water into the cabin in streams. Two dories which had been lashed on top of the house were torn off and swept overboard. Other dories nested on the deck were smashed to bits. Of the twenty-two boats the *McKay* carried, only two were left whole.

The schooner shipped many such seas after that, but the worst ones were striking her full on the bow, where she had been taking such punishment that it was no great surprise to the captain when one of the hands told him water was coming in forward. When he went to the bow, he found her badly shattered there, with several planks started outward.

The leak was enormous, but the *McKay* had two up-to-date pumps, and the skipper divided the crew into watches of three men to each pump, and gave the order to "keep 'em going full tilt to the last act." The spare man of each watch was stationed in the rigging, where he kept a lookout for the worst seas. When he saw one coming aboard, he yelled to the men at the brakes. They dropped their work then, and hopped up to the foregaff, which had been cleared for that purpose. If they were nimble enough, they could jump out of the wash along the deck, and escape being taken overboard; but there was also the danger of getting hit by one of the pieces of wreckage from the broken dories, which were shooting from side to side as the craft rolled.

In the early morning Captain Johnson saw a light, bobbing up, disappearing, bobbing again. Within a few minutes he recognized the oncoming shape as the hull of the big Portuguese bark *Navigador*, adrift under bare poles, and heading down squarely athwart the *McKay*'s hawser.

With such seas as were coming in over the bow, it was going to be bad business for anyone to get far enough forward to cut the *McKay*'s cable. But if the drifting bark should foul it, the *McKay* would be swung about broadside into a collision that probably would send both craft to the bottom. Captain Johnson turned to go for the axe. He met John Marshall already coming forward with it. When the skipper reached for it, John held on. Then both men made their way forward together.

They moved with their chances, reached the windlass, and hung on there while sea after sea fell over them. John watched the cable. The skipper watched the Portuguese vessel.

"Just as we were on the point of cutting, the tide gave a sheer to the Portuguese that carried him a little way from the line of his drift, and the next minute he flew past us, right in the trough of the sea. He went out of sight as quick as he had come. While he was swaying by, the yards barely missed our own rigging. It was a narrow escape – the narrowest I have ever known."

Through the night and the day following, the men kept the pumps going without a stop except to jump clear of boarding seas. At 2 o'clock in the afternoon the *McKay*'s cable parted. At the same time, the oakum had been washed out of several places in the after part of the hull, and she began to settle by the stern.

"The water was rising in the hold despite our steady pumping. That night [Thursday] no man knew whether he would see the dawn of another day. But all knew that it depended on work at the pumps, and nobody required urging.

"On Friday morning the wind moderated but the sea was very wild and the craft set low in the water. Her bowsprit was twisted and loosened, standing out of line with the hull. Her rudder had been torn off during the night. Thinking we might be able to work her to land, we hove in what was left of the cable, to use it in rigging up a makeshift rudder.

"At 6 A.M. Friday we saw the *Talisman*, Gloucester, lying under bare

Chapter XI: Big Wind on the Grand Banks

poles, far away but dead to leeward. The leak in our own vessel was worse, the cabin and forecastle full of water, and she was surely doomed. We hoisted three-reefed foresail and the forestaysail, and with our ensign hoisted Union down, kept off for the *Talisman*.

"We ran down close to her and hove to windward. Her people saw our need of help, and got dories over. We started to get over our own dories, but we had only two left, and they were in bad shape. The sea was very rough, and they filled as soon as they were put over alongside. This was the first time we abandoned the pumps for 28 hours.

"We did not get the last of our crew away from the *McKay*'s side until 8 A.M., as only three men could go safely in a dory, and we had 24. As I was going up the *Talisman*'s side, the *McKay* went down.

"If we had not sighted the *Talisman*, we would have tried to make for land, but the nearest point was 150 miles. We were blown sixty miles to the southward after we struck adrift. We would have had to pack into the two dories that were left. A dory will not carry half a dozen men safely in that kind of a sea.

"We consider that our rescue was a miracle."

One by one, schooners of the Grand Banks fleet came home to Provincetown, to Gloucester, to ports down east; and the "unknown American fishing schooner" which had been reported at St. John's, Newfoundland, as having foundered with all hands, remained a puzzle. The *Cora S. McKay* hadn't come back yet, but she was even bigger than the *Willie A. McKay*, and the people of Provincetown were not letting themselves get excited about her.

"No anxiety is felt for the *Cora S. McKay*," said the *Boston Globe*, "as she is the staunchest and best-equipped craft in the whole fleet. It does not seem possible that this vessel could suffer serious injury in a gale that has spared smaller and weaker ones."

Three months later, Provincetown officially gave up hope for the return of the "staunchest craft in the whole fleet."

> No such calamity has befallen the poor of this town since November, 1897, when the trawling schooner *Susan R. Stone* disappeared with her entire crew of 19. The *McKay* leaves 15 widows and 54 orphans. She sailed last May for the Grand Banks with a crew of 28 men. Since the gale that began at Galveston last Sep-

tember, Provincetown women have been going daily to the hills behind the town to watch for the big schooner.

From the *Gloucester Times*, September 27, 1900:

> News has been received at Drummore, Luce Bay, of a hurricane at Oflord, Iceland, September 20. The wind, it is said, blew 120 miles an hour. Nearly all the fishing smacks were driven ashore. Houses were razed and several persons killed. There was great destruction of property.

September 20 was seven days after the Grand Banks fleet was struck, and twelve days after the wind known as the Galveston Gale had destroyed that city, distant by air line thirty-eight hundred miles.

Chapter XII
The Crowning of Captain Joe

"I AIN'T THE ONE TO BELIEVE in no furriner's miracles. You know that. But what I seen, I seen. And I say that vessel never should have stayed afloat by rights, never *would* have, without it was just a plain and simple miracle!"

They were yarning in the Master Mariners' clubrooms. While rubber-shod feet kept up a constant shuffle through the metropolis-in-little that was Gloucester's main street, the select group of skippers up here in "the Rooms" spent their evenings ashore in the dignified piracy of cutthroat whist or "swacker," and occasionally in making statements of "fact," plain and fancy, which nobody dared question.

Just now Captain Frank Hall, Captain Joe Mesquita, and half a dozen others had tilted back for a session, and old Captain Bob McEachern was getting under way on the subject of St. Elmo's fire – those eerie lights that sometimes appeared out of nowhere on a vessel's rigging.

Queer balls of fire, they were, which showed at the masthead or the bowsprit or the tips of the booms; but only once in a great while, in the worst part of the heaviest gales, and not always then. Sailors had given them the name "corposant" (*corpo santo* – saint's body), but Captain Bob added that professors and high-toned people like that said 'twas only brush electricity that come to roost somehow on the ironwork of the rigging.

"P'r'aps so, p'r'aps so," Captain Bob conceded. "But in the gale of '73, when we seen that Frenchman rolling in the trough, with everything carried away but the split stump of her bowsprit, I watched two of them lights dancing along the hull, and it didn't look like no electricity to me.

"I yelled down to the captain that we had a Frenchman afire almost alongside. He come on deck, and a feller named Louis Veneau, which we'd shipped in Judique, Nova Scotia, come up too when he heard it was a French vessel.

"The minute the Judiquer looked at her, he give a laugh like he was tickled to death. The skipper stared at him and said he didn't see nothing funny in it – them poor devils with their vessel afire and in such a gale, and with their craft already the saddest-looking wreck you ever seen! And what kind of a man was he, to be laughing when it was a crew of Frenchmen – his own people – that was dying out there on the Queero? But the Judiquer just grinned.

"'No fire, no fire!' he says. 'That vessel, she safe, Captain, she safer as we are!'

"Well, the Judiquer had always seemed to me like a good, level-headed sort of a feller, so when my watch was over I went below to see what 'twas that had throwed him off ballast like that. He told me the light I'd seen on that vessel was St. Elmo's fire. She was from Brittany, and St. Elmo is them fellers' patron saint. When that kind of fire shows on a vessel, they know their saint has come to watch over her, and they quit worrying then, no matter what shape she's in. St. Elmo will see her through.

"I told him I still didn't see no reason to laugh. Even if that craft wasn't afire, she was in such desperate bad shape that all the saints in the catalogue wasn't going to save her. I'd never seen a gale like this one, and that vessel was just about the completest wreck that ever had the nerve to show herself out of water on Queero bank.

"Through the night it blowed harder and harder. I didn't know whether we was going to see daylight ourselves, and we had one of the best sea boats out of Gloucester. For that other craft, there wasn't a chance in a thousand to keep afloat through them next twenty-odd hours of gale!

"But she did. Yes, sir, so help me God, we sighted her again the next night, and we took off her crew and towed the wreck to Canso! Eighteen of 'em, there was, and they was in pretty bad shape. But after he'd jabbered with 'em awhile, the Judiquer told me there wasn't none of 'em really worried through the worst of the blow, because when they seen that fire on their wreck, they knew St. Elmo was going to see 'em through. Their saint had hoisted his colors on their craft. They knew there was going to be a miracle, and – well, there was!"

Captain Joe Mesquita nodded when the old man was finished.

"I know this fire," he said. "But you talk miracles, Bob. I tell you one miracle too."

It was getting late, but no one got up to go. Captain Joe was Portuguese, and these fellows at "the Rooms" were all Yankees and Nova Scotians –

Chapter XII: The Crowning of Captain Joe

seafaring aristocrats who did not ordinarily admit the Portuguese into their inner councils. And yet, Captain Joe was one of the most popular members the Master Mariners had ever enrolled. With a pack of cards he was the toughest "pirate" in the club, and therefore much sought after at the tables. As a fisherman, he had few equals in the Gloucester fleet.

But Captain Joe was a peculiar fellow, too. He not only commanded the respect of the other skippers up at the Rooms and mixed as one of them; along with this, he was one of the leaders among his own people on Portygee Hill, and he was keenly aware that they were his people. You couldn't talk that out of him. If any greenhorn from the Azores was looking for a berth in the Gloucester fleet, he was sent to Captain Joe. And if the cooperation of the people on the Hill was wanted by other groups in town, Captain Joe was the man to see.

Now, while he is telling in his own words the story of the miracle of Isabel, I shall give you the same in mine.

In all Europe, never was ruler more beloved than *Diniz Re Lavrador* – Dennis the Farmer, of Portugal, and when he married Isabel of Aragon a nation approved, and people went rejoicing through the streets.

To the war-sick, priest-ridden, tax-enslaved peasantry of that country, what a change had come with the accession of this farmer-king! – this lover of peace and the arts of peace, defender of the man with the hoe, builder of schools and of homes for the orphans of the field! And now that he was wed to Dom Pedro's lovely daughter, the kings to be could bring no ill, the children and the children's children would be safe from a return to the old ways of war and fruitless conquest, of costly alliance, and intrigue. Yes, in that year of 1281, when the royal farmer took his wife, there was reason for the peasant folk from Algarve to the Rio Minho to dance and sing and thank the God that had given them this monarch with a farmer's heart!

Through the years that followed, the promise of peace was kept. For the rich man, the merchant and shipper there was wealth enough; but for poet and peasant there was absolute bliss, prosperity unheard of! Only the elders shook their heads and clucked out their dismay at the way Dennis and Isabel were tampering with the old laws, with the courts, with the very workings of nature. For was not the King encouraging strange, untried methods of farming, had he not laid out a huge pine forest at Leiria, was he not appointing corregidors and otherwise interfering dangerously with the feudal courts, and was he not making commercial treaties with other nations that might bring on no end of tangles? And Isabel, too! Had she not induced her lord to set up a school of poets for the court, and to establish – at great expense – a university at Coimbra?

Yet these things were done, and more, and only the elders shook their heads and clucked on. The people learned to love Isabel quite as much as they loved Dennis. It was fitting that a queen be beautiful; but it was a lovely surprise when she was anything more. And Isabel was. She was deeply religious; yet her thoughts, to the puzzlement of tonsured politicians of her day, had a way of going astray – of dwelling upon the status of the poor in this world as well as in the next – which confusion caused her to do strange things.

At Alenquer, for example, she revived the ancient "king-for-a-day" tradition in a Whitsuntide ceremony that spread to great popularity throughout the country. She called it the *Festa do Imperio* (Feast of the Emperor), and in the ritual she inaugurated, her own crown was placed with much pomp and ceremony upon the poorest farmer in the neighborhood. For that one day, the man was spiritual "emperor" of the land. And to salt the occasion with a little realism, Isabel gave him the power to free one condemned prisoner.

Back in the world of Dennis and Isabel, the thought behind this crowning on Whitsunday was a daring one, sentiment dangerous to toy with even in symbolism. "Kings for a day" there had been, in play-acting older than the memory of man, but none with this sponsorship! None upon whose head rested a crown of real jewels! Yes, a dangerous play it was for queens to stage!

So said the tacticians. But if it was that, it was also a spectacle that strangely moved her lowlier subjects. And so, Portugal lived on at peace within itself and at peace with the world.

But even before the death of Dennis the Farmer, his people knew that they had hoped for too much. After him, there was to be no line of defenders of the peace, friends of the peasant. Affonso, the heir apparent, was an ambitious young man who listened to the head shakers, the tongue clickers, and at one time even got his own army of tin-shirts together in an attempt to overthrow his father. Only the intervention of Queen Isabel herself spoiled the scheme.

Two years later in 1325, Dennis died; Affonso became king of Portu-

Chapter XII: The Crowning of Captain Joe

gal, and the peasants went back to starving. Isabel tried to help her people, and it was during these dark years that the miracle took place which qualified her for canonization three centuries later. Because it was a good, practical miracle, concerned with the empty stomachs of people at large, it remains as one of the few such events that seem worth retelling today.

Actual starvation had come to such a pass in Lisbon, so the story goes, that Isabel, though deprived, now of her former powers, improved her time by smuggling loaves of bread from the royal pantry to the street, where she handed them out to needy passers-by.

It was dangerous work. Affonso was just looking for some excuse to do away with his mother. The crime of smuggling bread would have served admirably. But Isabel got away with it by hiding the bread under her cloak; and with a cooperative kitchen force, she was getting things organized nicely.

Then there came a time, while she was on her way out with an almost embarrassing load, when King Affonso saw her and called her back. He asked her what she was carrying, there under her cloak. Isabel said it was just a very large bunch of roses. The King jerked the cloak open. And from its folds there fell – not bread for the despised poor, but just a very large bunch of roses! Whereupon, Isabel went her way, and thereafter passed unmolested through the hall – with more bread.

So goes the old story. Afterwards, people remembered. Long, long afterwards they remembered, too, the crowning ceremony she had inaugurated at Alenquer; and as a tribute to their most appealing saint, people of both the mother country and the Azores revived the old rite of Whitsunday crowning. Only now, rich and poor alike could kneel while the spiritual crown of Portugal was held over their heads; and in honor of St. Isabel and her miracle of roses, it was especially for those whose lives had been spared at some time during the year – as by a miracle.

The tide brings in the wreckage, and like a catch-all for the discards of Davy Jones, the long "back beach" of Cape Cod stands out to sea. Wood of broken ships comes home, and "the mourners go about the streets."

On the morning of October 24, 1900, Surfman Bassett of the Old Harbor Life Saving Station at Chatham, saw two badly smashed dories on the beach. They were merely skeletons of lapstreaked boats, and upon them was left no mark to identify the schooner that had carried them. But the next tide bore in a third dory on those sands, and two more appeared at Peaked Hill, twenty-five miles away on the same beach. All three boats were marked *Mary P. Mesquita.*

A dory fisherman in Cape waters found a steamer's life buoy a few miles offshore. The name was no longer legible. One of the men at the Highland Light Station picked up a foghorn marked *Mary P. Mesquita.* And then the days passed, and nothing was heard from the trawling schooner of that name which had sailed from Gloucester on October 20 for Georges Bank.

People at home, the boys up at the Rooms and the folks on the Hill, refused to resign themselves to the thought that Captain Joe was not coming back. Leaves were brightly coppered under the Indian summer sun, visitors stayed on to enjoy the beaches at Pigeon Cove and Halibut Point, and vessels from the banks were one and all reporting good weather.

"The safety of the schooner *Mary P. Mesquita* is creating much anxiety," said the *Gloucester Times* on October 31; and next day the *Boston Globe* added, "Fear that disaster has overtaken the crack Gloucester fishing schooner *Mary P. Mesquita* is now shared by all fishermen."

Disaster to the schooner, yes. But still not the loss of Captain Joe and his crew. Gloucester clung to its hopes for them:

> Fishermen here believe she has been cut down in collision with some outbound steamer, but they are loath to believe that the crew went down with their craft. Such telltale evidence as has come in on the waves hints that the *Mesquita's* men gained the deck of some craft after the supposed collision. They point out that while the painter was coiled in the bow of one dory, the stern-strap had been cut in two, evidently while the dory was still in the "nest," as a hurried means of getting it over the side.

Then, on November 5, a cable was received from Queenstown, Ireland: "Run down by steamer. All saved except Alfred Brown, killed. – Joseph P. Mesquita."

Each year the steamers were getting to be a greater menace on the fishing banks and along the course to Boston. Schooner after schooner went down during the nineties – rammed and sunk by towering bows of the great power-driven "tinpots." In the fog, there is no certain means, even today, of keeping out of a steamer's path, and collisions still send Gloucester boats to the bottom.

Chapter XII: The Crowning of Captain Joe

There is now, however, some regard for the lives of men on the fishing vessels; and there is also a comparatively strict enforcement of rules of the road, whereas four decades ago those who officered the steamships showed a curious indifference to the safety of these little workaday craft. Contempt, sometimes outright hostility, towards the sailor-laborers who manned them came to be something in the nature of a tradition.

I do not mean to say that the fishermen felt any kindlier, on their part, toward the steamers; but when the two met in the fog, it didn't matter what the fishermen might have felt; it was always their craft that went down, and it was the iron ship, proceeding at full speed through waters crowded with these helpless little schooners, that was running hand in hand with Fate.

Sometimes the collisions occurred even when there was no fog. On the night of November 27, 1894, the steamer *Reading* crashed into the fishing schooner *Gracie H. Benson* of Provincetown in moonlit waters near Boston Light. Within three minutes the *Benson* started settling. Twenty fishermen clung to the rigging and called out, begging the *Reading*'s crew to lower boats for them. The steamer's officers refused. A near-by tug put out a boat and took off ten men. Four swam to the *Reading*'s side, and lines were cast to them. Six drowned. Said Charlie Foss, one of the men who managed to get aboard the steamer:

"The captain only came near us once – to ask the name of our schooner."

Passing over the Grand Banks on the night of August 20, 1898, the steamer *Norge* suddenly sighted the French fishing schooner *Coquette*, dead ahead. In reporting the collision that followed, Captain C. B. Knudsen of the *Norge* said:

"I saw at a glance that collision was inevitable. The *Norge* must run into the schooner or be run into. As the *Norge* had a large number of passengers, I preferred to take the former course. I ordered the *Norge* ahead at full speed." Sixteen fishermen of the *Coquette* were drowned.

In the crew of the schooner *Mary P. Mesquita*, on the night that she was rammed and sunk, was a man named Alfred Brown. Alfred Brown was born in the Azores. Once, when he was in the crew of the *Sarah H. Prior* fishing on the Western Banks, he had a dream. Next morning he told two of his shipmates, Manuel Palha and Manuel Shuma, that he had dreamt they went out in their dory and got astray in the fog. He advised them not to go out that day. Palha and Shuma shrugged. It was his dream, not theirs! And that afternoon, Monday May 13, 1895, Manuel Palha and Manuel Shuma got astray in the fog. Four days later, in desperate condition, they were picked up by the Canadian coaster *Sophia* and landed at St. John, New Brunswick.

Another time, the skipper of the Gloucester schooner, *Lucania* couldn't make up his mind whether to try Georges Bank or the Western Banks on his next trip. Luck hadn't been too good on either ground.

"I don't know where we go," Alfred Brown remarked, "but we have one damn quick trip. Last night I dream we fish one day and we come back full."

"Mmph!" said the skipper. "When I need the help of your dreams, Portygee, I'll let yer know." Then he began thinking it over. He had heard of Alfred Brown's dreams. Well, if it was quick trips the man was dreaming, then it was likely Georges, that ground being hundreds of miles closer than the Western Banks. To Georges he went. And after one day's fishing, the *Lucania* was on her way to Boston with 60,000 pounds of haddock and cod.

On the morning of October 23, 1900, Alfred Brown shakily made his way aft on the deck of the *Mary P. Mesquita*. Speaking in Portuguese, he told Captain Joe he had had a nightmare. He had seen the huge bow of a steamer knifing out of the fog, coming down upon the *Mary P. Mesquita*, splintering through her side, and then leaving her to fill and go down. "*Ai, Capitão, Capitão! Estou agoniado!*"

Yes, Alfred Brown was sick, and he showed it. But for that kind of sickness, work was the only cure the skipper knew. The fishing was good in that part of Georges. He told Alfred to carry on at his work. Maybe the feeling would pass. And that night Captain Joe walked the deck of the *Mary P. Mesquita* and thought of many things.

Before dawn Alfred Brown awoke screaming. His noise roused out his already uneasy shipmates. He told them he'd seen it again. He begged Captain Joe to cut the trip short, to set sail at once for home.

The crew worked on shares. With the kind of fishing they had opened up in this berth, a few more days would have meant a big trip, a good share for all. Some of the men could see no reason why one man's whim, fear – whatever it was – should deprive all of the chance to make a big trip. But others remembered Alfred Brown's dreams, and were quite will-

CHAPTER XII: THE CROWNING OF CAPTAIN JOE

ing to humor him. Captain Joe knew pretty well how each of his men felt.

"All right," he said. "One more day of fishing. Then we go home." That night the schooner set sail for Boston with 80,000 pounds of fish. But the wind failed her, and for two days, and two very long nights, she was becalmed. On October 27 she was still sixty miles from market.

Alfred Brown was now keeping to his bunk. The man looked bad. That afternoon Captain Joe went forward and sat with him, and kept assuring him that the weather was clear, which was the only thing he seemed to want to hear. Then 'Bastião Rose came below, called the skipper aside, and whispered to him that fog had shut in. Captain Joe went back to sit beside Alfred Brown and told him again that the weather was clear. The sick man began to doze.

At six o'clock 'Bastião Rose heard a steamer's whistle, saw two lights bearing down on the *Mary P. Mesquita*, and screamed, "All hands on deck!"

Captain Joe rushed up, saw the lights brightening through the fog, and ran aft into the cabin. He came out waving a lighted torch.

"He's seen us! He's going clear!" he called to the men on deck.

For a moment it looked as if this were so, for the steamer was now showing her green light to the schooner's green. But then she suddenly swerved; and the fishermen stood helpless and watched the red light coming on. Collision was certain now. Captain Joe, standing by the house, ordered the men to cut the dories loose from the port-side nest and get off in them.

Before they could do this the steamer struck. The tall steel stem bore down on the starboard side, just forward of the main rigging. It tore into the schooner, clear through the hatch, all but cutting her in two. What was left, fore and aft, hung together by timbers that were cracking and groaning as the forward section began to settle.

Every man was thrown to the deck. But the steamer – she was the big Cunarder *Saxonia* – bore steadily ahead, keeping her stem in the gap she had made in the little vessel, and playing her searchlights on the men.

While the splintering fragment on the port side still held their craft together, Captain Joe and his crew cut at the dory lashings. They managed to clear one boat. Captain Joe held the painter while the men got in. As he was about to shove off, he took one last look at his craft. He saw Estulano Nunes climbing onto the boom. Nunes had mistaken the schooner's own mainsheet for a rope thrown from the *Saxonia*, and was trying to reach it. Captain Joe called him back, waited until he was in the dory, then got in himself. Less than one minute later, the *Mary P. Mesquita* fell apart, the fragments filled and went down.

Captain Joe counted the men in the dory. There were fourteen – two missing. An empty boat drifted near their overladen one, and the skipper and three men got into it and went on with the search for the missing. The *Saxonia* sent out a lifeboat.

Captain Joe found Antoine Rose swimming almost over the spot where the schooner had gone down. For half an hour more he searched for Alfred Brown. Then the steamer took the survivors on board, and hope for the missing man was abandoned.

For the last time, their terrified shipmate had dreamed the truth.

But the saving of fifteen lives within those few seconds after their schooner had been riven struck Captain Joe as a miracle. Against such odds as had faced those fifteen men, under the bow of the great ocean liner, the fact that they were now alive seemed to him quite wonderful – yes, a miracle, as much the work of a Higher Watchfulness as the roses had been in the old story of St. Isabel!

So he told his men. They knew that story. And they agreed with Captain Joe when he said it would be a fine thing to carry on the old-time crowning custom in their new country as they had known and loved it in the Azores. Certainly there could be no more fitting occasion to start it than that of their own miracle at sea!

A month later they arrived in Gloucester, and Captain Joe sent at once to Portugal for a silver crown. Men of the *Mary P. Mesquita* chipped in what they could to help pay for it. So did captains and crews of other vessels. On a Sunday in July, 1901, when people in Horta and Angra and Pico, and in Lisbon and Oporto, had formed colorful processions, each to bear a crown through the city, Captain Joe was busy arranging a march through the streets of Gloucester.

All were agreed – Captain Joe included – that he was to carry the crown this time himself. With him would march his fourteen shipmates, dressed in their yellow oilskins and sou'westers. They would end their procession at the church altar. There, while the choir sang through the short, joyous tune of the "Magnificat," over and over, once for each man, they would

Chapter XII: The Crowning of Captain Joe

kneel; and above their heads, for a moment, the shining crown of Queen Isabel would be held. For a moment, lowly fishermen were to be "emperors" – such emperors as no armies could enthrone!

Throats tightened that morning in the little Church of Our Lady of the Good Voyage, while fourteen fishermen in their oilskin clothes knelt and received the crown. Many who witnessed it were not of the fishermen's faith. There were Nova Scotian skippers, friends of Captain Joe; there were Yankee business men and officials of Gloucester and higher-ups from Boston; there were "summer boarders" from Manchester and Pigeon Cove, and artists from Rocky Neck. Those who did not know the precise meaning of what was going on had at least heard the story of the *Mary P. Mesquita*; and from the faces in that gathering while the bright symbol went from one man to the next, it was plain to see that the point of the crowning was not being missed.

But there were other things to be done too in St. Isabel's *Festa do Imperio*. There was a feast to be set out in a big hall on that Sunday afternoon, where the whole community could gather for *sopas* – a savory mixture of meat, bread, and gravy – and whatever else the women should concoct. And there were gifts to be offered to the poor in the manner of the good queen herself. Great doughnut-shaped loaves of sweet bread – *resquilhas* like those which she had smuggled out of the palace at Lisbon – were to be handed out to all who asked. After the supper there was to be an auction sale – an event Azorians dearly love – lasting into the evening. The auctioneer was to get extremely businesslike on this Lord's Day, quite hard-boiled in his dealings with low bidders – for the wares were donated and the proceeds were to go to the poor. Finally, there was to be a drawing of lots to see who should have the honor of carrying the crown in next year's procession and of bearing the special title of *imperador*.

At the crowning of Captain Joe, all these things were done. And since that time, on a Sunday in each summer, there has been a crowning and all that goes with it for the fishermen and their people in Gloucester. Thousands come to town on that day to watch the procession with its bright flags of America and Portugal, its religious banners, drum corps and bands, the little girls who carry *ramos* – sticks held foursquare around the bearer of the crown as he marches proudly along – and with its somberly clad line of sea captains walking two and two with a rolling gait better suited to deck planking than to the cobblestones of Gloucester streets.

It is a moment out of the Old World. But to this country it has come out of the fog sixty miles at sea, out of the hearts of men who have known terror.

Chapter XIII
Flying Fishermen

Provincetown, it seems, has the fastest schooners afloat. Our vessels are swifter than the greatest yachts, if our captains' statements are to be believed.

Often some resident captain, in speaking of a past trip, will nonchalantly mention the 21 knots rattled off in an hour by his vessel when close-hauled by the wind, and the captain who gives 18 knots as his best time has the sympathy of the crowd.

If our town skippers tell the truth – and of course they would not lie for eight or ten miserable little knots – it seems a pity that such vast amounts are spent defending the *America* cup when all this country need do in an international yacht race is to send to Cape Cod for any of our fresh-fishermen.

Suppose, for instance, that one of our vessels was pitted in a dead calm against the *Valkyrie*. Our home boat would get around the course inside the limit, for our captains can blow themselves to victory. They carry their own wind in stock.

– *Provincetown Beacon*, 1893.

IN THEIR NONCHALANCE towards a few "miserable little knots," these fishing captains were not unlike the proud owners of other kinds of speedy craft of that day. But for all their wind in stock, and for all the windy wordage that has since appeared in newspapers, magazines, and books on the subject of fishermen's races, the real racing they engaged in was not sport. If, in their sessions on the yarners' bench, these skippers made certain "adjustments for error" in their logline findings, it was not in the same pure and disinterested spirit which moves golfers, say, to omit a few miserable little shots from the score card. In their hearts they had little room for the love of sport. They did not fancy yachting caps. Sailing was not a hobby. With the uncertainty of getting a trip of fish on the one hand, and the certainty of getting cheated in the price on the other, the grim business of getting a living from the sea admitted of very little good clean fun as our jolly tars with the brass-buttoned jackets know it.

In short, when fishermen talked speed, they talked business. In New England's fresh-fishing industry of the nineties, which had been built up around Boston as the distributing point, almost every trip out meant a race back; for when vessels were gathered over a spot of "school fish," the first to fill and reach home for market got the best price. That best, I might add, was little enough. Fish prices paid by retailers and in turn by consumers, have not been low since Boston came into its own as the wholesaling center; but in relation to such figures, prices paid to the fishermen have been kept – by manipulation, collusion, and every device known to science, art, culture, and unctuous legal lore – at levels outrageously below what they should have been. In the struggle against such odds, the homeward run of fishing schooners was about as much a sporting event as a race between a couple of Boston lawyers after an ambulance.

Nearly sixty years ago, planned-course fishermen's races for prize money did come into being, but they came out of this background. In their main purpose, even these contests were distinctly non-sporting; they were not held solely for entertainment, either of crews or of spectators; skippers and owners were not trying to decide who should pose before the newspaper artist, loving cup in hand, nor even, primarily, who should get the prize money. What they did want was to see just how much chance they had of beating the other fellow from the banks to Boston. Under the varying conditions of the race, they had a chance to spot out shortcomings in their craft and note changes that might improve the performance – all to the end of leading the way to market.

Generally failing to take this grim background into account, writers have tried to get the public excited about fishermen's races by treating them pretty much as they treated college football games; and with the encouragement of the press, fishermen have been induced to go on racing long beyond the day when a fishermen's race still made sense.

It has been a quarter of a century since the fleet changed from sail to power. During that period, the business ashore also has taken to new ways. In 1908 the Fish Exchange was opened at T Wharf. Skippers no longer disposed of their fares to the highest bidders in the old informal

CHAPTER XIII: FLYING FISHERMEN

manner on the wharf. Prices set in the morning were stabilized for the remainder of the day.

In 1913, the New Haven launched its "Flying Fisherman," the fastest freight train in the country. Each evening at 5:55 she pulled out of Boston's South Station with fresh fish for New York. Sometimes, on Wednesdays, she carried as much as 300 tons, and often the last cases were hove on board after the cars began moving. She made the Harlem River yards at 1:50 A.M., and from there the East River boat rushed the cargo down to Fulton Market.

Two years later, the huge Boston Fish Pier was built; New York capital had bought those rascals, the fish buyers, out of their little holes on T Wharf and had set up piracy in the fishing industry on the scale it deserved; combinations were formed, and securities were peddled out; and with part of the proceeds, big steam-powered beam trawlers were set afloat, to bring in an ever larger part of the New England catch. In 1921, the public was offered packaged fresh fish and there was an immediate jump in the demand. This was followed by "quick-frozen" fillets, which were so well taken that by 1936 a fifth of all the fish landed at Boston was being processed by the quick-freezing method.

Thus within two decades the industry's primary producer, the fisherman, was not only using new tools; he was supplying a new sort of market, a market that no longer dealt strictly in perishables. It didn't mean that he was any better off financially, or even as well off, but hurrying now wouldn't do him any good. Where sail is carried today, it is not for adding to the vessel's speed, but only for steadying her.

Just as windjamming no longer has anything to do with the fishing industry, so fishermen no longer have any business getting into a sailing contest. This was how Gloucester men felt about it in the fall of 1938, when the big Lunenburg salt banker *Bluenose* came back to meet another challenge by the local trawler *Gertrude L. Thebaud*. For the race, the vessels had to be divested of the engines which both used in their everyday work; and canvas which neither ordinarily carried had to be dug out of the sail lofts. The whole proceeding, while it resulted in nice picture postcards, was about as realistic as a duel with broadswords on the stage of the Metropolitan Opera. The newspapers filled out columns of somewhat labored romanticizing; radio chains devoted hours to tack-by-tack accounts; yet the public was not ecstatic. When the fifth race was over, the crowds in Gloucester accepted the defeat of the American vessel with a rather unflattering amount of good sportsmanship, even of detachment.

No one could blame them. Through five performances they had been watching a couple of floating museum pieces.

Good sportsmanship, splendid virtue in the white-collar realm where it belongs, is the luxury of keeping one's temper while losing something one can very well get along without. On board a fishing schooner in real life there was precious little of this ethical delicacy; and yet, for excitement, maritime history holds up few highlights to outshine those races to Boston, few moments packed with greater danger and greater thrills. In their long and perilous races around the Horn, Boston to San Francisco, to fit out the great gold rush, the celebrated California clippers took no greater chances than these little craft of Gloucester and Provincetown. The risk on the banks was as large, and to the fishing crews, the incentive for winning was even larger. Foremast hands on the clipper ships stood to gain nothing in return for the risks they were forced to take. They worked for a flat wage, between eight and twelve dollars a month win or lose, and only the skippers and owners shared the benefits of a victory.

But the thrill of a race to the Boston market, with the best price for a fare of fish as the stake, was as real for the crew as it was for the skipper. Each man shared in the excitement because each would share in the stock the vessel was to make; if the schooner won, all hands on board won. And the skipper, fond as he may have been of his craft, did little to spare her. The greater precaution he took in favor of life, limb and property, once such a race was under way, the less respect his own men had for him. Around the turn of the century, in the period just before motorization of the fleet, spar and sail makers were doing a rushing repair business on vessels that came limping into Boston, all but wrecked for having cracked on more canvas than the standing rigging could bear.

Two of the best customers for new parts on this account were the Provincetown rivals, Captain Manuel Crawley (Santos) and Captain John Bull (Silva). Both were daring young men on their flying sloops of Cape Cod, and both later came to be known among the "killers" – the big money-makers – of the New England fishery. A man shipping with either skipper knew he was going to make money as long as the combined dangers of wind, sea, and the skipper's sailing habits spared his life.

Chapter XIII: Flying Fishermen

They were as unlike as Nature in her mighty versatility could make two men. Captain Manuel, body of many pounds and soul of few words, belonged body and soul to salt water, was quick to become landsick. To relieve the monotony of these shorebound intervals, he went in for charity work and civic reform, and pulled strings in the marionette show of town politics. Thanks to his mighty restlessness, the Portuguese community held its own fairly well against a contemptuous and usually corrupt Yankee town government.

Captain Johnny Bull, short, ruddy-faced, a "heller on the liar's bench," went to sea because his living was there, loved to meet up with the boys at the Nine Points, a little water-front shed where fishermen gathered from the eight known cardinal points of the compass and from a ninth, unknown one. There he would keep the gang on the edges of their "mackerel-kags" for hours on end with yarning on matters nautical, terrestrial, or celestial. But, at sea, Captain Johnny Bull was as restless and as desperately active as Captain Manuel Crawley was ashore. If it were humanly possible to get his fishing done in a "quick trip," Captain Johnny Bull did it; and when it was not humanly possible he tried it anyhow.

One day, as he dropped in at the Nine Points for a little session while a new bowsprit was being stepped into his twenty-two-ton sloop *Active*, Captain Johnny Bull was given warning that if he hoped to keep the vessel high-liner in her class that season, he'd better get her out there in the Bay and fish like hell. For Captain Manuel Crawley had just been given command of the *Lear C*. Everybody knew Crawley was a big fisherman, and the *Lear C*, also a twenty-two-tonner, had been able to outfoot everything in Gloucester, her home port up to now. She was a faster vessel than the *Active*, so Captain Johnny was informed.

"Huh!" he said. "You go on board my vessel and tell cook to lash up his pots and pans! We go fishing by 'm by!" And from that time on, the two men in their well matched sloops were deadly rivals – deadly one to the other, and about as deadly each to his own crew.

In mid-July, 1901, both vessels were fishing off the Chatham shore. They had been running honors-even in stocks and crew shares that season. In point of fast running for market, nobody, crews included, could win the argument for either craft, because too few of their races had been sailed without one or both getting partially disabled. The *Active* – had shown her heels to the *Lear C* at times when they were sailing by the wind, but the suspicion lingered in Captain Johnny's mind that his rival had the better ship for running off the wind with sheets started.

Fishing was big in the Chatham waters that afternoon. Both vessels were getting full fares on board. As the hour for the start to Boston drew near, a breeze freshened in from the southeast, and the scene was set for rattling off more than a hundred fast and furious miles.

But it wasn't set exactly to Captain Johnny Bull's liking, for it was precisely in that kind of breeze that he suspected Captain Manuel had the edge on him; and when he had battened down on the last of his fish and squared away the *Active*, it was already blowing a little harder than was healthy for either vessel as she was sure to be handled at night. Twenty minutes later, when Captain Manuel got the *Lear C* under way, the wind had shifted to sou'west, and was blowing even harder. But "smoky sou'wester" or no, both vessels carried not only their lower sails, but also gaff-topsails and ballooners.

Captain Manuel was happy, supremely happy and at peace with a careening, roaring, spume-filled world. While the *Lear C* went pounding along with her lee rail in the lather and with her crew beginning to think kindly thoughts of a life ashore, he stood at the wheel and smiled. What more could a man want? Here were a full fare of fish, a real scupper breeze, and a worthy rival – though Captain Manuel was, as always, quite confident that his was faster. If, of course, she would only hold together!

Captain Johnny was not peaceful, but he was even more determined. It was not his breeze, and there was a mighty choppy sea making. But handling counted for something too in this here ocean; and, that being so, he might still show that feller Crawley a straight wake. If, of course, the old girl didn't give anywhere!

Captain Johnny's *Active* had bearings to which she was easily listed, but beyond which even a gale-force blow wouldn't heel her over. Now, with everything but the skipper's shirt flown aloft, she was heeling her limit, bending her topmast like a whipcord, and going quite madly about her business.

But for the best that she could foot it, Captain Manuel's *Lear C* had a little better. Before they reached the Highland Light at Truro, the two wildly plunging sloops were bow-and-bow. Then, to Captain Johnny's surprise, he saw that the *Lear C* was taking in her uppers – yes, shortening sail! His hands tightened on the spokes.

Chapter XIII: Flying Fishermen

"*Filho do diabo!* (Son of the devil!) He don't make me douse no kites!" But it was high time that kites were doused. It was blowing a howler now, and even these sturdy craft could stand only so much. In discretion lay the only chance of winning this race. And when Captain Manuel had seen that, he had turned discreet. But Captain Johnny, with the strategy of desperation for which he was noted, kept his canvas on.

For a few miraculous minutes it worked. The *Active*, with her nose in white water and her crew in silent prayer, began to draw away. A few minutes, and then – crack! – down over her lee bow crumpled the gaff-topsail and ballooner. And with her topmast carried away, there was no more thought of trying to outsail the *Lear C*.

But Captain Johnny wasn't through. The tactics of desperation were not yet exhausted. As he skirted Race Point, at the tip end of Cape Cod, he observed that he was running into headwinds from over the Bay. At once he swung off and rounded into Provincetown Harbor. And while his crew were wondering if the strain had also caused something to carry away in the skipper's own upper rigging, he ran down to a vessel anchored in mid-harbor.

She was the steam tug *Peter B. Bradley*. Captain Johnny spoke her, had her skipper roused out, and asked him what he'd take for a tow to Boston. On being told that it would come to $140, he had the towline made fast at once. Within ten minutes the *Active* was again on her way to market – in the teeth of headwinds to which she gracefully curtsied as she glided along at the end of her towline!

Late the next morning when Captain Manuel luffed the *Lear C* in for T Wharf in Boston, after endless hours of tacking against the headwinds over Cape Cod Bay, there he beheld the disabled *Active*, peacefully creaking at her dock lines while shoresmen were taking out the trip of fish that Captain Johnny Bull had already sold!

Unhesitatingly Captain Johnny gave his colleague the details. On his arrival, he had had the market all to himself. His fish had stocked him $1,150. Since then a number of vessels had followed in with big fares, which had driven the price down to half the figure he had received. Had he kept on under sail, he might still be out there in the Bay somewhere – with a trip of fish worth about $600 less.

Thus happily ended Captain Johnny Bull's epic of the sea. Sportsmanship? Every fresh-fisherman on the Boston waterfront had something to say that morning about the conduct of the *Active* in her latest match with the *Lear C* – and for Captain Johnny there was nothing but the greatest admiration. In the years that followed, when small power boats were more often at hand, quite a number of fishermen's races were won by virtue of the power tug and towline – contests which have never been mentioned, so far as I know, by writers who have tried to superimpose on the fishermen's race a code of ethics better suited to an afternoon of croquet.

Our Cape Cod scribe's left-handed salute to the honest captains and their twenty-one-knot runs, as quoted at the beginning of this chapter, was a wholesome way of disposing publicly of much of this believe-it-or-knot skipper talk, a problem that had grown delicate for the Yankee press. All alongshore the editorial soul was constantly being torn between pride in the seafaring prowess of New Englanders and its own professed obligation to truth. Wonderful things were constantly happening, out at sea, far from the eyes of disinterested witnesses. And of course nobody could doubt a New England sea captain's word! But when a paper printed a story as news, folks held the *paper* responsible, not the captain, and – Well, you see how it was: when you got things down in black and white, there were limits.

But one schooner there was in the Cape Cod fleet about which nothing was unprintable. Newspapers from Provincetown to Boston could quote Manuel Costa, master of the *Jessie Costa*, and rest assured that anything he said about his vessel, or anything they said he said, would pass unchallenged – not because Captain Costa was more truthful than his fellow skippers, but because everyone knew there wasn't anything the *Jessie Costa* couldn't do. Fortunately, Captain Costa was not too communicative.

The same reporter for the *Provincetown Beacon* who could toss off raspberries for the rest of the fleet was lost in adoration of this queenly craft. She was a wonder, he declared, "the fastest thing afloat in any waters." In a dead thrash to windward, the birds of the air and the fishes of the sea gave it up and let her go; and so did all previous monarchs of the New England fleet, and their sisters and their cousins and their aunts. She pointed high and went where she pointed. And when a heckling reader wrote in to ask the *Beacon* if it thought the *Jessie Costa* could perform the physical impossibility of pointing right up into the wind's eye, the newspaper – circulation 2,100 – gave out its answer to the world: "Yes! And a point the other side!"

Chapter XIII: Flying Fishermen

What this statement lacked in accuracy it made up in terseness and fairness. The *Jessie Costa* was wonderful indeed – a worthy successor-queen to the old *Carrie E. Phillips*; and in point of speed this was saying a great deal, for the *Phillips*, during the years 1877 until she ran on the rocks at White Head, Maine, and pounded herself to pieces in 1899, had outsailed everything that was made to earn its living on the Banks.

The only fishing schooner designed by the great Edward Burgess, the *Phillips* was built with yacht bows instead of the clipper bows that had been the fashion. With the *Phillips,* Captain Al Miller of Gloucester had beaten the mighty Sol Jacobs in a race off the Jersey shore for the New York mackerel market, driving the schooner at thirteen knots – patent taffrail log, so help him! – and later Captain Joe Carlos had worked her up to fourteen.

The *Jessie Costa* was yacht-bowed too. Like the *Phillips*, she was "a livin' miracle" at sailing close-hauled by the wind, but she could do more than that; running off the wind with a deckload of fish, she could stand straight as a church steeple and leave the fleet to fight it out for second price at Boston.

Of all the officially sponsored races that fishermen have sailed, the greatest was that of six famous Gloucester schooners that went banging into a full northeast gale on the afternoon of August 26, 1892. Despite the screamer, which had set aboil the whole of Massachusetts Bay, they fought it out with all sail set, topsails spread, staysails "scandalized." One of them cracked her main gaff, another split her jib, a third had half her canvas blown out of the ropes, and one of the sailors suffered a broken leg when he was caught in the main sheet. But the six, top-rank flyers all, made the run from Eastern Point to Nahant to Minots Light Buoy and home without tying a reefpoint. As one observer described it, "In the midst of an extra heavy sea and a living gale of wind, the best of Gloucester's big fleet thrashed through the waters of Massachusetts Bay under a pressure of canvas which caused the few hardy spectators to look on in silent wonder."

To top off the drama, Captain Maurice Whalen's *Harry L. Belden*, a last-minute arrival for the start, came in winner – with a full trip of fish still on board!

Nothing like that race has ever been seen since, in the way of a planned sail, but there aren't many old-timers left alongshore who can still command the yarner's bench to silence by right of authority vested in them as eyewitnesses. That race, grand as it was, has been practically forgotten, and the event that history seems to have picked out for our grandchildren to hear about – and to see commemorated with a slab of granite and a huge silver loving cup in a glass case – was the race which the *Jessie Costa* lost to Captain Marion Perry's *Rose Dorothea* in 1907.

Marion Perry disliked talk and despised frills. An old shoe was not plain enough for him if it still had a tongue in it. Parades, brass bands, salutes, greetings, birthday cakes, even neckties and custard pie – to all such things, he had an emotional allergy. Yet from the day when he had come into the world naked and had seen that situation quickly corrected with silk, lace, ribbons, and rosettes, life was just one such annoyance after another. Fate had chiseled out an ascetic and handed him a bunch of balloons. His early years in São Miguel were a round of celebrations; and Boston, where the Perreiras became the Perrys, was not much better.

From this strange plight Marion Perry eventually found escape at sea. At sea, a man could work as hard as he liked and talk as little. He could wear what he liked, eat good plain food, think straight thoughts, and slip into dreamless sleep on the honest planking of a ship's bunk. What fools these fellows were to grumble and talk of getting a job ashore!

But the escape was short-lived. Marion Perry did not have many of the collateral yearnings of ambition, but he did like to work. In him, the affection for hard work was so deep-seated that he never even mentioned it to himself. As a result, before he could worry much about it, he was "kicked to the front" and made skipper at the age of eighteen; and he very soon discovered that the captain's cabin was not the same hide-away from human folly that the forecastle had been. There remained plenty of hard work, but life was no longer short-spoken nor free of frills.

For a couple of years as skipper of the little *W. B. Keene* of Provincetown he proved himself a big fisherman, working against older hands and better vessels. Then he was given command of the larger *Mary Cabral*, and soon afterwards of the still larger *William A. Morse*, in which his record was sensational.

Meanwhile, he married Rose Dorothea McGowan, a little Irish Rose who was not at all wild and who "liked nice things." At what stage of their romance the captain discovered this latter trait I cannot say; but he married her anyhow, and the fact that love is grand has seldom been better demonstrated to the people of Provincetown than in the skipper's grim

CHAPTER XIII: FLYING FISHERMEN

and silent acceptance of the plan and furnishings of an $8,000 house that went up in the west end of town under Rose Dorothea's direction.

Soon there were silk, lace, ribbons, and rosettes again; and after his infant daughter the skipper named his newest schooner the *Annie C. Perry*. In that vessel, which was built especially for him in 1903, he took his place among the big "killers" of the banks fishery: captains like Manuel Costa of the *Jessie Costa*; Johnny Bull Silva of the *Isaac Collins*; Joe Silva of the *I. J. Merritt*; and Manuel Crawley Santos, who in the *Philip P. Manta* was high-liner of all New England for the year 1903.

In the next two seasons, Captain Perry made a fine showing with his new vessel, but he wasn't satisfied. Speed wasn't everything, but it counted. He wanted a craft that was even faster, such a schooner as would place him on an equal footing with the skipper of the *Jessie Costa*. And so, in 1905, while keeping his share of ownership in the *Annie C. Perry*, he had the big schooner *Rose Dorothea* built for his own command.

With Captain Perry at the helm, no one doubted that the *Rose Dorothea* would rank among the high-liners; and with lines like the *Jessie Costa*'s own, she was sure to cut water with the fastest of the fleet.

When the skipper went to Gloucester to pick up his new craft, he took Rose Dorothea along because she begged him to. At the wharf, he looked the new schooner over, humphed and decided to send her back to the Essex yards at once. She was perfect in her lines, but in her carpentry below deck she was impossible. All that gilt and fancywork! What the hell did those fellows in Essex think they were building – a summer boarder's yacht, a pleasure boat?

Back she would have gone, then and there, for a complete refit of cabin and forecastle, but at this point Rose Dorothea herself stepped in to defend her namesake. Rose Dorothea loved nice things. And the *Rose Dorothea* was lovely, a little floating palace, a dream! As the *Boston Herald* described her:

> The cabin is a roomy apartment, with polished panels and gilded moldings and walls of handsomely grained hard woods. Opening off this cabin one finds a snug stateroom, equipped with toilet and other essentials, lighted, of course, with bulls-eyes of thick glass, and provided with a locker, bunk and ample store of good bed clothing.
>
> The forecastle is as unlike the quarters provided for the old-

time fishing crew as could be imagined. In fact, what was until recent years a "black hole" – greasy, pestilential and gloomy – is now a commodious cuddy, flooded with light, and bright with brass rods and flowered curtains that serve as screens to the rows of sleeping bunks.

Forecastle walls are stained a warm and sunny tint. Connecting with the after end of this cuddy, of which, in fact, it forms a part, there is another spacious apartment, what was formerly termed the "forehold," extending the full width of the ship. This is the stamping-ground of "cooky." It is filled with all the conveniences of a modern hotel kitchen.

And so, to please Rose Dorothea, wouldn't the captain keep the *Rose Dorothea* as she was? And also, before he took her out fishing, it would be nice if they held a little ceremony, or if they sailed her just once against the *Annie C. Perry* – a little race, just to show how much faster she was! When you were captain, you had to do those things. People expected you to. Here the newspapers had sent men all the way from Boston, reporters and photographers, and – and it would be so nice! To please Rose Dorothea, *wouldn't* the captain – just this once?

The skipper ground his teeth, kissed Rose Dorothea and took the *Rose Dorothea* out on a trial race with the *Annie C. Perry*, back to Provincetown. He "beat his former vessel handsomely in a smashing breeze" – and smashed the fore-topmast of his new one, which kept him ashore three more days before he could finally kiss Rose Dorothea good-by and get down to business with *Rose Dorothea*.

In the summer, of 1907 there were big doings in Boston. It was "Old Home Week," and one of the diversions was to be a fishermen's race off the North Shore, with the half-dozen top-rank schooners of Gloucester and Provincetown sailing in the first class.

A thirty-nine mile course was laid from Thieves Ledge, off Boston Light, to Davis Ledge, off Minots Light, to Eastern Point, Gloucester, and home. Although the race had no particular bearing on an "Old Home Week" celebration, such was the interest shown in it that in addition to the $650 first prize, a huge loving cup was offered by Thomas Lipton, at that time the most hopeful if not the greatest yachting enthusiast the world had ever known.

Chapter XIII: Flying Fishermen

Captain Manuel Costa agreed readily enough to enter the *Jessie Costa*, and so did the skippers of the *James W. Parker* and three other Gloucester craft. The cup alone, the newspapers said, "was valued at $5,000."

But that summer of 1907 was also turning out to be an excellent season for the fresh-fishermen. And when the famed *Rose Dorothea* was asked to race, her skipper tersely replied that he didn't have time. That was a lot of silver for a cup to have in it – $ 5,000 worth – but what the hell could a man do with a cup like that when he got it? It was too heavy to drink out of. And Captain Marion Perry didn't need a cup for anything else. No, the price of fresh fish was high, the skipper knew where to go for some big trips, and the *Rose Dorothea* would do all her racing between Boston and a certain stretch on Georges Bank.

That was what the skipper of the *Rose Dorothea* said, and probably he would have stuck to it, but again Rose Dorothea stepped in. She had seen a picture of the lovely cup Sir Thomas Lipton was offering. And she adored nice things.

Captain Perry explained to her that the other share owners in the schooner would be entitled to their shares in the cup, and so would the crew. But you couldn't cut up a thing like that cup into shares! And he repeated that you could not drink out of it; and as for him, if he won that big useless thing, he wouldn't give it house room. Rose Dorothea said all right now that he'd consented to race he could give the cup to the town. It would be a beautiful gesture. Captain Perry said he had *not* consented to race and as for the town, he had another gesture. Rose Dorothea said all right, that was a very good way to settle it – race without consenting. Captain Perry wrung his hands, kissed Dorothea, and took *Rose Dorothea* to Boston to race.

At ten o'clock on the morning of August 1, while thousands lined the shore from Hull to Cohasset and from Lynn to Gloucester, schooners *Rose Dorothea*, *Jessie Costa*, and *James W. Parker* were jogging about off Boston Light. The three other schooners had not arrived from fishing trips, but informed spectators knew that, barring flukes, this was to be a race between the *Rose Dorothea* and the *Jesse Costa*, and that whether the others showed up or not wouldn't make any real difference. The *James W. Parker* "presented the most festive appearance, having a band along, which banged and tooted bravely until the sea came up a bit, when the musicians lost interest." But that vessel's crew had small hope of figuring prominently.

After being held up an hour for the possible arrival of other entries, the three schooners were given the starting gun, and the *Rose Dorothea* crossed the line a minute ahead of the *Jessie Costa*. Then, with sheets slightly started, they went bowling along under a land breeze, everything drawing and scuppers level with the water.

After they had rounded Minots for the eighteen-mile run to Eastern Point, the two Provincetowners became involved in a fast and furious set-to at luffing. For the crowds, it was a grand exhibition, with Captain Perry finding himself neatly luffed out in one bout and then promptly serving Captain Costa some of the same crow in the next. While engaged in this, the *James W. Parker* tried to come up and steal the race, but she couldn't get near enough to be dangerous.

The two Provincetowners were still close together on rounding for the return. Whitecaps were going on a fair little jump of sea, and the *Rose Dorothea* had just flattened sheets when there was a rending crack aloft. Her foretop had snapped in the middle – just as it had done on her first run two years before!

For Captain Perry the race now ceased to exist. Race! What the hell was a race? That broken topmast meant three whole days ashore, doing nothing, while the wholesale fish market was at the best level it had reached in years!

He was furious at those pirates, the spar makers, who had supplied him with a pipestem for topmast; furious at the freak puff that had snapped it off; and furious at himself for letting Rose Dorothea talk him into this piece of foolishness in the first place! In fact, he was so thoroughly disgusted that he wouldn't even bother to have the broken spar taken down. His one object now was to make T Wharf and get those swindlers, the spar makers, on the telephone.

The *Rose Dorothea*, however, "appeared to be doing very well without her foretopmast, pointing higher than her rival, which continued to carry all her kites, and footing fully as fast." As a matter of fact, the *Rose Dorothea* was in better racing trim for the accident! While the broken stick hung at a crazy angle across the fore gaff-topsail and her jib topsail, or "flying jib," as the fishermen call it. But this same sail – the big "flying jib" – on the *Jessie Costa* now began to pull that vessel's head to leeward. And because of it, with only a dozen lengths between them near the finish, the *Costa* sagged off and had to make a tack.

Chapter XIII: Flying Fishermen

Captain Perry wasn't watching the *Jessie Costa*. He neither knew, nor cared what that schooner was doing. All he wanted was to make T Wharf, and make it quickly. It was at this moment that the *Rose Dorothea*, "headed higher than ever under the marvelous handling by her skipper," pinched past the flag, winner over the *Jessie Costa!*

> Somebody on board the victorious schooner produced a new broom, and as she was entering the harbor, a man went up her maintopmast to lash it to the truck.*
>
> When the *Rose Dorothea* arrived at T Wharf at 5:30 and was shoved into her berth by a tug, she was given a shrieking welcome by steam craft of all kinds. The salutes were begun by the Nova Scotia steamer *Yarmouth* and were taken up and repeated three times three all along the waterfront.
>
> On T Wharf a crowd had collected which cheered the *Rose Dorothea* and her crew.

Under other circumstances Captain Perry might have locked himself into his stateroom while all this fuss over nothing was being made. But now he had business to transact.

With his derby hat jammed down close over his ears – he had stonily refused to wear a beautiful gold-braided white cap Rose Dorothea had bought him especially for the race, and had worn the derby throughout – he jumped ashore now, straight-armed his way through the crowd, and made for the nearest telephone. And while the whistles were shrieking their three times three, those pirates, the spar makers, cringed under a volley in which there was no repetition.

But the sound and furor raised in Boston over the *Rose Dorothea* were as a pinfall in the wild welcome which the home folks of Cape Cod insisted on giving her skipper! Provincetown took her hero into her embrace – by the collar. This is how, in part, the *Boston Herald*'s reporter tried to do justice to the mingling of pleasure and pain on that memorable afternoon:

> Now, this Captain Perry is a combination of daring and timorousness – that is, he is all to the good when real dangers threaten and courage and brawn and brain are needed, but a veritable

---

* A new broom lashed to the mast, signifying a clean sweep of the fleet, was the traditional symbol of victory in races of the New England fishermen.

greyhound for the backwoods when men seek to haul him into the limelight of publicity. Then he shies like a terrified horse.

Captain Perry is not only modest, but silent. After winning the Lipton Cup, he was the recipient of an ovation such as had never before been given a denizen of the district, an ovation that continued from his landing at the steamboat pier until he escaped within the portals of his home, more than a mile away.

What he suffered during his ride through streets decorated in his honor and packed with shouting admirers, the town officials seated beside him, a full brass band preceding, and a rousing big band of new broom carriers constituting the rear guard, may never be learned; but he certainly endured an ordeal more to be dreaded by a man of his bashful makeup than the perils of a lee shore in a winter's smother.

During all that triumphal march, Captain Perry sat mute.

Three weeks after the Boston celebration there were big doings in Provincetown. On August 20 the cornerstone was laid for the Pilgrim Monument, a two-hundred-fifty foot granite tower which, after eighteen years of campaigning, Cape Codders were now putting up to remind the nation that it was at Provincetown – not Plymouth – that the *Mayflower* people first landed. The ceremony was gone through with speeches expressing the usual sentiments and containing the usual distortions of historical fact, but the duty with the trowel was performed by President Theodore Roosevelt himself.

The President's staff had carefully timed out a full program for him during his one-day stay in Provincetown. This included an address that same evening to the Cape Cod fishermen, just before his departure; and at the suggestion of his publicity expert, an hour was saved out of the afternoon schedule for a meeting and chat with the famous skipper who had recently won the fishermen's race at Boston.

The inspiration was not, as it turned out, a happy one. For this was Captain Marion Perry's busy day, too. While Cape Codders and summer people alike were jammed on Town Hill to see a President of the United States, the skipper was down at the wharf, checking over some requirements of new gear and rigging for the *Rose Dorothea*.

A messenger who called that afternoon at the Perry home was told that the captain was still down at the wharf. And when he finally located the

Chapter XIII: Flying Fishermen

captain and recited the invitation from the President, it was while several complex problems in strain and draw and chafe were being worked over. The messenger waited, decided the captain hadn't heard him, and recited the whole thing again, a little louder. Suddenly the captain bit through the pencil he was chewing, and at the same time dropped a couple of sheets of paper, which were wafted lightly down in the space between the wharf and the side of the vessel. Then he turned upon his annoyer.

"All right, all right! Tell the President if he wants to see me, he knows where he can find me!"

The story got around, of course, and that night the captain "got plenty hell" from Rose Dorothea. Did he realize what he'd done? Was that any way to treat the President of the United States? How would *he* like it if *he* were President, and a great sea captain had just won a big race and . . .

And on and on, during all of which the captain sat meekly enough, silent, abashed. He was too embarrassed to go to the Odd Fellows' Hall that night to hear the President's speech to the fishermen. No, he couldn't do that. But he kissed Rose Dorothea and told her he'd write a letter to try and make it up with President Roosevelt.

During the next two days, while riggers were at work on the *Rose Dorothea*, the captain knuckled down with pencil and paper, then had the following edited and typed out for him:

PROVINCETOWN, MASS., August 23, 1907

To Theodore Roosevelt
President of the United States
Washington, D.C.

Honored Sir: –

A report is current that you said to the fishermen assembled in Odd Fellows' Hall, at Provincetown, Tuesday, Aug. 20: "Mr. Connolly has said that it was a sacrifice to meet you. It is no sacrifice. On the other hand, I am glad of the opportunity of seeing you. I would like to go out on the Banks to have a chance to talk to you."

As master and part owner of the trawling schooner *Rose Dorothea* of Provincetown – the craft which won the Lipton cup in the Fishermen's race, off Boston, Aug. 1st – I cordially invite you to be my guest on that schooner during a trip to the fishing banks, the date of departure from port to be of your own selecting.

Speaking for myself and crew, we shall be glad to have you with us; and we will do our level best to make your stay on board ship both pleasant and profitable.

Yours, with respect,
MARION AUGUSTINE PERRY

Mr. Roosevelt couldn't go. But for once, Rose Dorothea had guessed wrong. For when it got into the newspapers that Captain Perry had "stood up" the President of the United States, she read:

> President Roosevelt was somewhat shocked but inwardly pleased when the messenger returned to inform him that the Provincetown sea captain had declared, "If he wants to see me he knows where he can find me."

Chapter XIV
Tollgates of Davy Jones

... I used to be lonely when you were away. I used to think Homeport was a stupid, monotonous place. Then I used to go down on the beach, especially when it was windy and the breakers were rolling in, and I'd dream of the fine free life you must be leading. I used to love the sea then. But now – I don't ever want to see the sea again ...

ON THE BARE OUTER SHORE of Cape Cod, three thousand miles due west of Spain, a young man once sat at a table in an abandoned lifesaving station, and wrote and wrote. Whenever he paused, he was sure to hear the break and boom of an incoming comber on the sand, a toss beyond his shack; and while he worked, whether he heard it or not, the break and boom, the spread and hiss of foam, went on and on. It was the surf at Peaked Hill.

The young man was writing plays of the sea, little heartbreaking dramas of men who came back from the sea, and of some who did not. And when those plays were produced, people said they could feel a curious rhythm in them, roll and pitch, "muffled monotone of breaking surf," cold stealth of fog. From the sea and from life on the sea, the young man's plays had caught something authentic. They were good plays, so good that even after longer and more ambitious works had won the Nobel Prize for Eugene O'Neill, many people insisted that those short early works were still his best.

O'Neill hasn't gone back to Cape Cod, but people there remember him. Provincetowners describe him as a "close-hatched kind of a feller that was shy of folks in general," and they will explain that he chose that out-of-the-way spot, two miles across the dune lands where the old Peaked Hill Lifesaving Station stood, because he could work there uninterrupted.

Certainly "folks in general" didn't bother him there. From Labor Day until the following June, those wind-whipped sands on the "Back Shore" of Cape Cod offer more seclusion than most of us need – enough, so the boys of the Coast Guard say, to "drive a man right nuts." The wheeling and screaming of mackerel gulls, the wind's moody clamor, the fine hailbeat of sand that can frost glass panes on the windward side of a house in half an hour – these and the surf make up the whole of the repertory – in that place not so much sounds as variations on the silence.

But, to O'Neill, I think that Cape Cod shore must have meant something more than a refuge from the great swirl of life in Provincetown (population, 4,000). Where he wrote of men whose "hair is matted, intertwined with slimy strands of seaweed," whose eyes, "as they glide silently into the room, stare frightfully wide at nothing," and whose bodies "sway limply, nervelessly, rhythmically as if to the pulls of long swells of the deep sea," – there, within a few hundred yards of his shack, more ships had been wrecked, more sailormen drowned or frozen to death in the rigging of stranded vessels, than at any other point on the New England coast. To a dramatist of the sea, that spot was "copy." There he was brought face to face with the sea at its rawest, its starkest. There it had shown, times without number, how merciless it could be.

In the sands of the whole thirty-mile beach from Peaked Hill to Monomoy, at the "elbow" of the Cape, broken timbers and ironwork have lain covered for more than three hundred years. When Champlain saw the sinister strand in 1602 quite probably even then the skeletons of French and Portuguese fishing smacks lay buried there. Champlain knew nothing of its past, but he may have had some inkling of its evil future, for he recognized hell's handiwork at once and called it Mallebarre. It was from the breakers of this same shore, too, that the people of the *Mayflower* turned their little craft and made their run for Provincetown Harbor, "againe to set their feete on ye firme and stable earth, their proper elemente."

How many craft were wrecked there, how many lives lost, no one knows. Ships with iron rails from England, with jute from India, palm oil from Africa, lumber from Canada, all were broken up. Cargoes of the coalers from Perth Amboy blackened the sands under the beams of nearby Highland Light; "stone sloops" littered the bottom with granite blocks from the quarries of Cape Ann; strands of algae were twined alongshore with bamboo sticks from the West Indies; salt from Spain was

Chapter XIV: Tollgates of Davy Jones

dissolved in the sea. During a sixteen-year period in the middle of the last century, five hundred vessels ran aground and were dashed to pieces between Peaked Hill and Monomoy. And more and more, the nameless graves were dug in "Judgment Lot."

But from the fishermen Peaked Hill took heavier toll than from all other mariners together. It lay directly in their course to and from the Banks; and while they knew its treachery, and skirted it as a skater passes thin ice, still the combination of dangers there was often too much for even these schooners and the "local knowledge" of the men who sailed them. Through the eighteenth and nineteenth centuries, schooner after schooner was swept into the trap, crew after crew perished.

Engine-driven craft of our own time are not the match of that shore. As this is being written, the ninety-five-foot Diesel-powered beam trawler *Andover* of Boston, built of steel and modern from stem to stern, is fast on the beach in heavy surf. As of old, the breakers are tearing their prey to bits where she lies abandoned; and as their forefathers did, Cape Cod "wreckers" are out there, busily stripping her of everything movable before her rightful owners can get around to it. By the time you read this, the *Andover* will have become a battered mass of metal, settling to gather rust and to share the graveyard of the centuries-old procession. But also, while you are reading this, she will have been forgotten, my story of the Back Shore already outdated, and the sea and the Cape Codders at work on still another broken ship.

For sailing vessels, Peaked Hill was a piece of the devil's own architecture. In the first place, the prevailing wind in winter was northeast, and in a northeast gale, that whole stretch of the Cape was a "lee shore." Once caught in the combined forces of wind and tide sweeping landward, the stoutest vessel was like a straw in a sluiceway. She could neither claw off with sail nor expect the heaviest cable to hold her. And in the second place, offshore at that point were the Peaked Hill Bars – hidden shoals that trapped the craft swept in by the gale, and held her there until there was nothing left but scattered wreckage.

There were two lines of these sandbars, lying just far enough below the surface to remain unseen at low tide. They ran parallel to the coast for about six miles, the outer bar about fourteen hundred yards offshore, the inner one about six hundred. Most vessels that came ashore ran over the outer bar, but they had small chance of escaping the inner. To go anywhere near them, even with a depth chart for guidance, was dangerous, for they were not stationary; like the rest of Cape Cod's sandy shore line, the bars were constantly shifting. A chart made in one year was of little use the next.

In the nightmares that an inlander has of drowning at sea, his dread tends to heighten in a sort of ratio with the depth of the water and with the distance from the shore. That is natural. That is the way it works in a swimming pool. In the nightmares of the seafaring man, the whole conception of danger is reversed. His fear is not of the depths out on the open sea. His craft has been built to take care of herself there. But she has not been built to withstand the tremendous leverage the sea brings down upon her when her keel is held fast in the shallows inshore. In an article captioned "Death Knell of the Pounding Surf at Peaked Hill," a writer for the *New York Herald*, February 19, 1911, thus described the terrors of those invisible bars:

> Vessels which ground upon the outer bar during an on-shore gale never escape. The giant billows which pound that shoal almost invariably destroy vessels stranded there within a few minutes of the stranding.
>
> The stoniest hull is as matchwood when exposed to the titanic blows of the seas, and in the inability of the hull to long withstand the pounding lies the greatest danger to the crew, since a certain time must elapse after the stranding before help can come, if at all, from the shore, and in the event of immediate or nearly immediate collapse of the vessel's fabric the only hope remaining to the mariner is that of being swept ashore or within reach of the lifeboat men.
>
> The struggling man who is washed ashore at a gale-lashed point not guarded by surfmen or others has not one chance in a thousand of escaping alive, for the cruel sea of the Peaked Hill beach region clings tenaciously to its prey. The horrible surf not only pounds and wrenches its victim, but it flings him headlong far up the strand, only to drag him back and roll him over and over, as if in sport, in the undertow, and this alternate casting and drawing continues until death mercifully intervenes.
>
> Two sailors who were swept swiftly ashore on a plank from the Italian bark *Giovanni* on the afternoon of April 4, got within

Chapter XIV: Tollgates of Davy Jones

thirty feet of the land. There the 'longshore current seized the plank, completely checked its shoreward progress, and bore it sidewise, parallel with the beach. The two men were overridden repeatedly by the seas. One man was swept away but swam back and got a fresh grip on the plank, only to be washed off anew and perish in full view of the horrified spectators.

Until 1872, despite the fact that hundreds of ships had been lost, many with all hands, no lifesaving stations had been provided by the federal government at Peaked Hill or at any of the other bad spots along the Back Shore of Cape Cod. In those places were only a few miserable little huts, built by the Massachusetts Humane Society as refuges for such sailors as could get ashore from their wrecked ships. Once a man had made his way up on that lonely beach on a winter's night, he might still have frozen to death before any help reached him.

Lifesaving stations were dotting the coast lines of New Jersey and Long Island more than twenty years before the government started to equip Cape Cod's busy Back Shore, with its more treacherous shoals and its much heavier toll of men and ships. Although Congress appropriated $20,000 for lifesaving service in 1849, all the stations were built elsewhere; and through those fearful winters of the fifties and sixties, death was left a free hand on the Cape.

For this delay there was a curious reason; and to get at it, one must tamper with the locks of local lore, and trot forth a rather grisly skeleton which Cape Cod historians have been at some pains to leave undisturbed in its closet. So many craft had been cast on that shore, with valuable cargoes from all over the world, that the industry known as "wrecking" – recovering these cargoes and stripping abandoned ships of everything that would come away – was highly profitable almost from the beginning of commerce.

To people who had been profiting in this way for generations, the rules of salvage were so much legal fancywork, and during the law's delay, while gales blew and the tide came and went, the simple tradition of finders-keepers worked as a quick salve to the New England conscience. That which was too bulky to cart off for himself, the wrecker dutifully "salvaged" to the rightful owner – for a good-sized fee. The rest disappeared as by magic. And the profession, though it was loudly deplored by the up-Cape towns which had no such shores to trap the wealth of the world, was considered more or less honorable by those who lived where they could profit by it. In short, it was considered nice work, and Cape Codders could get it.

But such things as lighthouses and lifesaving stations threatened to bring on depression in the wrecking industry. Therefore, nearly two hundred years ago, Cape Codders were telling the government it ought to keep its hand out of business.

Boston Harbor had a light in 1716, but the Cape managed to face down all agitation and keep dark o' nights until 1797, when the big primary beacon known as "Highland Light" was built on the bluff in Truro, near the Peaked Hill Bars. It was built over considerable protest. Years before, the Massachusetts Humane Society had begun urging it. "It is a serious truth," the society declared, "that in each revolving year seamen are forced on shore with nothing left them but the liberty of complaining."

"Off-Cape furriners" were responsible for finally getting Congress to act at last on the proposal to build the light. The only local figure to champion it publicly had been a poor impractical minister, who nearly got himself into trouble by this meddling in other folks' affairs. As late as 1854, when Ralph Waldo Emerson went to Orleans and visited the Nauset Light, another Back Shore beacon, he wrote:

> The keeper Collins told us that he found obstinate resistance on the Cape to the project of building a lighthouse on this coast, as it would injure the wrecking business.

While the wrecks kept piling up and the corpses floated ashore during post-Civil War years, another impractical soul, a young schoolteacher, also began interfering in other people's business. As a result, in June, 1872, Congress suddenly trampled all over the constitutional rights of Cape Cod's minority, ordering nine lifesaving stations to be built along the Back Shore. And from that time on, the history of Cape Cod is brightened with the courageous work of a force assigned to save men's lives, rather than their property. The daring rescues these men succeeded in making, and their equally brave failures, all sum up as a stirring offset to the doings of their neighbors alongshore, who continued in the wrecking business despite the new interference. In the last quarter of the century, lifesavers of the Peaked Hill district alone rescued more than a thousand mariners.

Chapter XIV: Tollgates of Davy Jones

"You've got to go but you don't have to come back." That is the unofficial motto handed down to our present-day Coast Guardsmen from their predecessors on Cape Cod. Something of the dramatic story enacted in those waters, a sort of last chapter of the whole era of sail, is told in a little book now out of print – *The Life Savers of Cape Cod*, by John Dalton, shore correspondent for Boston newspapers around the turn of the century. He had witnessed much horror, many thrilling rescues.

Writing in 1902, Dalton called the Cape Cod shore "the most dangerous winter coast of the world," and added:

> Death has often claimed the life saver at his work. Or as a result of his gallant, unselfish toil for the safety of others in the rigors of winter, one life saver after another is compelled to retire from the service on account of shattered health.

The pay of a surfman at that time was $65 a month, with no compensation if he had to be dropped because of disabilities.

The profession, Dalton pointed out, was "entirely different from that of a sailor." The training a surfman needed could be acquired only by coast fishermen or others who had had years of experience of taking boats in and out through the breakers and in handling them in rugged water. The lifesaving service therefore drew on the fishery for nearly all its personnel; and before 1900 the majority of those who manned the stations of lower Cape Cod, including the dreaded Race Point and Peaked Hill districts, were Portuguese fishermen of Provincetown. These fellows had cut their teeth on belaying pins, they had quit fourth grade to "go cook" to the Grand Banks, they had ridden out of the gales of Georges Bank in trawling dories; they had rattled the dice with Davy Jones and knew which side was loaded.

The job of these men was hardest at Peaked Hill, because there they were seldom able to use the gun-and-breeches-buoy apparatus which facilitated rescue elsewhere alongshore. The Lyle gun used in the late nineteenth century fired an eighteen-pound shot carrying a linen thread whip-line, and it had an extreme range of six hundred ninety-five yards. But the line sagged, and the currents were usually so swift that the crew of a stranded vessel couldn't haul the whip on board when too much of it lay in the water. About two hundred yards was considered to be the working range of the gun. As against this, the inner sandbar at Peaked

Hill was six hundred yards offshore. Therefore almost all rescue work had to be done by surfboat. Of the way it was necessary to carry out this job, the writer for the *New York Herald* has this to say:

> If life-saving bands from neighboring stations are on the scene, the launching crew spring to the thwarts and the oars. The crews of the other boats – brought to the spot on wheels – now cluster at the "launcher's" after end, and holding the gunwales, "meet her" – that is, force the stern to right and left along the sand – in an endeavor to keep the bow pointed directly at the seas that rush upon her, and thus avoid swamping and overturning.
>
> As soon as a favorable opportunity offers, the keeper gives the command and the forward oarsmen ply their blades, while the swarming, half-submerged fellow life-savers at quarters and stern push vigorously. Then, while the shore surf curls overhead and cascades down upon boat and men, the boat, waterborne but standing almost straight on end, moves slowly ahead, clears the shore sands, dives through the first of the breakers, and if successful emerges half full of water beyond the shore seas at length, to be followed as soon as possible by another boat – the one to aid the other in the event of a capsize . . .
>
> On the occasion of the wreck of the three-master *Willie Higgins*, March 31, 1898, the writer saw one particular bit of Peaked Hill Bar water leap suddenly skyward, bearing on its bosom the Race Point lifeboat and crew, and fall with such abruptness as to leave the boat suspended in midair for just the briefest space of time. For an instant, boat and crew were wholly out of water, enabling the onlooker to view the entire foreshortened craft. Instantly thereafter she was lost to sight in clouds of sea spray.

At times the seas of Peaked Hill were so overgrown that no boat could live in them, and it would have been foolhardy to do anything but wait for them to subside – or for what they would wash ashore. It was on that sort of night, in January, 1895, that the eleven-hundred-ton four-master *Job H. Jackson*, coal-laden from Norfolk for Portland, was trying to weather Race Point and run for shelter in Provincetown Harbor. While she was off the Point her fore and main sails blew out of the boltropes and she fell to leeward. With her decks full of water and with ice making

Chapter XIV: Tollgates of Davy Jones

rapidly on the hull and spars, she became unmanageable. In the darkness she drifted down on the Peaked Hill Bars. She struck head-on just outside the inner bar, and at once was battered broadside to the shore.

She carried two boats, but they were torn away before the crew could reach them. Within an hour from the time when she was hung up, the deckhouses forward and parts of the deck itself were gone. While the men were huddled in the cabin, which was heated, the seas broke the roof in, and the last man to reach the ladder was up to his waist in water.

The craft had heeled offshore, and now every sea was falling full on her deck. No man could have remained there long. And so, though it was blowing hard and so cold that the salt spray froze as soon as it fell, the six men had to climb into the rigging. The jiggermast was swaying crazily as each sea struck, but it was the only one they could reach, so all six took to it There, while ice crusted their clothes and the breakers rocked their perch back and forth, they hung on and waited for daylight.

Surfman William Carlos of the Peaked Hill Bars Station was on beach patrol that night. Near the eastern limit of his beat, at a little after three o'clock, he heard above the surf the snapping and pounding of canvas offshore – familiar sound at Peaked Hill, which meant only one thing. He fired his Coston signal, a flare to notify the distressed crew that their plight had been discovered ashore, and then ran back to the station. From there the neighboring Race Point and High Head stations were telephoned, and men and equipment went out from all three.

Boats were brought down on beach carts and made ready for launching as soon as the sea should allow, and the "sand anchor" for the breeches-buoy gear was set up. In another hour, the vessel could be seen against the graying east.

Some of her canvas was streaming in rags, some wrapped in long strings around spas and rigging. The main gaff hung banging across-deck, with a broad strip of sail floating halfway aloft. Ice had formed in strange shapes on her bows, and long needles of it hung from the shrouds. Away aft, in the starboard rigging of the jiggermast, the six men still hung on:

> High above the howling of the wind and the roar of the surf sounded, occasionally, the voices of the apparently doomed men. It was a fearful scene. Their craft was going to pieces, hull and rigging were covered by ice, making their clinging a thing of difficulty, and at any moment their frail mast might go by the board.

But it was still impossible to launch a boat from shore. The *Jackson* lay about six hundred yards off, and rather than stand idle, the lifesavers tried firing a line to her. The shot fell just inside. So did another. A third passed over the taffrail of the schooner, but the line had parted. Again and again they tried the guns, but it was obvious that the schooner lay too far offshore for this method.

The question of whether to launch a boat was always left for the station commanders to decide. Those men knew what was expected of them, but they also knew the difference between an act of courage and a spectacular suicide. The Peaked Hill Bars Station was then under command, of Captain Isaac G. Fisher, one of the greatest old heroes Cape Cod ever produced, and also, strange to say, one of the soonest forgotten.

Captain Fisher saw small chance for a boat to survive the row out to the *Job H. Jackson* — so small that he told his men he would wait until ten o'clock. But the water didn't subside. And the station commander kept his gaze on the crew of the schooner, still up there in the rigging, freezing before his eyes. At a quarter to ten, Captain Fisher broke the rules. He couldn't stand aside and watch those men any longer; and so, he ordered the boat out, in a sea in which no boat should have been ordered. And, of course, he took the steering oar himself.

As she became fully water-borne, a nasty sea struck her before the oars had given her headway, knocking her bow to one side, while water flew over and into her. A second and larger sea struck her an instant later on the port bow and whirled her half around, while she reared straight on end on a roller that came in to break on the beach. But a sharp eye and a crafty hand were aft. A quick sweep of the steering oar and a good pull by the rowers started her ahead, and like a racer she plowed her way through the sea and was fairly afloat. With spray flying clear over her, off she went.

Straight for the *Jackson* they went, all the way meeting ugly breakers, now hidden from the sight of those ashore, now thrown against the skyline. They came up on the starboard bow of the wreck to escape the swirls about the head and stern. But rough water was everywhere; the boat stood on end or went splashing down, and to those watching from ashore she seemed doomed every foot of the way.

Chapter XIV: Tollgates of Davy Jones

All at once she appeared out of the crests and whirled in amidships, alongside. A shout rang in from the men up in the rigging, and they tumbled down to the rail. The trip back to the beach was made in good time.

This account, which I have borrowed from columns of the old *Provincetown Beacon*, ends with the remark: "'Twas a gallant rescue, effected by gallant men." And as the record of more than threescore years attests, 'twas one of many such at Peaked Hill.

To the fishermen especially, a lifesaving station at such a place was a godsend. And because of their own training, the crews of these schooners could give their rescuers better cooperation than any other class of mariner, either in rigging up the line for the breeches buoy or in getting ashore in a surfboat. As a result, Davy Jones often got the surprise of his long life just when he thought he had a crew of these men well on the way to his locker. By sheer magic, feats of marine sleight-of-hand that made shore watchers gasp, rescuers and rescued worked together, and sometimes came out of it with whole skins. Many a man living out his old age today in some port that once sent schooners to the banks owes his survival to the daring work that was done on Cape Cod.

One of these spectacular rescues, as good an example as any, occurred on the morning of February 17, 1896, when Provincetown's "hard-luck schooner," the *Gertie Winsor*, struck at Peaked Hill, climaxing a woeful career. She had sailed five weeks before on a fresh-halibuting trip to the Western Banks. There she found very little halibut, but plenty of heavy weather. The grounds were being swept that winter by some of the wildest and long-windedest storms the fleet had seen in years.

On February 3, the *Winsor* reached Liverpool, Nova Scotia, with four thousand pounds of fish on board and with her sails blown to rags, a couple of broken sticks, and other miscellaneous injuries. She repaired there and went back to the banks for more fish. She got more gales. Blow after blow overtook her, making it impossible to set the trawls. After two more weeks of this, the men were discouraged, and Captain Manuel Enos agreed that the thing to do was to call it a broken voyage, go home, and forget about it as quickly as possible.

A northeast gale accompanied the *Winsor* homeward. All through the day on Sunday, February 16, the schooner was banged about mercilessly somewhere off the Back Shore, as she tried to beat westward and round

Race Point. That night it blew harder than ever, and the mercury went to five degrees below zero. At three o'clock, when the crew believed they still had an offing of several miles, they started settling down the mainsail to take in a reef. While they were struggling with the frozen canvas, one man raised the cry, "Breakers!"

At the same time the *Winsor* hit the outer bar at Peaked Hill. She struck so hard that it looked as if she had come there to stay; and knowing what that meant, the crew promptly gave up all hope for themselves. Waves were sweeping the deck and giving the hull such punishment as no craft could have stood for more than a few minutes. The men climbed into the rigging. They would stay there until the schooner broke up. Then they would be dropped into the sea.

But it was only an hour past high water, and the long seas were making in so heavily that from the time she stranded, they had been jarring the schooner's hull, inching it along the bar. Then came one that lifted her clear. For a couple of seconds the *Winsor* faltered; then she was swept over, and into the narrow channel between the two lines of shoals. At once she ran down on the inner bar, stuck there and swung broadside to the shore. The water was still making a clean breach over her, but with less punishment to the hull than before; and the place where she was now aground, a sandspit extending shoreward from the main body of the bar, was only about two hundred yards from the beach.

Still hanging on aloft, the crew took heart from the fluke that had brought their craft closer inshore. If they were seen before they froze to death, they would have a fighting chance, as they were now within the working range of the beach gun. A few minutes later, they saw the red flare of a patrolman's Coston signal. And across the sand, a man went running for the station.

The lifesavers tried their first shot when the schooner was still only a few black scratches on a murky field – literally a shot in the dark – but the line passed straight between the masts! Men on the vessel made their way down and grabbed it, giving a few tugs to signal ashore. The lifesavers then tied a "tail-block," or pulley, to the shot-line, and the men on the schooner hauled this on board. Through the block an endless pulley-line was rove, and attached were the printed instructions:

> Make the tail of the block fast to lower mast well up. If the masts are gone, then to the best place you can find. Cast off

shot-line, see that rope in the block runs free, and show signal to shore.

When this was done, and the signal given, the lifesavers tied a three-inch hawser to the endless line, which was now running through the pulley on board the schooner. Then they hauled away, paying out the heavy rope, until the end of it was carried on board by this pulley system. Further instructions went along with it:

> Make the hawser fast about two feet above the tail-block; see all clear, and that the rope in the block runs free; show signal to shore.

At this signal from the schooner, the lifesavers made the shore end of the hawser fast to the strap of a sand anchor, placed a crotch of heavy timbers under the rope, and raised it. This drew the hawser taut, making a bridge of rope between the stranded vessel and the beach. They put on a traveler block, carrying the breeches buoy, and by the same pulley system, whipped it out to the schooner.

Then back and forth the traveler block went on its track of rope, each time bringing a man in the breeches buoy. Within half an hour, all seventeen of the *Gertie Winsor*'s crew were carried, one by one, safely over the surf. In less than an hour, the schooner went to pieces.

Three hundred years after the Pilgrim Fathers began talking about a Cape Cod Canal, that 'cross-Cape channel connecting Cape Cod Bay and Buzzards Bay was dug through, and opened to commerce. But commerce wisely gave it a wide berth. For it was a rather puny little ditch that August Belmont's company had finally completed in 1914, a ditch with a lightning current caused by the tides, and with not enough water to see any fair-sized craft safely through.

Four years later the federal government took it over, spent many millions of dollars in widening and deepening it, and gradually made it a workable passage for vessels of any draft. Then commerce started using it.

The importance of the Canal, which in future years will repay many times the millions that have been poured into it, lies partly in the saving of time and distance – about seventy miles – between New York and Boston, and even more in the greater safety at sea between those points.

Long after coastwise shipping had changed over to power, freighters were still being wrecked, passenger liners were still stranding, on the Back Shore of Cape Cod. Between 1900 and 1920 there were more than nine hundred shipwrecks there. But the Cape Cod Canal ends for all time the threat of the Back Shore to the big freighters and passenger boats. For such ships, Davy Jones will have to think up new troubles.

Because the traffic has thinned out, the United States Coast Guard, which succeeded the Lifesaving Service in 1915, has started to cut down the forces stationed along the Back Shore. In September, 1937, over the protests of Cape Codders and fishermen from all ports, the Peaked Hill Bars and near-by Pamet River stations were closed. The fishermen wanted the stations kept open, because they still fished in those waters, and the waters were still dangerous.

But all appeals failed. The sea keeps eating away at the bluff overlooking the Peaked Hill Bars. Several times in its long career the station has had to be rebuilt, farther inland. But this has been done, now, for the last time; and the breakers will keep on eating away, and one day, to the ghosts of wrecked ships that haunt the beach at Peaked Hill, will go the ghost of the old shore lookout. The sea will have the last word.

Chapter XV
Nets and Trawls and Six-Inch Guns

SWOOPING DOWN ON THE FISHING FLEET and burning five unarmed vessels on a night in June, 1863, the Confederate bark *Tacony* made news that startled New England and caused the citizens of Gloucester to bite through their pipe-stems when they heard it next morning.

Before burning the vessels, the "rebel pirate" had taken off the crews, and eventually the men were landed on northern soil. But, for all that, her raid got up the dander of 'longshore Yankees, to such a pass that when the Navy refused to do anything about it, they armed their own craft and sailed out for revenge. The pirate, scared off into southern waters, was never seen on the fishing grounds again.

Her disappearance only made the Yankees madder. A wave of new enlistments followed, and even the elders on Cape Cod, who were not yet finished fighting over the War of 1812, wanted to forsake the cracker barrel then and there and take up arms for Abe Lincoln. The *Boston Transcript* remarked:

> Fishermen, in war times, are regarded as neutrals or noncombatants, and free from attack or seizure. It remained for the rebel pirates to violate this usage and wantonly destroy the property of an industrious and defenseless class, whose vocation is hazardous enough always to exempt them from savage assaults on their unarmed craft. They never dreamt of needing protection!

Lesser outrages than the "contemptible and reckless acts of this gang of pirates" have enticed our newspapers off the straight path of accuracy, before and since the *Tacony*'s raid; and we may forgive the *Transcript* if that wave of righteous wrath swept out all memory of "savage assaults" on fishermen during the Revolutionary War; or if, in striking while the editorial iron was hot, the paper had not time to brush up on its history of the War of 1812 and review such exploits of its own Yankee privateers as, for example, those set forth in the 1814 log of schooner *Harrison*:

> November 11. Took and destroyed [British] schooner *Mary* with fish from Halifax, which had before been taken by privateer *Portsmouth* and retaken by the *Juno*.
> November 18. The small boat returned with schooners *Seaflower* and *Lucy Ann*, both with dry fish; burnt one and gave the other to Prisoners.
> December 31. Off Lisbon captured the British schooner *Britannica*, from Newfoundland with fish; burnt her. Same day, British brig *Race Horse*, from Newfoundland with fish; burnt her.

And of course there was not time to check up with the Yankee sailors who had gone out to do this work, men like Thomas Thompson, of the crew of the Gloucester privateer *Macedonia*, who later reminisced:

> We had orders to burn, sink and destroy. We took a new schooner bound to England, which we burned. We captured a ship in ballast, bound to the Provinces, and we scuttled her because she would sink easily . . . Then we took another ship loaded with Newfoundland codfish. We then had so many prisoners aboard that we made a cartel of her, putting the prisoners on board, and let them go off where they wanted to. We captured and destroyed quite a number of small vessels.*

Fifty-five years after the rebel pirate slapped Gloucester's wrist and scooted off to the southward, a sinister fleet of sail-less, stackless enemy craft from across the Atlantic made, its presence known on the fishing grounds – craft which 'longshore Yankees could not scare off.

In the summer of 1918 America's "war profiteers" were out to make a financial killing at home commensurate with the killing then in process abroad, and for this purpose the Boston wholesale fish market was admirably equipped

As the price of meat rose, the government began urging people to eat more fish, to eat it for personal economy and as a patriotic duty, whereupon the remotely controlled but closely cooperative companies that did the wholesaling at Boston Fish Pier began applying their talents to the

---

*History of Gloucester, by James R. Pringle, Gloucester, 1892.

Chapter XV: Nets and Trawls and Six-Inch Guns

opportunity. Fish followed up meat and other food prices, and then, in percentages, outran them. The profiteering machinery in Boston was thrown into such high gear that the rest of the country couldn't keep up with it. Fish in salty Massachusetts was higher than fish in inland Kansas!

To make the most of their situation, the Boston wholesalers had to ensure for themselves a steady and plentiful supply. But with man power now in extraordinary demand, fishermen saw many kinds of work open to them ashore, work less dangerous and better paid than any they had ever known. The wholesalers were therefore obliged to make it worth while to these men to keep on going to sea. Accordingly, "ex-vessel" prices for fish, though still far behind the soaring prices to dealers, were lifted to average levels they had never attained before.

Meanwhile the government was bringing heavy moral pressure to bear on the fishermen. In calling for a speed-up, the Food Administration said it could not doubt "that the fishermen, than whom there is no more patriotic body of men in the country, will flock to the Hoover standard and fish for victory over the Kaiser." And despite this somewhat overdrawn imagery, it *was* important to keep on fishing, so important that the French had mounted guns on the decks of their big St. Malo fleet and had been sending these vessels to the Grand Banks each season.

From the American ports, many of the younger hands had gone to France or enlisted in the Navy, and a number of unnaturalized Portuguese residents of Provincetown, Gloucester, New Bedford and other ports had gone over to join the army of Portugal. Those left at home were not exactly spellbound with the sentimental picture of themselves flocking to the Hoover standard when this meant going far out to sea, unarmed, in wartime. But they went, partly because of loyalty, partly because they saw a chance at last to earn a decent living in their own work, and mainly because they had been assured that the United States Navy would protect them.

"The regular fish supply is of so much importance," said the *Gloucester Times*, that the Government feels the need of giving adequate protection to those engaged in procuring it." So anxious, in fact, was the Navy to protect the fishermen that its authorities even gave them psychological protection. Navy censors were annihilating fear – and the truth along with it.

As for the danger of submarines – well, yes, we were at war with Germany, but Germany was a long way from the Grand Banks or Georges Bank. And the United States Navy was on the job. Hadn't it already ordered a hundred "sub-chasers" (authorized March 4, 1917), and wouldn't these swift armed vessels be enough to safeguard a few dozen fishing craft in one or two small spots on the Atlantic? When one U-boat actually had dared to show up in our half of the ocean, sinking a couple of steamers in southern waters, hadn't Senator Henry Cabot Lodge of the Naval Affairs Committee told folks not to get excited?

"Everything that can be done is being done," the Senator had announced after that raid. "The Navy has been expecting just such an affair and was adequately prepared. We needn't worry one bit about what is being done to cope with them."

Just what the Navy was adequately prepared to do was not clear, since it did nothing and the submarine continued its raids, but in saying that the Navy had been expecting such an affair, the Senator was quite correct. A month before, on May 1, advice had been relayed by cable to the United States Navy from the British information service at the North Sea base that a German submarine, the *U-151*, had left on a long cruise, and was bound for the coast of the United States What the Navy was prepared to do, and did, on May 27 was to issue this press release:

> WASHINGTON – Navy Department officials said tonight there was nothing to indicate the presence of enemy submarines on this side of the Atlantic.

Before this story was sent out to the newspapers, wrecks of three vessels sunk by the *U-151* had already been found!

Early in June, two poor old New Bedford whaleships, ghostly remnants of the century-old fleet of "blubber boilers" which had come as hand-me-downs to impoverished Portuguese skippers, were creaking their homeward way together from a last-gasp voyage to the Hatteras grounds. Off the coast of Virginia they met up with the *U-151*.

Neither the *Ellen Swift*, nor the *A. M. Nickerson* had arms, neither had power, and in fact, neither was sure of reaching home port intact even if no serious obstacles were encountered. The United States Navy wasn't around. All things considered, it looked to the Portuguese whalemen, as they gazed on the gleaming steel of the submarine, like a pretty one-sided war as far it concerned them.

CHAPTER XV: NETS AND TRAWLS AND SIX-INCH GUNS

At the submarine commander's bidding, the *Nickerson* put over a boat, and a few minutes later Captain John Gonsalves of New Bedford, faced Korvettenkapitän von Nostitz Janckendorf of Prussia.

The commander of the German craft could speak English fluently. The commander of the American couldn't. But in spite of this unfortunate reversal, Captain Gonsalves did his best to make it clear that he and his fellow whalers were all poor men, and that the loss of their ships would mean ruin to them, and could scarcely be of any large benefit to Germany.

The Korvettenkapitän heard him out, then went on deck and took another look at the whaleships. He was inclined to believe Captain Gonsalves. The industries of America would be only very moderately crippled by the disappearance of these two vessels; and deciding that together they weren't worth the powder it would take to blow them to Davy Jones, he told Captain Gonsalves to get back on board his ship and beat it.

Captain Gonsalves rowed back in all haste, the two whalers crowded on sail, and at the rate of three knots an hour, they beat it.

The whalemen had a hard time making folks at home believe their story, but a month later, when survivors of the sunken Norwegian bark *Manx King* were brought to Boston, having been picked up from their lifeboats by another craft, they declared their vessel had been torpedoed by a German submarine. The *Manx King* had gone down about three hundred miles off Cape Race, Newfoundland. Newspapers in Massachusetts ran the story under headlines like this:

U-BOAT HANDY TO FISHING BANKS

But Gloucester and Provincetown were still skeptical, and the United States Navy was still very reassuring. Kiel, base of Germany's submarines, was on the Baltic Sea – thirty-five hundred miles away! Even with such an incredible cruising range as would have been necessary for them to work along our shores from that remote base, how could the craft carry enough supplies to sustain their crews after they got here? The whole idea was preposterous (and Navy officialdom had a convincing and explosive way of saying words like "preposterous"). Besides, the *Manx King* was on the Grand Banks when she was sunk, and all the American fishing, or almost all, was being done at that time several hundred miles to the westward, off Nova Scotia and on Georges Bank.

On July 21 the skepticism of the fishing ports and the reassurances of the Navy were blown to smithereens with six-inch shells, and so were four barges of the Lehigh Valley Railroad – by a submarine only three miles off the shore of Cape Cod!

The barges were in tow of the tug *Perth Amboy*. On board the five craft were forty-one persons, mostly Portuguese from New Bedford, and among them three women and five children. At half-past ten on that tranquil Sunday morning, the string was passing by the town of Orleans on its way around the Back Shore. Ashore, "summer people" were bathing and lying on the beach. Half a dozen sail of pleasure craft were in sight, waiting for a breeze. The Atlantic was keeping the Sabbath. Everybody knew there was a war; but there were a time and a place for all things, and war at that moment seemed more like three million miles away than three thousand.

Suddenly a deck hand on the *Perth Amboy* saw a strange streak in the water, shooting past the bow. He yelled, and Captain J. H. Tapley came out of the cabin. The deck hand thought it was a torpedo. The skipper didn't see how it could be. While they were staring at the water, another narrow gray wake silently streaked across the tugboat's bow, then a third.

Out of a fog bank four miles offshore, the submarine appeared. She glided to within four hundred yards of the tug and then, while the tug and barge crews were still standing nervously on deck, without further ado she began a furious bombardment with her two six-inch guns.

The gunning was very wild. Had it been otherwise, the Americans would certainly have been blown to bits within a few minutes. One of the guns did score a hit, and fire broke out forward on the *Perth Amboy*. The men ran astern. Then one of the shells burst near the pilot house, tore one man's arm open and blew a hand off another. The crew of the helpless tug, unable either to fight or run, decided now to risk getting off in the boats, for the wounded men had to be taken care of at once.

Meanwhile the terror-stricken people on the barges were also putting over their boats. Jack Ainslee, eleven-year-old son of one of the barge captains, had raced out with his father's .22 rifle, and was "returning the fire" when the captain grabbed him by the collar and put him into a boat.

The boats made the beach without further casualty. But for an hour and a half the submarine carried on its one-sided engagement with the derelict string, disabling the tug and sinking the barges one by one. The

Chapter XV: Nets and Trawls and Six-Inch Guns

people on the beach at Orleans were interested spectators, thinking all this was some sort of Navy target practice, until one shell came ashore and the truth dawned upon them in a rain of sand, sending all hands scurrying for cover. That German shell, incidentally, was the only one to land on American soil during the World War.

Thirty-five miles from the scene of the "battle" a fleet of Gloucester schooners was seining for mackerel. On her way to join these vessels, the little schooner *Rosie* was met by the U-boat. Five shots were fired at her, one missing by about ten feet.

"We didn't stop to do no fishing," the *Rosie*'s skipper explained. "When I seen that sub, looking like a big tin whale spouting hellfire, I hollered to Tony down below for full speed ahead, and we got into the first fog we ever appreciated."

The undersea boat that had blasted away so mercilessly at the *Perth Amboy* and her inoffensive barges, and then at the *Rosie*, was the *U-156*. She had sailed from Kiel on June 15 – a departure of which the United States Navy also had been immediately advised by the British information service. From the same source the Navy was again informed on July 26, when a third craft, the *U-117*, left for American waters.

Washington also knew – though the fishing crews were at a complete loss to figure it out – just why the Germans were going after these small, harmless craft. On July 31, when the first submarine had come back to Germany from her raid in American coastal waters, the Cologne *Volks Zeitung* published her commander's report, in which he made the point: "The appearance of the U-boat before their very coast will hardly tend to improve the morale of the Americans."

He was right. Morale was not improved. Among the fishermen, the knowledge that a submarine was cruising the waters where they worked – a submarine that seemed eager to turn her six-inch guns on anything in her path – did not add to that morale.

But the German's report missed an even better point. For even more dismaying to the American fishermen was the knowledge that their own navy, after so many assurances, was letting them down when it came to action, was doing nothing to guard the shores, or was guarding them so poorly that a bold above-water attack had been possible, in broad daylight, and in heavily trafficked waters three miles from the coast.

Even among the folks who stayed ashore, there was uneasiness. While the submarine commander was writing up his achievements for the Cologne newspaper, the *Gloucester Times* editorialized:

> There was a time not so many months ago when Americans were thinking of the great war as being 3,000 miles away, and therefore a contest from which they might entirely keep themselves free.
>
> But since then, distance has been abolished . . . We received last Sunday a very vivid reminder of the nearness of the battle when barges were sunk in sight of the summer residents of the town of Orleans.
>
> We know now if we never did before that no nation can live a life apart from others. And we who have thought ourselves safe from foreign entanglement do well to see how close this war has come to us. Victory is absolutely necessary.

The day after the shelling of the *Perth Amboy*, schooner *Robert and Richard*, high-liner of the Gloucester halibut fleet, was homeward bound from the Western Banks with a big fare. On Cash's Ledge, about seventy-five miles from Gloucester, a U-boat suddenly broke water two miles off and sent a shot across the fisherman's bow. The schooner hove to, and her crew, all unarmed, stood on deck with their hands in the air as the raider drew alongside.

The German commander was taken on board in a dory. He asked Captain Robert Wharton for the ship's papers and flag, and then ordered him to abandon the vessel at once. While this was going on, two of his aides had tied a bomb to the schooner's sounding-line, swung it over the stern, hauled it forward, and then made it fast on both sides amidships.

The fishermen were told that the bomb was timed to give them ten minutes in which to row the Germans back to the submarine and then get off themselves, in their dories. In their haste the men took no time to stock the boats with food or water. When they had returned the Germans, and had rowed a mile off, the bomb exploded. It sent the schooner to the bottom in two minutes.

The twenty-two men of the *Robert and Richard*'s crew were adrift in six dories. One sailed to Cape Porpoise; two were picked up by other fishermen; and three, after drifting nearly twenty-four hours, were sighted by the steamer *Snug Harbor* and brought in to Boston.

Chapter XV: Nets and Trawls and Six-Inch Guns

The men thought themselves very lucky to have come out of it alive. The weather was calm, the hold-up was staged in waters that were frequented by other fishermen, and the submariners were in a somewhat more merciful mood than they had been in the attack off Cape Cod. Had any one of these three circumstances been otherwise, the men pointed out, they would have been lost.

Although the United States Navy kept Germany's own secrets faithfully as it was informed of each new submarine that left Kiel, American fishermen now knew that more raids were coming. Submarines were on the grounds – nobody outside the American Navy's inner council, and the Germans themselves, knew how many – and they had not made that long trip across the Atlantic to sink four barges and one fishing schooner! The raids would go on unless something stopped them, and although naval authorities came out with further denials of danger, assurances of aid, and much other verbiage of the same caliber, the fishing fleet had had pretty convincing evidence, not only that it had been let down, but also that it had been picked out to be sent down. And now, even upon the newspapers, the truth began to dawn. As the *Boston Transcript* fatalistically sized up the situation: "To bring the [fishing] vessels home or to relax mid-ocean vigilance would be to do the Germans' work. So we let our fishermen take their medicine."

Our fishermen could take medicine, but they balked at poison. When certain non-seagoing Congressmen thoughtfully proposed that the fleet be fitted out with guns as the French were, so that they might sink the submarines, craft for craft – a plan against which the Navy made no audible protest – Gloucester and Provincetown themselves objected. French craft on the Grand Banks were being sunk, guns or no guns; and the fact that they were armed only subjected them to worse treatment. Besides, most American vessels were too little to fight submarines. Except for the Boston beam trawlers, they were small wooden schooners. A gun big enough to dent a U-boat, the men said, would do even worse to the schooner from which it was fired! Having no other choice, the fishermen preferred the mercy of German commanders to the ingenuity of American politicians.

They did ask for war-risk insurance, however, and early in August this was arranged. Nobody knew who was to be next, nor what that next would mean.

It came on August 3. The *Rob Roy* of Gloucester, the *Muriel* of that port, and the *Annie C. Perry* of Provincetown, were getting ready to fish at the mouth of the Bay of Fundy when the "Hun Sea Horror," as the newspapers were describing the then unidentified *U-156*, struck again. The men of the three vessels were set adrift in their dories and the schooners blown up by keel-hauled bombs in the same procedure that had done away with the *Robert and Richard*. The dories, though scattered, all reached the shore of Nova Scotia.

After this day's work, the submarine lay off Seal Island all night, her deck awash, and displaying a bright light which could be seen plainly from the shore. She was still there, shore witnesses said, through the next forenoon. But she got busy again that day, sinking a Nova Scotian schooner, and another the next, and then joining the *U-117* on Georges Bank, where a fleet of thirty Gloucester craft was swordfishing.

When the *U-117* left Kiel, American naval officials received advance information that she was expected to operate among the fishing vessels working between Cape Race and Halifax. That section was east of Georges Bank; but the submarine, learning that the American swordfishermen were concentrated on Georges, and finding no armed opposition anywhere, went on to join the *U-156*, in raiding the swordfishermen. And on August 10 the two U-boats were busy indeed, sinking nine American schooners within a few hours.

As the *U-117* was about to blow up one of these – schooner *Kate Palmer* of Portland – Kapitänleutnant Droscher told the Americans:

"We are not baby killers. Don't tell any lies about us when you reach land."

But this was true of his colleague, Kapitänleutnant Oldenburg of the *U-156* only because fishing schooners did not carry babies. Bearing down on a group of three of the little craft, the *U-156* gave no warning, but began banging away at them just as she had banged at the tug and barges off Cape Cod.

Within five minutes schooner *Old Time* was on her way to the bottom, and almost as quickly schooner *Cruiser* followed her. Men of the third vessel, the *Mary E. Sennett* of Rockport, were getting ready to leave in dories, as the other crews had done. The cook put a box of biscuits and two bottles of water in each of the *Sennett*'s two dories. Shells from the submarine began falling around the schooner while the men were trying

Chapter XV: Nets and Trawls and Six-Inch Guns

to get the second dory over. One burst on the deck forward, and two men were thrown off their feet. They got up, jumped into the dory, and started rowing away. According to Captain Manuel Dias, two shots were fired at the dories while they were in the water, but both missed. The submarine then applied herself to the task of demolishing the schooner.

The *Sennett*'s crew lashed the two dories together and went on rowing. The boats were 160 miles east of Cape Cod. After twenty-four hours, the men were picked up by the schooner *W. M. Goodspeed* and brought home. One of them, Antoine Silva, describing the attack, said:

> "They wouldn't give us a chance. Manuel started to yell for the Americans to come on and help us. The Americans didn't come, but God did. I guess God must have been with us, and He didn't want to take us so soon. Maybe that's why the Germans are such bum shots."

One by one, through several days following, dories of the eight other schooners sunk in that raid were accounted for. Crews of two of these vessels rowed one hundred eighty miles before they were picked up near Nantucket. But somehow and somewhere, all the ninety-odd shipwrecked men reached shore. They had lost everything but their lives, and for those God alone received a unanimous and exclusive vote of thanks.

Hoping that He would continue to protect them, and knowing that if He didn't nobody else would, the men went on fishing. Receipts of groundfish at Boston in the month of August were above those of August a year before, when there had been no U-boat campaign on the banks; and through later periods they continued "about normal."

Morale, however, was now depressed to a level below the Germans' fondest expectations. On August 11, the Massachusetts Public Safety Committee sent a wire to the U. S. Food Administrator in Washington:

> ACTION OF U-BOATS IN SINKING NINE FISHING VESSELS ON GEORGES BANKS YESTERDAY HAD BROUGHT CONSTERNATION TO RANKS OF FISHERMEN AND THEIR FAMILIES. WE URGE THAT STRONG STATEMENT BE GIVEN OUT BY THE NAVY DEPARTMENT THAT ALL NECESSARY PROTECTION BE GIVEN AT ONCE . . . WE FEEL IT IS UP TO YOU TO ACT PROMPTLY.

Five days later the Navy Department announced that "steps had been taken" to protect the fishing fleet. "You are authorized," the Department told the Food Administrator, "to give this matter general publicity."

The publicity went out next day:

> Recent raids by undersea pirates have done little actual damage to the fishing fleet, taken as a whole, but much uneasiness among the men has resulted. Wives and families in some cases have induced them to remain on shore. But the American fisherman is not easily kept from the sea, and it is expected that his courage and the knowledge that the Jackies are on guard will keep the fish catch up to normal.

The steps the Navy had taken were those necessary to order one small patrol boat to "Georges Bank and adjacent banks" – an area of several hundred thousand square miles.

Meanwhile, the *U-156*, moving on to the adjacent Western Banks, captured the 125-foot Nova Scotian steam trawler *Triumph* while she was on her way to Portland with a fare of fish.

In a conversation with the *Triumph*'s skipper, Kapitänleutnant Oldenburg said Germany was to have a fleet of six submarines operating in near-by waters, and that the purpose was "to destroy the fishing fleets." And to further that purpose, instead of sinking the trawler, the Kapitänleutnant had one gun transferred to her, put a crew of twenty-one of his own men on board, and supplied them with rifles and a number of time bombs. The fishermen were set adrift in their dories.

Early that same afternoon the crew of the *Triumph* – the fishermen who were in their dories – sighted a schooner hull-down beyond the horizon, a schooner that any bankerman would have recognized at once as the *Francis J. O'Hara, Jr.*, of Gloucester – Joe Mesquita, master.

Everybody knew what Captain Joe thought about the war. A fisherman's job, Captain Joe had said, was to fish. The Germans knew that. The newspapers called them "Huns," but after all, they were men, just like the rest of us. They had had jobs before the war, those Germans, just like anyone else. They knew a fellow had to get out and earn his living if he wasn't fighting; and they knew the fishermen weren't fighting. Germans themselves must have done a little fishing, somewhere. They must have known what a tough life it was, even without a war. And if they knew that, what was there to be afraid of?

Chapter XV: Nets and Trawls and Six-Inch Guns

No, you couldn't show Captain Joe where the danger was any greater than getting run down, say, by a steamer in the fog, or being wrecked in a gale; and fishermen took such risks every day of their lives. You couldn't tell Captain Joe any seafaring man – even a German in his submarine – really meant to hurt a fellow! And as this had seemed, under the circumstances, as serviceable a view as any other, many had listened to Captain Joe, and had sailed out to danger fortified with his homely, human, but wholly unfounded faith in the immunity of honest labor.

Now, when the schooner *O'Hara* was sighted from the *Triumph*'s dories, she was heading directly for the shoal known as the Middle Ground, where the submarine and her prize trawler were cruising. The men in the dories tried to warn the *O'Hara*. They yelled, waved their coats, and rowed as hard as they could. But the *O'Hara* was too far off to see or hear them, and was going fast.

Off Sable Island, where he intended to start fishing, Captain Joe saw two other schooners and a beam trawler – the *Triumph*, which he knew well – steaming between them.

"I think we run down to speak her," Captain Joe told Tony Braga, who was at the wheel. "I better ask George Myrrhe [the *Triumph*'s skipper] if he's got any luck here before we try a set."

"Better ask him if he's seen any submarines too," Tony suggested. "It's going to be a tough night to spend adrift in a dory!"

"*Ai*, submarines!" sighed Captain Joe. "You fellers, always talking submarines, submarines! I wish you stay home tonight – with the women! *A mulher e a gallinha, com sol a casa!*" (Women and hens should be at home when the sun goes down!)

As the *O'Hara* drew near, Captain Joe, seeing no signs of work on board Captain Myrrhe's vessel, cupped his hands and gayly called out:

"Hey, you beeg steef! Why you don't get beezee and do sometheeng? Is too rough for you fellers here?"

From the *Triumph*, a voice came back in broken English: "Heaf to! You vill see vee do someting!"

"I didn't get it! What's a matter, George?" Captain Joe shouted solicitously. "You catch yourself a cold?"

"Heaf to! Vee are going to zingk your vezzel!"

"There's something wrong over there," Tony Braga explained. "He says he's going to sink our vessel!"

Captain Joe's deep laughter went booming across to the mystified enemy.

"Go ahead, sink me, George! But look out, when I'm down there I tell these U-boats to get after you!"

Men of the *O'Hara's* crew had come on deck. They were looking puzzled, and Tony Braga, white-faced, was tugging at the skipper's arm.

"I tell you, Captain, there's something funny over there! That ain't Captain Myrrhe!"

"Eh? Sure it is! He's a beeg josher, that Myrrhe! You fellers – "

Just then a shot whizzed across the *O'Hara's* bow. Then another. Captain Joe looked at his men. His smile was gone at last. "Better lower the jib and jumbo, boys," he said quietly, "and let her jog."

The *Triumph* now drew alongside, and her new commander ordered Captain Joe to come aboard and bring his papers, "and quick, too!"

The German, it seemed, was "real mad" with Captain Joe about something. He strode across the deck, stood before him and demanded to know why the *O'Hara* hadn't stopped when she was ordered to do so. Captain Joe, still a bit taken aback, gave the commander a faint, apologetic smile and said:

"To tell you the truth, Captain, I figure we are just joking, you and me. I know thees vessel and her skipper, long time now. She is not German, thees vessel – "

Yes, but hadn't he seen the German flag on her?

Captain Joe was very sorry. He hadn't noticed the German flag. Naturally, if he had – and his smile faded again with the recollection of the things he had been yelling across the water.

But the German commander "didn't seem so mad" now. In fact, he was beginning to grin!

Nevertheless, the *Triumph* meant business, and she went about it forthwith. She gave Captain Joe five minutes to get back to the vessel and take his crew off in the dories. Then three Germans were sent on board. They did their work and got off, and a few minutes later the *O'Hara*, with scarcely a sound, lifted slightly out of trim, and then went down.

Next day Captain Joe's wife received a telegram informing her that the skipper and crew of the *O'Hara* were safe ashore in Nova Scotia, and six days later all were back in Gloucester.

When newspapermen asked Captain Joe what the Germans looked

Chapter XV: Nets and Trawls and Six-Inch Guns

like, he said they all wore leather coats and long boots, but they looked human – just like the newspapermen themselves. The only one who hadn't looked quite human was the commander, and that was because he "wore a Charlie Chaplin mustache."

Two days later Captain Joe Mesquita took command of the Gloucester schooner *Muriel* and went haddocking to the Western Banks.

For the armed trawler *Triumph*, that first day of raiding – August 20 – had been a busy one. She was not a fast vessel; she had only one gun; and any encounter with the smallest American or British war craft probably would have meant her destruction in short order. Yet her commander had boldly cruised the banks, getting miles away from the convoy submarine during the course of the raid! And by nightfall, in addition to the *O'Hara*, he had sunk five fishing schooners.

That same night, Navy Department officials "confidently awaited a wireless dispatch telling of the capture or destruction of the British trawler *Triumph*." It was declared in Washington that "a cordon of ships" surrounded the fishing region. The Navy, said Admiral W. S. Benson, had "taken steps."

But the Navy Department, sitting tight on its isle of self-composure, was gradually being left alone there. In an editorial on the chances of removing the *Triumph* as a permanent menace to the entire fishery, the *Gloucester Times* concluded: "The only hope seems to lie in the French fishing fleet, all of which are armed with guns of fair calibre this year, as they were last."

Congressmen who owned shore property had been taking an interest in the submarine warfare ever since the *U-156* had landed a shell on Cape Cod; and because the Navy was continually announcing that it had taken steps, the legislators began to wonder why the steps were so ineffective. On August 26 the atmosphere in the Senate registered several degrees of excess temperature, in a sudden realization that the U-boats had come to America. The five-weeks-old Cape Cod affair was taken up as news; and when someone wanted to know where the United States Navy was when the submarine came out, the only answer was an unofficial and offensive murmur from the gallery: "Down in the cellar eating sauerkraut!"

Then Senator Gerry of Rhode Island called attention to what had been happening to American fishermen. Of the raid by the *Triumph* he said: "Here a single submarine appears in our waters, puts German sailors aboard a trawler that it captures off the coast, puts some guns aboard it, and now for more than a week this converted trawler has been destroying fishing smacks. Where is it all to end? Where are the swift U-boat chasers we've been hearing about?"

The swift U-boat chasers were not on the Banquereau – or "Quero Bank," as Gloucestermen called it – but while the Senators were talking the *U-117* was. The United States Navy had been informed in advance by transatlantic cable that that was where she was scheduled to go; and after lending a hand in the raid on Georges Bank, that was where she went.

Also on Banquereau was the Boston steam trawler *Rush* – Captain Alvro Quadros. At a little before six o'clock on the morning of August 26, Cook Joe Telles was peeling potatoes in the galley of the *Rush*, when one of the hands called down, and in a trembling voice told him the skipper wanted him. Joe hurried on deck.

He saw the crew gathered aft around the pilothouse. A hundred yards off to starboard lay the long, low-riding form of a submarine, gray steel with blue waves painted sloppily on it. Two men of the *Rush*'s crew had stepped out from the little group aft, and were standing beside Captain Quadros The skipper beckoned to Joe.

"We got to go aboard that feller, Joe. He says we got to – all the officers of this vessel!"

Joe, who had taken out American citizenship papers, gazed across at America's deadly enemy.

"I'm no officer," he said.

"Sure you are. Cook is an officer. Don't argue, come on!"

The skipper himself didn't look delighted with this invitation from the Germans. Neither did the other two men whom he had picked on the spur of the moment to be "officers." But all four got into the dory and rowed to the submarine.

There they were searched for arms and then courteously led below to the quarters of Kapitänleutnant Droscher.

The submarine commander was unexpectedly chatty. He spoke English well; and once, when Joe turned and muttered to Captain Quadros, *"Quanto tempo paramos aqui?"* ("How long are we going to be kept here?") the commander smiled and promptly replied, "Not long, senhor. Maybe one hour, maybe two." Joe was flabbergasted, and tried no more asides.

Chapter XV: Nets and Trawls and Six-Inch Guns

But the German talked freely. He said the *Rush* would have to be sunk. He didn't like to set men adrift in dories so far from the shore, but there was no other way. In fact, he disliked this whole business of attacking fishing craft, he said, but – he had his orders.

"And if you want to know the reason why we are doing this, here it is!" He slammed his hand down on a newspaper lying before him.

To the amazement of his visitors, it was an American newspaper, with the date line August 13, 1918 – only thirteen days old! At the top was the headline:

HUN SEA TERROR STRIKES AGAIN – FISHERMEN VICTIMS

"When we left Germany," he went on, "we had instructions to sink only three-masters. But after stories like this came out in the American press – stories of shooting down unarmed men at sea – we got orders later by wireless to sink everything in sight. You see what comes from such lies? Is it so hard to understand now?"

Joe Telles lived in Gloucester. He knew Gaspar Silva, one of the men on the sunken schooner *Mary E. Sennett*, and he had heard Gaspar himself tell how the submarine had fired two shots at their dory after they had put off from that vessel. The newspapers had said four shots. Well, there were two. But Joe wasn't in a mood to argue with Kapitänleutnant Droscher. Instead, he asked how the submarine had come by the newspaper.

"This? Oh, we go ashore, sometimes. Last Sunday I went to a dance hall in Boston." He laughed, and Joe couldn't decide whether he was joking; but there, before his eyes, lay the, thirteen-day-old newspaper.

While the commander was entertaining his guests, men were bringing loads of stuff below – stores and equipment from the *Rush*. They were taking practically everything movable. The officer pointed towards the men as they passed the open doorway.

"Those supplies ought to keep us another month," he explained.

As one fellow went bumping through with something heavy, Joe peered after him, and his heart skipped a beat. They were taking over the phonograph from the *Rush*'s forecastle! If those fellows started playing it, there might be hell to pay. That was a bright trick Joe Goulart did, all right! – bringing all those records of war songs on board, last time they were in port! Joe Telles had heard that Germans were funny people that way – didn't have much of a sense of humor. And if they started playing that phonograph . . .

Sure enough, they were going to play it, and at once. In fact, they seemed more delighted with it than with any other item in their haul! One of the officers took charge, wound the damned thing up and put on a record; then, while four Portuguese fishermen quaked in their boots, the machine squawked out:

> Oh, we'll get the Hun,
> The son-of-a-gun . . .

The officer who had commandeered the phonograph sat solemnly, listened hard. He seemed disappointed at the harsh ragtime tune, but it was also clear from the look on his face that he wasn't catching the meaning of the words. Kapitänleutnant Droscher went over to him and explained the song briefly in German. The two men grinned at each other. As the piece went on, they guffawed, and in their heavy boots, went into a little dance to the song some dead-serious patriot was bellowing at them through the wax disc from their enemy's shores.

The four fishermen relaxed, sat back, and grinned sheepishly. Joe Telles wondered where it was that he'd heard the Germans didn't have much of a sense of humor. Well, there was nothing like the things people did when they got into action – any people – to pitch a man's ideas about them keel-over-maintruck!

Three hours later Joe, the skipper, and the two other men were sitting in a dory, adrift on Banquereau, waiting for a passing fisherman to pick them up, and wondering whether they would presently awake from some strange nightmare of having been prisoners on board a German submarine.

Ashore, news of the raids kept coming thick and fast. On August 27, Gloucester learned that the *J. J. Flaherty*, one of the high-liners and the largest sailing vessel left in the North Atlantic fleet, had been sunk on the Grand Banks. On September 20, the new steam trawler *Kingfisher* was torpedoed.

The Navy, realizing that nobody would listen any more to denials that war was being waged in American waters, at last took a new tack. Admiral Benson issued this statement:

Chapter XV: Nets and Trawls and Six-Inch Guns

The [Navy] department would suggest that information be disseminated among fishermen that during the war they confine their fishing as much as possible to waters outside of frequently used sea lanes, and that the department cannot be held responsible for loss to individuals from naval operations which it considers necessary to protect shipping.

This statement came out October 18. After sinking thirty-four schooners, all German submarines had been recalled from the fishing banks more than three weeks before.

Chapter XVI
Today

The "adventure of the sea" dies hard. For years it has been lamented that the old quality of danger has disappeared from seafaring; but then something happens like the foundering of the Brava packet *Frank Brainerd* to show it isn't so.

Two months ago the *Brainerd* was fitting out here, and Captain Benjamin Costa was proud of his staunch three-master. "We expect to make the [Cape Verde] Islands in about thirty-five days," he said.

Three weeks ago, when the tanker *Vancolite* found her, the *Brainerd* was in as desperate condition as any doomed Spanish galleon ever was. Her masts had gone. Rigging, sails and yards covered the sea-swept deck. Her seams were opening under the savage pounding of the gale. If such a scene constitutes the adventure which is passing from the sea, we are glad to see it go.
– *New Bedford Standard-Times.*

THERE WAS EVEN MORE to the scene on board the *Frank Brainerd* than is disclosed above. On that day in August, 1936, when the oil tanker came to her aid in mid-Atlantic, she had been drifting three days in her state of complete wreck; and huddled on deck were her crew and passengers, among the latter a child of less than a year and a woman of sixty-five.

But the "adventure of the sea" has gone on; so have the Brava packets; and so have the wrecks. From New Bedford, where the Cape Verde Islanders came into this country before the mast on the old whaleships, and where their descendants live now, people still make the three-thousand-mile voyage to the islands in ancient little sailing ships ships that are fairly palsied with the "old quality of danger."

Little has been said, and still less written, about these quaint and deadly passenger vessels known as the "Brava packets," which have continued

CHAPTER XVI: TODAY

their strange comings and goings under sail while, faster and faster, the world of travel sweeps by them in mighty ocean liners.

I call their voyages strange because they are not larks, nor sporting cruises, nor transatlantic yachting contests; nor are they the anachronistic whims of people who can think of nothing saner to do with their leisure than to try living over the "great old days of sail" by venturing on long voyages in obsolete craft. In the life of the Brava packets there has been no such counterfeit romance, there are no hobbyhorse mariners setting out deliberately to tempt Davy Jones with vessels that belong in museums, merely as an escape into "adventure." Nor is. there any of the fake heroism of "stunt crossings" for publicity. No, these are simply freight and passenger ships. They sail the Atlantic because their people – a few each season from among the 30,000 Cape Verders living in New England – want to get on the other side. That has been their purpose for seventy years.

Time was when packets sailed to the Azores as well as the Cape Verdes. From the southwestern quarter of New Bedford, which came to be known as "Fayal," there were people who wanted to go for a visit to the island homes of their forefathers, or to bring over relatives, or to send back gifts.

The packets of those days were more prosperous, and accordingly, better found; but still they were little craft, as passenger vessels went; most of them had seen other kinds of service before they went into packeting, and among them were ex-whalers, a few hand-me-downs from the short-lived clipper fleet, and some of the more venerable three- and four-masted schooners. Skippers and crews were usually ex-whalemen, and there was a gay and sometimes exciting informality about the voyages, which one was not likely to find in any other transatlantic passenger service, even of those times. A New Yorker who decided to go a-voyaging in one of the Fayal packets back in the eighties has left an account of her two weeks at sea, which began like this:*

> The ship, scarcely moves. The sails are altered every half-hour, in vain attempts to catch a breeze. A great steamer, brilliantly lighted, passes dangerously near us, outward bound. We hail a schooner drifting near with, "Schooner ahoy! Which way is the tide setting in the Sound?"
>
> At midnight I wake, burning with fever, and begging for ice:

* C. Alice Baker, in *A Summer in the Azores*, Boston, 1882.

at sunrise creep on deck for air, – but alas! there is none. We lie becalmed off Block Island. A boy in a rowboat comes alongside. He lives near the post office, and will take letters.

"I didn't expect to send back a mail every day on this trip," says the captain with grim facetiousness.

"Light, baffling airs," continues the log. We are learning meaning of that word *baffling* as we never could have done on land. Tediously tacking all day and all night, from Long Island to Nantucket Shoals light, the end of the second day's voyage finds us, after two hundred and fifty miles of sailing, but fifty miles on our journey, scarcely one-fortieth of the whole distance. For all we have gained, we might as well have been sleeping in quiet beds at home.

But things happen on this voyage to take the writer's mind off the disturbing matter of distance run:

The morning of the third day is ushered in by the cry of "Porps! Porps!" The sailors harpoon a porpoise; and the sound of the poor creature, flapping in its death-agony on the deck, I shall not soon forget.

"A strong breeze, wind south-west, and all sail set to best advantage." The passengers revive, and aim to become nautical . . . July 2, at sunset, the cry of "There she blows!" which often rings through the ship, rousing the old whaling instincts of captain and crew, is suddenly changed. "It's no whale!" cries the mate. The captain runs to the masthead. The crew, press on deck. The excitement is intense. "A boat, keel up!" say some. "A wreck!" echo the others. The ship is put about. Preparations are making to go to the scene of the disaster. Imagination is busy depicting possible horrors, – men starving, dead – "It's only a whale's carcass!" shouts the captain, coming down. The crew disperse, and all are relieved.

I haven't any doubt that if it had been a live whale, the skipper would have lowered for him, and as a matter of fact, it is a little surprising that he didn't stop to investigate the dead one. In 1902, when the skipper of the Azores packet *Freeman* took time out to do that, inside the carcass, he found a 145-pound lump of ambergris, which sold for $37,000.

Around the turn of the century, this traffic between New Bedford and the Azores had become so heavy, and the ties between the two places so close, that the islands tried to make an international issue of their liking for America. As relayed here by the *Boston Post*, this rather surprising suggestion was made in 1902:

> The *Telegrapho* [of Horta, Fayal] has been for some time publishing a series of articles under the heading, "Separation Idea," showing considerable dissatisfaction over the obstinate disregard displayed by Portugal toward the islands, and recommending annexation to the United States.

As the *Telegrapho* conceded in its choice of heading, the "separation" was just an "idea." The Azores were never officially recognized as a suburb of New Bedford. But the traffic between Fayal and "Fayal" has continued lively to this day, and is now handled by a little steamship line.

After the old-time packets were displaced in the Azores trade, freights and fares could still be collected, on a modest scale, between New Bedford and the Cape Verde Islands. Steamer service to the Cape Verdes consisted of one boat a year; and so, between these arrivals, decrepit little sailing craft carried on, and occasionally do so now.

People who go in them are very poor. They can't afford steamer tickets. But if they have a little money – from thirty to forty dollars – a great deal of time, and a very great deal of fortitude, the wind will still take them across. At least it will take them as far as the packet can get before she falls apart (a misfortune which must be taken into account seriously because it has so often befallen packets).

In the abandonment of the *Frank Brainerd*, the ship and her cargo – which consisted of one used automobile – were the only losses. In July, 1913, the old whaling schooner *William Grozier*, then relegated to the packet trade, was battered to pieces in mid-Atlantic, and again all hands were saved by a passing steamer. But most of the wrecks ended more tragically. When Captain Anthony Benton, Cape Verde whaleman, took out the forty-six-year-old Gloucester schooner *Florence Nightingale* in January, 1901, as a Brava packet, neither the ship nor any of her people survived. The *John R. Manta*, after seven years' service between Providence and the Cape Verdes, sailed in November, 1934, and was never heard from again. The following year two more were lost – the *Winnepesaukee*, fate unknown; and the *Trenton*, which ran on a reef off the African coast. In 1939, the *Stranger* went aground and was wrecked, and so was the three-masted schooner *Thomas H. Lawrence*.

There have been others. And there were so many because by the time a ship was brought to the lowly estate of Brava packet, she was likely to be no more than a poor, enfeebled ghost of her old self. In the way he chooses to dispose of has-beens – men and ships alike – old Father Neptune shows a distinctly elfin streak A few years ago, for example, one could find on Cape Cod many a shipmaster whose name might once have been known in ports all over the world, living out his last years as keeper of the town cemetery. That had long been a favorite way of taking care of retired sea captains on the Cape, men who had earned fame and fortune but had preserved only the fame.

So it has been with ships. Tracing down craft that once bore great names of the sea, one finds them at strange chores in their old age. Among the many such that spent their declining years in the Cape Verde line were the bark *Coriolanus*, crack sailer of the foreign trade in the days before steel hulls replaced iron ones; schooner *Stranger*, once winner of $15,000 in a fishermen's race; the *Joseph P. Johnson*, unsinkable Provincetowner, of whose many adventures I have related only a couple; the *I. J. Merritt*, which stocked nearly half a million dollars in her sixteen years of banks fishing; the Grand Banker *Gracie Benson*, which was rammed and sunk in Boston Harbor, then salvaged and refitted as a packet; and the eighty-foot yacht *Corona*, which had been launched at Newport in 1896 by Harold B. Vanderbilt as a possible defender of the *America*'s Cup.

The *Corona*, last of the Brava packets, went into that service in 1930. Captain Joseph de Souza, her skipper, navigates with a quadrant and an alarm clock. In 1938, he brought her safely into New Bedford on September 19 – two days before the great "New England Hurricane." In the spring of 1939, the *Corona* sailed again, making Fogo, Cape Verdes, in the scheduled time of thirty-five days. She carried six passengers, two secondhand automobiles lashed to the deck, a pen of live pigs atop the fo'c's'le, and a hold full of general cargo. On September 16, 1939, she arrived back in New Bedford after a forty-five-day voyage, in which she had serenely made her way through seas infested with mines and submarines. She was unaware that war had been declared!

Though this one-time racing yacht is all that remains of the Brava packet fleet, she is not typical. For most of their ships, the Cape Verde line had drawn on the old Yankee whaling fleet. In their last years, the sperm whalers of New Bedford were manned and skippered almost entirely by these half Portuguese, half African Cape Verde Islanders. The few exceptions were Azorians. And the employment of both men and ships in this archaic little transportation line of the twentieth century was really the last chapter in the story of New Bedford whaling.

That industry had been a long time dying. The discovery of large petroleum pools in Pennsylvania in 1859 was the beginning of its troubles, but by no means the end. Whales were getting scarce – or at any rate, harder to find. As soon as the ships began to have difficulty showing the huge profits they had once made, New Bedford capital, which was accustomed to huge profits, began shifting into the textile mills. Things went from bad to worse, and by the end of the century it looked as if the sperm whalers were finished forever.

But in December, 1900, a new type of whaling vessel, a "revolutionary" type designed to solve the industry's biggest problem by operating at lower cost, came into the port of New Bedford to be coppered for a cruise to the Charleston grounds.

She was the *Joseph Manta*, named after her owner, a continental Portuguese who had come to Provincetown some years before and had made a fortune as owner and outfitter of banks fishing schooners. Manta was an adventurous operator, and the "Manta fleet" had already been credited with several important innovations in the fishery. Now he was sending a ship to show New Bedford how to catch whales!

The tired old town, still harboring the foul-bottomed relics of a fleet that once had led the world, took one look at the whaling schooner *Joseph Manta*. Then it tossed its hat in the air, and without waiting to see what the wonderful new vessel could do, ordered more like her and went back to sea.

A few years later such headlines as this were appearing in Massachusetts newspapers:

NEW BEDFORD WHALERS AGAIN VEX
THE DISTANT SEAS
Revival Made Profitable by Improved Weapons
and Abandonment of Primitive Methods
and Traditions of Other Days

It was no flash in the trypot. With Cape Verde crews, and in most cases with Cape Verde skippers, ships of Bedford port were going back to the Charleston grounds and to many other parts of the Atlantic; they were killing whales, they were coming home with oil and bone, and sometimes with ambergris. When we think of whaling at all now, we are likely to think of it either as an old story – a story that happened once upon a time – or as a new story of the great "floating factories," which do everything but smell the whale by machinery. As a matter of fact, there was no gap in time between the old whaling and the new. They overlapped by many years. For the last of the "old-time" New Bedford whalemen did not climb ashore and march up Johnnycake Hill for home until 1925.

What the schooner *Joseph Manta* did after she left New Bedford on her own voyage, however, is another story – a curious and a short one. It seems that her main mission on earth was to spur New Bedford to take this last twenty-five-year lease on life as a whaling port. As a newspaper described this vessel:

> Her model and rig are radical departures from old-fashioned custom. Her bowsprit is of the "pole" variety, her masts are of unequal length, her forward and aft overhangs are pronounced, while her stern tapers in, yachtlike.
>
> Patterned closely after the newest and speediest of the New England fresh-fishing fleet, and painted a glossy white, she appears, despite the try-works structure of brick on her main-deck and the array of whaleboats suspended from her lofty cranes, like a yacht masquerading as a whaler.

Among the unwieldy hookers in the Acushnet River, she looked like a midget, for she was only a "three-boater," taking a crew of twenty men. But her size itself was an innovation in deep-water whaling, giving the old-timers much to think about. The smaller the vessel, the smaller the crew and the expenses all 'round. A good fast craft, built without a care for carrying capacity, would be a better whaler than the leisurely old bluff-bowed tubs that had served in the days when whales were so plentiful they could be stumbled upon, and didn't have to be run down in a long chase. Now, if a fleet of these smaller, faster craft were to get together and pool in on their own transport ship to take home the oil (a plan later carried out), old New Bedford might hang on yet a while longer.

CHAPTER XVI: TODAY

On December 10, 1900, the *Joseph Manta* sailed with Captain John Frates in command, on a three-year cruise for sperm whales.

The time allotted for the voyage was almost gone, and the schooner had taken and sent home 1,900 barrels of sperm oil, when on October 13, 1903, Manta received a cable from his agent in Fayal: "Reported *Manta* and crew total loss at Pico. Will furnish full particulars as soon as received."

Next day another cable confirmed the report. The particulars were that a hurricane had very suddenly overtaken the *Joseph Manta* while she was passing through the channel between the Azorian islands of Pico and São Jorge on October 9; that the schooner had been dashed on the rocks of Pico; and that all hands had been lost with her!

Later it came out that Captain Frates had gone out of his way to pass through that channel; and that if he had taken the logical route, between the islands of Pico and Fayal, the vessel would have been out in the open sea when the hurricane struck, with a much better chance of saving herself. Still later, it came out that the reason Captain Frates had not followed the logical course was that his own home was along the route he sailed, and that he had told his wife he would wave to her!

One year after the loss of the *Joseph Manta*, another schooner of the Manta fleet sailed from New Bedford. She was built along the same lines, and was named *John R. Manta*, after the owner's son. Of her the *Boston Globe* said:

> This craft, though 35 tons larger and not quite so "lean" as the *Joseph Manta*, is the handsomest, costliest and best constructed vessel of her inches ever built for whaling work.

First commanded by Captain Henry Mandly, who had gone into whaling from the Azores at fourteen and who had become one of New Bedford's best known skippers, she brought in handsome returns over many years. In the spring of 1925, under command of Captain Mandly's son, Antonio Mandly, she sailed on her last whaling voyage, cruised the Hatteras grounds, killed enough whales to pay her way with a little left over, and then came home to end the last "old-time" whaling voyage from the port of New Bedford.

Of the men from the Cape Verde and Western Islands who commanded the whaling fleet in its later days, few remain. The generation is passing that produced whalemen like Captain Mandly, of the *Quickstep* and later of the *John R. Manta*; or Captain Antoine Edwards, who brought the bark *Wanderer* home in 1917 with the biggest catch of whale oil ever made on a voyage out of that port. Shore business – the mills of New Bedford and neighboring towns, the stores, offices, and a thousand and one places far from salt water – has drawn away their descendants.

Out of "Bedford port" today go the chugging "draggers," "scallopers," and "sworders," a well found fleet that fishes on Georges and sometimes on the Western Banks; but of her older business in great waters, there is no seafaring remnant making that port today, not even among the occasional craft that still hobble across to the Cape Verde Islands. Of those many long years in pursuit of the whale, all that remains is one or two fortunes now invested elsewhere, a few heaps of old iron and other keepsakes carefully labeled in the museums so that new generations in New Bedford can tell folks what they were for, a stack of yellowed ship logs, a whaleship kept high and dry with her bottom forever in a plaster cast, and an inaccurate statue in front of the public library.*

Provincetown, too, has come ashore for the bigger part of its living. Cape Cod babies no longer insist on belaying pins to cut their teeth on; gone is the schoolmarm who made her incorrigibles box the compass twenty times as their punishment; men sleep soundly on Cape Cod now without setting the garden hose to play against their bedroom walls.

The decline of seafaring here had cast a long foreshadow. Time was when this town, like its neighbors on the Cape, carried on "shore whaling" as a steady business, with several schooners engaged, and with a factory on the beach to try out the catch. But when a thirty-five-foot whale came into Provincetown Harbor one morning in the winter of 1909 and couldn't find its way out, there was only one man on hand who was ready to tackle it. Captain Joshua Nickerson dusted off a few bomb lances, went out after the whale, and killed it. But instead of cutting in his whale and trying out the blubber, "Cap'n Joshway" gutted the creature, filled up its main hold with empty barrels, towed it to Boston, and sold it.

The purchasers loaded the whale on a flatcar and took it on an exhibition tour. Strictly an open-air attraction, it played to large crowds, even

---

* A bronze figure of a whaleman standing in the bow of his boat, harpoon in hand; but the harpoon line is too short. It would be almost impossible for him to iron a whale with so little free line; and if he should succeed, Heaven help him!

on Cape Cod; and at Provincetown, the end of its itinerary, one beheld not only the depressing phenomenon of the whale, but the equally depressing one of Provincetowners paying ten cents a head to see it!

As a port for deep-water whalers, Provincetown closed its career with the still unsolved riddle of the schooner *Carrie D. Knowles*. After many seasons as a Grand Banker, the vessel was rerigged for whaling, and in January, 1904, she sailed with a crew of thirteen under command of Captain Cohn Stephenson. She was to go to Dominica for more hands, but she never reached that island, nor was she heard from again in any port.

Five years later a man all tattered and torn who said he was Elisha Payne of Provincetown, turned up on the island of St. Vincent, in the British West Indies. What was left of his clothes was recognized as a prison uniform, and authorities of Kingstown arrested him as a fugitive.

Payne told a wild story. He had been a last-minute addition to the crew of the *Carrie D. Knowles*, he said, when she sailed out of Provincetown five years before. While en route to Dominica, the schooner had been blown far off her course by southwest gales, and had found refuge in "a small obscure port on the Venezuelan coast." Payne said he didn't know the name of that town, but that the vessel was boarded immediately by Venezuelan officers, who took the men ashore and clapped them into "the damp vaults of an old stone fortress overlooking the harbor from a promontory." He went on vividly about his sufferings in prison, and about his lone escape when he struck down a guard with a water jug and fled into the great swamps. Hunted by soldiers, starved and weak from exposure, he had eluded them at last and made his way to St. Vincent.

Because incidents of the kind had not been unusual in the high-handed administration of the Venezuelan military leader, Cipriano Castro, Kingstown was inclined to believe the story. Payne knew the names of the *Carrie D. Knowles*'s crew, and when he was confronted by Captain Stephenson's daughter, who lived in Kingstown, he gave a description of the skipper which she said was accurate.

Provincetown was "electrified by Payne's story." Though George Knowles, owner of the schooner, had been dead two years, half a dozen Portuguese families and the relatives of a few Yankees in the crew were much concerned with the news. On May 6, the Provincetown Board of Trade telegraphed Senator Lodge, asking him to demand an investigation by the Department of State.

Four days later, a cable from Barbados informed Washington that Elisha Payne of Cape Cod was a liar. In the course of further questioning, his story had capsized. He had not been in the crew of the *Carrie D. Knowles*; he had been in prison, but for reasons which he decided were better left untold to the Kingstown authorities.

After many weeks, the interested families in Provincetown were advised that they had been the victims of a "cruel hoax." People recalled that shortly after the *Carrie D. Knowles* sailed, the Atlantic was swept by fierce gales, and that early in February of 1904 the steamer *Lancastrian* reached Boston from London with the report that she had sighted a wreck, unidentifiable and floating bottom up, "a schooner of the old Grand Banks type."

Among the older skippers in Provincetown's banks fishing fleet, there were a few die-hards for canvas who put off installing those mysterious, greasy "put-puts" in their vessels as long as they could. To fit out with an engine meant to strip the craft of her mainsail; and who ever heard of a schooner without a mainsail? She wasn't really a schooner at all when you did that to her! It changed everything, all the old ways. And it made her look like hell.

But the schooners without mainsails that looked like hell were bringing in the fish. With Boston sending big steam trawlers to the banks, these hybrids were the only small craft that could still hold their own. One by one, the old-timers installed power, or else retired and sold their schooners. In reporting that Captain Manuel Crawley Santos was having a new vessel built at Essex, the *Provincetown Advocate* of November 6, 1913, explained:

> The *Mary C. Santos* has been very successful . . . but this is a gasoline age, and in order to compete with vessels employing steam and other modern speed devices, Captain Santos wants a craft not wholly dependent on canvas.

Captain Santos did compete. The next year, with his new power "schooner," he made the largest stock of the New England fleet, steamers included. A few years later he retired, and his last vessel, the *Mary P. Goulart*, remained as the only banker of the old Cape Cod port that had once sent out a hundred sail. In 1938, five years after the death of Captain Santos, the *Mary P. Goulart* was sold to Gloucester; and with the

Chapter XVI: Today

banks and all that they had meant through three centuries, Provincetown now was finished.

Today, the "queen of the fleet" is a little "dragger" which confines her voyaging to Cape Cod Bay or waters close along the Back Shore.

But from the wharves of Gloucester, men still go "down to the east'ard" for fish, in stanch little schooners that still hold their own against the giants of Boston. The struggle, for them, is a desperate one. Only by going with them, to the Western Banks, to La Have, or to treacherous Georges, can one know the hardships they go through, the chances they take, to carry on.

On a Gloucester trawler there is no time off. There are no work shifts. Sometimes these schoonermen will go through a solid week of back-breaking labor, day and night, with no regular hours for sleep and precious few irregular ones – naps of fifteen or twenty minutes, snatched between "sets"– keeping up the work until the hold is fulL The landlubber, returning from such a trip, feels as if he has waked on the good earth out of a nightmare, a remote and awful fantasy of iced-up rigging, of stinging spindrift, of decks reeling to crazy angles and made treacherous, with fish gurry, of wind and fog, and of everything else that is wicked in the weather man's catalogue.

The same Atlantic that has closed over great "unsinkable" liners has always behaved at its incredible worst in the parts where these tiny craft must go to do their work. Whether they have engines of a hundred horsepower or three hundred, they are riding out to lay themselves at the mercy of forces which cannot be measured in horsepower. Gloucester still loses vessels on the banks, and alongshore in their comings and goings. Few seasons pass without some contribution to the long tale of tragedy. There will always be another "great, gale"– the sort of storm that every few years overtakes a big part of the fleet many miles from home and spreads destruction in wholesale lots.

In the "August breeze"– another Gloucester term for hurricane – of 1924, a score of vessels came home from Georges in various stages of disintegration. Somehow, by the mercy of Fate and the blessing of engine power, these craft had managed to drag themselves out of it.

But in the very same gale half a dozen other vessels, which also had engine power but which had not found Fate so merciful, were wrecked. And for their ill luck in those few hours, a score of fishermen paid with their lives.

In May of each year, the Gloucester schooners tie up for a week or two while their rig is changed for the summer season of swordfishing. Topmasts are fitted to the stubby foremasts, with places for five lookouts to perch aloft; a bowsprit is stepped into the vessel, and at the tip of this stick a little braced stand known as the "pulpit" is rigged. Here the "striker" rides, harpoon in hand, ready to iron the "blue gladiator of the sea."

This swordfishing is hair-raising business from start to finish. From their posts seventy-five feet above deck, the lookouts can see a fish even though he may be swimming deep below the surface, and when he is "finning"– basking and showing his long half-crescent dorsal fin out of water – their trained eyes will spot him a quarter-mile off or more.

But the "swords," even when they are traveling in a school, keep themselves off, one to a classroom, so to speak; and the lookouts may put in hours at a stretch of tense searching while the vessel crisscrosses the shoals, without raising a fin *"Paciencia, paciencia!"* groans the skipper. Then, when it seems as if the last fish must have been taken out of the ocean, one of the masthead men suddenly raises the cry, and the chase is on.

"Starboard!" he yells, keeping his eyes on that wandering telltale fin. And then, "Port!" Now, "Steady!" And again, "Starboard – *starboard!*" And he fairly screams in frantic falsetto, and writhes on his uncertain perch at the crosstrees.

The fellow at the tiptop has at hand a pushbutton which is connected with an electric horn down on the deck. The horn relays the directions to the wheelman, above the noise of the engine exhaust. When the call is "Starboard," the topman gives two sharp toots on the horn; for "Steady," one toot; and for "Port," a second single toot.

Below, the whole craft suddenly springs to life. To ears that have been waiting for its welcome squawk, that automobile horn packs as great a thrill as the old whaleman's cry of "Blow!" from the crow's-nest. No word is spoken, but there is the quick thud of rubber-booted feet on the deck. Each man has his own part to carry out, and the performance must be timed to the second. A slip on the part of anyone may cost the vessel her fish, which may mean $75 or $100, and this in turn means $2 or $3 in the share of each man.

The wheelman, husky fellow with plenty of grease in his elbows, spins away at the tooted directions as if he were trying to avoid a collision. The

Chapter XVI: Today

engineer rushes up to lend him a hand. Cook has come out of the galley to see that buoys and buoy lines are in order, and spare darts ready.

The vessel runs down her fish at last, and at this moment all depends on the striker. His harpoon is set in a ten-foot pole, ending in a short shaft of soft iron which will bend but not break. A bronze barb is slipped on the end of this shaft. The idea is to jab the dart deep into the fish without doing a number of other things at the same time. Mainly, one should remember not to fall out of the pulpit. That is very bad, because of the chance of getting run through by a four-foot sword, or of engaging in an equally one-sided bout with the propeller.

It takes a quick eye, a steady hand, and a strong arm for the job of striker. The vessel is moving ahead at the moment he must strike, and the fish may be moving, too. The fish may be directly under the bowsprit, or it may be off to one side. But in that split second it must be hit, and hit hard. I have seen many a striker draw back his harpoon, after ironing a fish, with the metal shaft bent nearly double. Once I kept tabs on Captain Joe Rose of the schooner *Magellan*, who comes from the Azorian island of Pico, and who is generally acknowledged along the Gloucester waterfront to be the best striker in the fleet. Of a total of ninety-eight tries made during the three-week trip, Captain Joe Rose succeeded in ironing ninety-six fish. Many of these were under the surface when they were struck; and to get some of them, the captain had to heave his harpoon eight and ten feet off to one side.

When a fish is struck, it goes tearing away with the barbed dart fast in its flesh. To this dart is attached the end of a six-hundred-foot line, which cook has laid in neat coils on top of a keg-buoy, or small barrel painted in bright colors and marked with the vessel's initials. The other end of the line is fast to this keg. The buoy line is now zipping out over the starboard rail, and the wheelman is swinging the vessel hard astarboard to keep the propeller clear of the fish. Cook heaves the remaining coils of line overboard, and after them the buoy. He handles this gear gingerly. Such lines snag easily, and if by mischance cook's wrist should catch a bight of the whizzing rope, he could be flipped overboard and drawn under by the two hundred to six hundred pounds of blue fury which is streaking astern.

To get the fish on board, a doryman now puts out from the vessel and rows for the keg-buoy, which is retarding the fish but may still be bouncing over the water at a merry rate. When he has caught up with the buoy, the doryman lifts it into his boat. Then, over a roller set in the bow, he starts hauling in. It takes from half an hour to an hour to bring the fish up, depending on its size and the life left in it. It must be played, as in sport fishing. If the doryman pulls too suddenly, or too long at a time, the iron may draw, for the flesh is soft. Or it may aggravate the pain, until the fish, in an agonized flurry, turns and dashes sword-on at the dory.

Many a dory has been run through by an up-rushing sword. When a doryman's line suddenly goes slack – a sign that trouble is coming – he hops up on the gunwales and straddles his boat. There he remains until the sword has come splintering through the bottom, or until the fish turns down again. If one forgets to jump, the possibilities are obvious. In August, 1938, Doryman Frank Ferreira suffered a badly torn leg when a sword with six hundred fifty pounds of fish behind it came ripping through the bottom of his boat. In the summer of 1899, Auguste Sylvia, doryman of the Gloucester sloop *Klondyke*, was killed by a sword.

To make up for the risk of getting thus impaled, or of going astray in a fog, or of falling from the masthead, or of being shipwrecked in a gale, this swordfishing game offers a man his chance to earn a few extra dollars each summer – unless the imports from Japanese "hellships" have glutted the market and taken that chance away from him at the outset.

After September, the vessel changes back to trawling rig. Foretopmast, bowsprit, and pulpit are stored away for next season; the "gallowses," or steel hoists for beam trawling, are bolted back on the deck, nets taken aboard, and out she goes for haddock and cod, for redfish, winter flounder, or other cold-weather tenants of the shoals. Each year, a few days after Christmas, part of the Gloucester fleet goes south, to bring scup and fluke, butterfish and tilefish, into the Fulton Market, and to work in southern waters until the following April.

Others, dorymen sticking to the old way of laying their trawl lines on the banks and hauling them back by hand, carry on through the winter "down to the east'ard;" and among these are still a few hardy crews who can stand the gaff of fresh-halibuting away down on the Grand Banks.

> *Ser pobre a casar com pobre*
> *É remar contra a mare . . .*

Chapter XVI: Today

In those lonely waters nine hundred miles from home, Tony Gonsalves of Gloucester stands in the bow of his dory and hauls on the trawl. And as he hauls, now slapping off a dogfish with a whack against the gunwale, now snubbing up a big halibut, bringing the gobstick down on its nose and deftly gaffing it into the dory, he sings.

When news is good, Tony bends a two-fathom grin between his ears and sings. When it's bad, Tony shakes his head – and sings anyway. For like all men who must tax the muscles of arm and shoulder to win their bread, he often calls on his lungs as well.

Casar com mulher sem dote
É andar so com um pé.

Just now the news is bad. And the songs that Tony Gonsalves sings have been sung in the same doleful tones by men from across the sea who have fished these same waters before him, for how many years no one knows. Roughly translated, this one goes:

To be poor and marry a poor girl
  Is like rowing against the tide;
A fellow can get along on one foot,
  But not with a dowerless bride.

Yes, just now the news is bad. The price of fish, coming over the radio from Boston – very bad. In a way (Tony thinks as he sings and hauls and slaps and whacks), in a way it ain't such a miracle after all, this radio!

Take yourself, now. You come way down here to this God-forsaken stretch of water off the Newfoundland coast in mid-February. It's so rough that a ride in your dory would leave a blue shark bilgy in the stomach. And cold? *Aiee!* Frozen bait won't thaw in this water!

But, cold or no cold, you and your dorymate must row out from the vessel, to set for fish. Then you row back. By 'm by, maybe the sea makes a little more, maybe the wind is a little stiffer. But out you go again; and while the other feller in your boat coils the trawl into the skates and keeps the dory's head to the sea so she won't capsize, you haul back the trawl. Salt spindrift whips your face and trickles down under your oil jacket. Your hands are freezing to the cotton flippers that you have slipped over your palms to protect them from chafe. But haul you must, and haul you do – the better part of a mile of line – arm over arm, until you feel as if you are going to snap cables in those sore spots abaft your shoulder blades.

And all the time you're at it, you know it ain't going to stock you a dime, not a dime for the whole of it! Because, you see, before you came out this time you were listening to the radio in the skipper's cabin; and you heard today's ex-vessel price for fresh halibut in Boston – five cents a pound!

Five cents, the damned thing tells you! And if it keeps on that way, the skipper won't get no kind of a price for his fish, and you won't get no kind of a share. A broken trip! Then all *you* get for your three weeks at sea in this weather, is a five-dollar bill from the skipper, because he's big-hearted; you ain't got *that* coming to you!

But them fellers ashore, them fish buyers – they'll get theirs, all right! They always get theirs. They'll tell you the market's glutted with fresh fish, and they'll cut you way down on your price. Then they'll freeze your fish, and hang on to it until the glut is sold out. Then they'll get theirs. *Aiee!* Them fish buyers! Them pirates!

Yet, like a *toleirão* – how you call it, a dope – you still go out and set for fish. *Ai, Deos!* – better not to have a radio, Tony thinks. Then you wouldn't know what a dope you are making of yourself! And still, a man has got to try. He has got to try like hell when there are three little kids to feed back in Gloucester, and a wife – a wife who says they got to have real butter on their bread, not the stuff that grocery feller told her was cheaper.

Tony Gonsalves pauses for breath and gazes over the sharp blacks and whites of heaving water. For himself, he parades his three little *crianças*, one by one, across the bow of his dory, and he laughs and shakes his head and thinks again of the wife who insists on giving them real butter. Then, with a long sigh, he takes up his trawl and starts hauling, arm over stout arm. Again he sings of the consequences of marrying a girl without a dowry; and now and then he shakes his head and mutters: "*Aiee!* Them pirates!"

www.ingramcontent.com/pod-product-compliance
Lightning Source LLC
Chambersburg PA
CBHW060512100426
42743CB00009B/1294